Lecture Notes in Computer Science 1936

Edited by G. Goos, J. Hartmanis and J. van Leeuwen

Springer
Berlin
Heidelberg
New York
Barcelona
Hong Kong
London
Milan
Paris
Singapore
Tokyo

Paul Robertson   Howie Shrobe
Robert Laddaga (Eds.)

Self-Adaptive Software

First International Workshop, IWSAS 2000
Oxford, UK, April 17-19, 2000
Revised Papers

 Springer

Series Editors

Gerhard Goos, Karlsruhe University, Germany
Juris Hartmanis, Cornell University, NY, USA
Jan van Leeuwen, Utrecht University, The Netherlands

Volume Editors

Paul Robertson
Dynamic Object Language Labs., Inc.
9 Bartlet St # 334, Andover, MA 01810, USA
E-mail: probertson@doll.com

Howie Shrobe
Artificial Intelligence Laboratory
Massachusetts Institute of Technology
545 Technology Square (MIT NE43-839)
Cambridge, Massachusetts 02139, USA
E-mail: hes@ai.mit.edu

Robert Laddaga
Artificial Intelligence Laboratory
Massachusetts Institute of Technology
545 Technology Square (MIT NE 43-804)
Cambridge, Massachusetts 02139, USA
E-mail: rladdaga@ai.mit.edu

Cataloging-in-Publication Data applied for

Die Deutsche Bibliothek - CIP-Einheitsaufnahme

Self-adaptive software : first international workshop ; revised papers /
IWSAS 2000, Oxford, UK, April 17 - 19, 2000. Paul Robertson ...
(ed.). - Berlin ; Heidelberg ; New York ; Barcelona ; Hong Kong ;
London ; Milan ; Paris ; Singapore ; Tokyo : Springer, 2001
    (Lecture notes in computer science ; Vol. 1936)
    ISBN 3-540-41655-2

CR Subject Classification (1998): D.2, F.3, I.2.11, C.2.4, C.3

ISSN 0302-9743
ISBN 3-540-41655-2 Springer-Verlag Berlin Heidelberg New York

Springer-Verlag Berlin Heidelberg New York
a member of BertelsmannSpringer Science+Business Media GmbH
© Springer-Verlag Berlin Heidelberg 2001
Printed in Germany

Typesetting: Camera-ready by author, data conversion by PTP-Berlin, Stefan Sossna
Printed on acid-free paper   SPIN 10781242   06/3142   5 4 3 2 1 0

Preface

This volume emanated from a workshop on Self-Adaptive Software held at Lady Margaret Hall, Oxford in April, 2000. The aim of the workshop was to bring together researchers working on all aspects of self-adaptive software in order to assess the state of the field, map out the research areas encompassed by the field, develop a research agenda, and enumerate open issues.

The papers presented at the workshop were in some cases revised after the workshop.

The first paper in the collection: "Introduction: The First International Workshop on Self-Adaptive Software" provides a brief overview of self-adaptive software and a description of the layout of the volume.

November 2000   Paul Robertson

Organizers

Paul Robertson   (Oxford University)
Janos Sztipanovits   (DARPA, Vanderbilt University)

Program Committee

Paul Robertson   (Oxford University)
Janos Sztipanovits   (Vanderbilt University)
Howie Shrobe   (MIT)
Robert Laddaga   (MIT)

Table of Contents

Introduction:
The First International Workshop on Self-Adaptive Software

Paul Robertson, Robert Laddaga, and Howie Shrobe

MIT

1 Introduction

This collection of papers was presented at the international workshop on self adaptive software (IWSAS2000) held at Lady Margaret Hall at the University of Oxford between April 17th and April 19th 2000. They represent the state of the art in a new evolving field of research that attempts to build software systems that are more robust to unpredictable and sometimes hostile environments than we have managed to produce by conventional means.

As we try to solve increasingly difficult problems with computer software we develop new architectures and structures to help support our aggressive endeavors. It is in this light that the need for and the potential benefits of "Self-Adaptive Software" have become apparent.

2 What is Self Adaptive Software

The traditional view of computation is one in which a computational process executes within a fixed and well defined environment. Traditionally computers have existed in isolated environments with minimal contact to the outside world. On occasions the real world has leaked into the equation. Input and output is an example of such leakage. Programs that (say) have to read characters typed by a human operator are operating in an environment that is not well defined or predictable. Writing robust programs to perform input is notably hard. When the environment becomes even slightly unpredictable it becomes necessary for the programmer to carefully consider all possibilities and program them in to the code. Programs that are coded only for what is wanted as input rather than the full range of what might be presented are brittle and such program often fail badly in practice.

If writing programs that robustly perform input is hard it is only the tip of the iceberg. Increasingly we are taking computation away from the tightly controlled environments that have characterized the early development of computer science – away from the machine rooms and trained expert users – and putting them into situations where the environment is unconstrained. Computers are now often connected to a network which provides many additional forms of interaction with the outside world and the incredible reduction in both size and cost of computers

P. Robertson, H. Shrobe, and R. Laddaga (Eds.): IWSAS 2000, LNCS 1936, pp. 1–10, 2000.
© Springer-Verlag Berlin Heidelberg 2000

now allows us to embed processors throughout our homes, cars, and workplaces in ever widening and inventive roles.

Where we have done well with these embedded applications of computation have been precisely those areas where the environment can still be constrained. For example Digital Signal Processors (DSP's) are embedded into a wide array of devices (such as cell phones) where they can perform simple repetitive operations on an input signal that may be voice or image. Where the range of unpredictability is limited to the sequence of button presses on a cellular telephone keyboard or a microwave oven the computation can be adequately addressed using traditional techniques.

Gradually our ambitions are drawing us to use computation in situations where the unpredictable nature of the environment poses a formidable challenge. Obvious examples include robot navigation in unconstrained environments, the interpretation of human speech in noisy environments, the interpretation of visual scenes by mobile robots and so on. In the cited examples there is a significant domain specific component to the problem – such as visual feature extraction – that is unique to each domain but there is also a shared problem. The shared problem is that of writing programs that operate robustly in complex environments.

It is already the case that embedded systems represent the majority of our use of computers and it will never be less true than it is today. Most current embedded systems involve rather simple processors with highly limited memory and computational power. Until recently the limitations of what these embedded systems could do has constrained them to being rather simple and manageable. That picture however is changing rapidly. The new breed of embedded systems can expect to have enough computational power and memory for them to get themselves into some serious trouble. Over time these complex embedded systems will come to dominate.

While the model of computation as operating within a fixed and well defined environment has served us well during the early phases of development of computer science it now seems likely that in order to move forward we must develop a less restrictive model for computation and along with the new model, new methodologies and tools.

In a sense the kind of computation that we developed in the last century was a peculiar and even unnatural one. Nature is full of examples of computation. Most of these examples like the orientation of leaves towards the sun and the opening and closing of flowers in response to changes in light and temperature are fixed computation but many involve what is more recognizable as a programmable capability – such as the ability to learn exhibited by many animals. Whatever degree of learning these computational devices may have virtually all of them are involved with direct interaction with the real world. These natural examples of computation work in the presence of complex and often hostile environments. Indeed they exist precisely because the environment is unpredictable and hostile.

At a fundamental level computation is not different in these unconstrained environment situations. We can still describe them in terms of Turing machines and in principle we can program them using traditional techniques by carefully considering at every turn the full range of possibilities that the environment can present and programming for each case. On the other hand the traditional approach arguably missed the point. The notion of a computation halting is uninteresting in many of these applications and while it is theoretically possible to consider every possibility when programming a system it makes for unmanageably complex software that challenges our ability to build and test them.

When the environment is constrained we can develop an algorithm traditionally, whose complexity is a function of the problem being solved. If the environment must also be considered, again using traditional technology, the complexity of the program must mirror the complexity of the environment, because the program must consider every possibility... If a program's complexity is a linear or worse function of the complexity of the environment, then we are clearly in trouble because the world is a complex place.

Computation may be a much wider concept than we have historically believed it to be. In the future computation that operates in tightly constrained environments will represent a tiny fraction of computation as a whole. The Computer Science that we have developed to date may turn out to be a very special case of computation that occurs only when the environment is very tightly constrained.

For the time being those building systems involving sensors and effectors and those developing systems that must navigate robots, missiles, and land vehicles through complex and often hostile environments share a need for new approaches to building robust applications in these domains.

This need for a new approach was recognized by DARPA in 1997 when it published its Broad Agency Announcement (BAA) for proposals in the area of "Self-Adaptive Software". The BAA [14] describes Self Adaptive Software as follows:

"Self-adaptive software evaluates its own behavior and changes behavior when the evaluation indicates that it is not accomplishing what the software is intended to do, or when better functionality or performance is possible."

2.1   Benefits of a Self Adaptive Approach

The principle idea behind the self adaptive approach to achieving robust performance is that it is easier and often more efficient to postpone certain decisions until their need is evident from the circumstances. It is often easier to make a program that monitors its performance and recovers from errors than it is to make a program that goes to great lengths to avoid making any errors. This notion is already familiar to us in our use of errors and exceptions in languages like Common Lisp [24] and Java. Exceptions allow simple code to be written that expects the environment to be well behaved. The code must also include checks that everything is as expected. If things are not as expected an exception is raised. Elsewhere an exception handler contains the code that decides how the exception should be handled. For example if the code was trying to read a number and a non numeric character was detected a 'non numeric character in number' exception may be raised. The handler could then clear the input buffer, caution the user against using non numeric characters and retry the read. In this example the program has a 'model' of what it expects (a sequence of numeric digits). The program checks for differences between what it is getting as input and the model and when such differences occur the program tries to deal with them robustly–in this case by issuing a warning and trying again.

While the exception mechanism is invaluable for a certain class of problems and is suggestive of a general approach it does not easily extend to the full range of problems that can occur in complex systems. When a robot encounters difficulty in understanding a visual scene it could be for a variety of reasons: a sensor may be functioning incorrectly or have failed completely; the lighting may have changed so as to require a different set of algorithms; the contents of the scene may have changed requiring the robot to update its model of the environment; and so on. In general the environment cannot be given a warning and asked to try again! The program must deal with what it gets as best it can. In these situations when a sensor fails or an algorithm doesn't work or some other assumption about the environment turns out to be untrue the solution will often require reconstituting the program to deal with the actual environment rather than having enough complexity to deal with all possible environments hidden within exception handlers.

Self adaptive software therefore involves having suitable models of the environment and of the running program, the ability to detect differences between the models and the actual runtime environment, the ability to diagnose the nature of the disparity, and the ability to re-synthesize or modify the running program (or its models) so that the program can operate robustly.

The notion of programs that can manipulate their own representation is not new and has been a key characteristic of Lisp [24,12] since its inception although the full power of that capability has not often been used. The idea of programs that reason about their own behavior and modify their own semantics is well developed. Programming languages that support self reasoning and self modification are called 'reflective' a term coined by Brian Smith in his original development of the idea of reflective programs [4,5]. Reflection has been around long enough for efficient implementation methodologies to be developed [7,2,11, 8] and some level of reflective capability is now available in CLOS [12] and Java. Reflection makes it possible (and convenient) to write programs that can reason about the state of computation and make changes to the semantics of the running program. Self adaptive software can clearly benefit from such a capability but there is more to self adaptive software than reflection. Self adaptive software must have a model of what the computation is trying to achieve in order to have something against which to compare the current computation. Having determined some difference between the intended program state and the actual one a self adaptive program must be able to automatically adjust the semantics of the program so that the difference is reduced. Reflection provides the tools for writing such programs but it doesn't provide any guidance in how it should be done.

Managing complexity is a key goal of self adaptive software. If a program must match the complexity of the environment in its own structure it will be very complex indeed! Somehow we need to be able to write software that is less complex than the environment in which it is operating yet operate robustly. By keeping the program code separate from the code the diagnosis and synthesis code the core code can remain simple and the synthesis can be performed by a purpose built synthesis engine. Such an architecture makes writing the core code much less of a tangled web. In essence the total runtime program may be a sequence of different programs each one individually simple. The complexity of the program as a whole is moved into the architectural mechanism that maintains models, checks models against performance, and re-synthesizes new programs.

There are many advantages to this approach beyond making it possible to write programs that operate in complex environments. Correctness of our programs may be easier to establish whether by testing, proof, or other means because at any point the operating program should be simpler than a program that considered every possibility would be. To some extent correctness testing may be guaranteed by the synthesis engine or may be checked automatically because there is a model of the program against which it may be tested. Greater efficiency may also be achieved through the self adaptive software approach. Greater efficiency occurs when a crude but fast program that may not always work is substituted for a complex but slow program that tries to guarantee that it always works. By making decisions at run time when much more is known about the actual environment than could have been known when the program was originally designed it is possible to select more suitable procedures for achieving the intended goal. this can result in a more direct solution with less failure and less backtracking. Having better information about the environment allows better decisions to be made which can result in more efficient and successful execution.

There are also concerns and difficulties evident in the approach. A program that changes itself at runtime may in some sense be a less well understood entity than a program that remains unchanging during its execution. The notion that it may be more robust than its fixed counterpart should make us feel more comfortable about its behavior but the notion that the program changes at runtime is unsettling to people responsible for building complex missile delivery systems (for example). How can we trust a smart missile that may reprogram itself in mid flight? There are (at least) two answers to this. The first is that if the program fails in mid flight because it was unable to deal with its complex environment it may do a very bad thing in its failure mode so the self adaptive version that is less brittle should be less of a concern. The second is that we must develop a better understanding of self adaptive software and new approaches to software testing, debugging, and semantics that allow us to be confident about the systems that we deploy either through a proof theoretic framework or through a testing regime.

Today self adaptive software draws upon a great many technologies that may be used as building blocks. Reflection and exception handling mechanisms have already been mentioned but there are a great many other candidate contributing technologies including model based computing, theorem provers, models for reasoning about uncertainty, and agent based systems to name a few. The papers in this collection begin to address many of the issues described above as well and explore how many of these technologies can be harnessed to realize the goals of self adaptive software.

3   About the Papers

Self adaptive software is a relative new idea and the approach involves taking a significant departure from established software development methodologies and potentially requiring a rethinking of some basic concepts in computer science. Self adaptive software will be achieved by taking small steps from what we currently know. Some people are attempting to build self adaptive software solutions to solve existing problems, some are experimenting with existing technologies to see how they can be used to achieve self adaptive software, some are working with systems that interpret the world through sensors, and some are directly studying aspects of self adaptive software ideas in order to extend our understanding of their semantics. The papers in this collection provide examples of all of these areas of activity.

3.1   Understanding Self Adaptive Software

Robert Laddaga's paper on 'Active Software' [15] provides a good definition of Self adaptive software and a survey of related concepts and technologies.

One of the more ambitious self adaptive software projects that brings together a wide range of technologies is being being conducted at the University of Massachusetts at Amherst. Two papers from the University of Amherst project appear in this collection [19,6]. Osterweil et. al. describe a process of perpetual testing in 'Continuous Self Evaluation for the Self-Improvement of Software' as a means of achieving self improving software.

The environment in natural systems as well as artificial ones is not only complex but in many instances it can be hostile. Information survivability attempts to deal with systems that come under attack from outside agents. Shrobe and Doyle [23] consider how self adaptive software can provide software services in an environment that is actively hostile. Rather than considering issues of information survivability as a binary affair in which the system is either compromised (and useless) or not compromised (and useable) they consider how survivability can be achieved by self-testing to detect that the system has been compromised in various ways and then adapting so as to be able to provide the best level of service possible given the compromised state if the system.

There is a bone fide need for formal methods in a number of places in building self adaptive software. Formal methods may be involved in the automatic synthesis of the program when adaptation is required. Formal methods may also be useful in understanding the range of behaviors that a self adaptive program may exhibit. Dusko Pavlovic's paper 'Towards semantics of self adaptive software' [20] provides a first attempt at building a theoretical basis for self adaptive software.

3.2   Self-Adaptive Software Compared to Control Systems

The straightforward characterization of self adaptive software as continual runtime comparison of performance against a preset goal and subsequent adjustment of the program so that performance is brought back towards the goal is very similar in structure to a control system. The task of building self adaptive systems may be much more like building a control system than it is to conventional software development. We are trying to develop new methodologies for building software that is robust to changes in the environment within certain limits and we have observed that systems characterized as self adaptive are more control like in structure than conventional program like. Since control systems and their design are well understood it is hoped that some ideas can be borrowed from control system design and adapted to self adaptive software. Two papers in this collection deal with attempting to understand self adaptive software in terms of control systems and the subsequent borrowing of ideas from control systems. Alex Meng's paper 'On Evaluating Self Adaptive Software' [16] makes explicit the relationship between control systems and self adaptive software and discusses terminology and issues surrounding viewing software as a control system. The Kokar et. al. paper entitled 'Mapping an Application to a Control Architecture: Specification of the Problem' takes a radar-based target tracking problem and shows how it can be mapped onto a control system architecture [17].

3.3   Technologies for Self Adaptive Software

When a system is reconfigured at runtime such as by the replacement of one set of sensors with another set undesirable transient effects may occur at the point of switching. Gyula et. al. [9] investigate the management of such effects in 'Transient Management in Reconfigurable Systems'.

A key notion of self adaptive software is that the software contains some embedded account (or model) of its intention and of its environment. In 'Model-Integrated Embedded Systems' Bakey et. al. [1] describe a model based generative technology they call 'Model-Integrated Computing' and show how the technology is applicable to self adaptive software.

In 'Coordination of View Maintenance Policy Adaptation Decisions: A Negotiation-Based Reasoning Approach' Bose and Matthews [3] develop a negotiation based reasoning model for adapting view maintenance policies to meet changes in quality of service (QoS) needs.

While much attention has been given to robotic, sensor based, and embedded applications for self adaptive software there is a role to be played in the network computing environment. Network computing provides all of the attributes of a naturally complex environment within a man made network. In 'Dynamic Self

Adaptation in Distributed Systems' Ben-Shaul [10] describes two implemented architectures that provide support for self adaptive software in Java.

Since the need for self adaptive software derives from running applications in an unpredictable environment many of the applications of self adaptive software involve real-time issues. One paper in the collection specifically addresses the real-time issue. Musliner [18] describes in 'Imposing Real-Time Constraints on Self Adaptive Controller Synthesis' a system that can adapt by dynamically re-synthesizing new controllers. Musliner shows how the synthesis process can be managed so that reconfiguration can meet real-time deadlines.

3.4   Systems that Interpret Their Environment through Sensors

The remaining papers describe implemented self adaptive software systems that involve sensors.

In 'Software Mode Changes for Continuous Motion Tracking' Grupen et. al. [6] describe a self adaptive motion tracking system that has redundant sensors and the ability to adjust which sensors are best suited to tracking.

In 'Port-Based Adaptable Agent Architecture' Khosla et. al. [13] describe an architecture that supports self adaptive software through an agent architecture. They go on to demonstrate the architecture on a multi-robot mapping problem.

In 'An architecture for self adaptation and its application to aerial image understanding' Robertson [22] describes a self adaptive architecture that is tailored to image understanding. The systems learns models from expert annotations of images from a corpus and then uses those models to monitor performance of the system on other images and to re-synthesize the program code when necessary in order to produce good interpretations of the images.

In 'Self Adaptive Multi-Sensor Systems' Reece [21] describes a system that utilizes redundant sensors for image interpretation. Sensor performance is learned from test sets and qualitative reasoning (QR) models of the imaged environment's physics allows a theorem prover to synthesize interpretation code.

3.5   Conclusion

The workshop brought together a wide range of researchers involved in the projects described above and provided an opportunity for us to collect our thoughts and experiences and access how far we have come with self-adaptive software, what problems remain to be solved, and how to characterize self-adaptive systems in terms of a set of capabilities.

The final paper summarizes some of these discussions and provides a taxonomy of capabilities and technologies and suggests areas where more research is needed.

References

1. Arpad Bakay Akos Ledeczi and Miklos Maroti. Model-integrated embedded systems. In Robert Laddaga Paul Robertson and Howard E. Shrobe, editors, *Self-Adaptive Software*. Spriger-Verlag, 2000.
2. Alan Bawden. Reification without evaluation. In *Proceedings of the ACM Conference on LISP and Functional Programming*, pages 342–351, 1988.
3. Prasanta Bose and Mark G. Matthews. Coordination of view maintenance policy adaptation decisions: A negotiation-based reasoning approach. In Robert Laddaga Paul Robertson and Howard E. Shrobe, editors, *Self-Adaptive Software*. Spriger-Verlag, 2000.
4. C. Smith Brian. Reflection and semantics in a procedural language. Technical Report 272, MIT Laboratory for Computer Science, January 1982.
5. C. Smith Brian. Reflection and semantics in lisp. In *Proceedings 11th Annual ACM Symposium on Principles of Programming Languages, Salt Lake City, Utah*, pages 23–35, January 1984.
6. Elizeth Araujo Yunlei Yang Gary Holness Zhigang Zhu Barbara Lerner Roderic Grupen Deepak Karuppiah, Patrick Deegan and Edward Riseman. Software mode changes for continuous motion tracking. In Robert Laddaga Paul Robertson and Howard E. Shrobe, editors, *Self-Adaptive Software*. Spriger-Verlag, 2000.
7. Jim des Rivieres and C. Smith Brian. The implementation of procedurally reflection languages. In *Proceedings 1984 ACM Symposium on Lisp and Functional Programming, Austin, Texas*, pages 331–347, August 1984.
8. G. Daniel G. Kiczales, J. des Rivieres. *The art of the Metaobject Protocol*. MIT Press, 1993.
9. Tam s Kov csh zy Gyula Simon and G bor P celi. Transient management in reconfigurable systems. In Robert Laddaga Paul Robertson and Howard E. Shrobe, editors, *Self-Adaptive Software*. Spriger-Verlag, 2000.
10. Ophir Holder Israel Ben-Shaul, Hovav Gazit and Boris Lavva. Transient management in reconfigurable systems. In Robert Laddaga Paul Robertson and Howard E. Shrobe, editors, *Self-Adaptive Software*. Spriger-Verlag, 2000.
11. P. Cointe J. Malenfant and C. Dony. Reflection in prototype-based object-oriented programming languages. In *Proceedings of the OOPSLA Workshop on Reflection and Metalevel Architectures in Object-Oriented Programming*, 1991.
12. S. E. Keene. *Object-Oriented Programming in Common Lisp: A programmer's Guide to CLOS*. Addison-Wesley, 1989.
13. Theodore Q. Pham Kevin R. Dixon and Pradeep K. Khosla. Port-based adaptable agent architecture. In Robert Laddaga Paul Robertson and Howard E. Shrobe, editors, *Self-Adaptive Software*. Spriger-Verlag, 2000.
14. Robert Laddaga. Self-adaptive software sol baa 98-12. *http://www.darpa.mil/ito/Solicitations/CBD_9812.html*, 1998.
15. Robert Laddaga. Active software. In Robert Laddaga Paul Robertson and Howard E. Shrobe, editors, *Self-Adaptive Software*. Spriger-Verlag, 2000.
16. Alex C. Meng. On evaluating self-adaptive software. In Robert Laddaga Paul Robertson and Howard E. Shrobe, editors, *Self-Adaptive Software*. Spriger-Verlag, 2000.
17. Kenneth Baclawski Mieczyslaw M. Kokar, Kevin M. Passino and Jeffrey E. Smith. Mapping an application to a control architecture: Specification of the problem. In Robert Laddaga Paul Robertson and Howard E. Shrobe, editors, *Self-Adaptive Software*. Spriger-Verlag, 2000.

18. David J. Musliner. Imposing real-time constraints on self-adaptive controller synthesis. In Robert Laddaga Paul Robertson and Howard E. Shrobe, editors, *Self-Adaptive Software*. Spriger-Verlag, 2000.

19. Leon J. Osterweil and Lori A. Clarke. Continuous self-evaluation for the self-improvement of software. In Robert Laddaga Paul Robertson and Howard E. Shrobe, editors, *Self-Adaptive Software*. Spriger-Verlag, 2000.

20. Dusko Pavlovic. Towards semantics of self-adaptive software. In Robert Laddaga Paul Robertson and Howard E. Shrobe, editors, *Self-Adaptive Software*. Spriger-Verlag, 2000.

21. Steven Reece. Self-adaptive multi-sensor systems. In Robert Laddaga Paul Robertson and Howard E. Shrobe, editors, *Self-Adaptive Software*. Spriger-Verlag, 2000.

22. Paul Robertson. An architecture for self-adaptation and its application to aerial image understanding. In Robert Laddaga Paul Robertson and Howard E. Shrobe, editors, *Self-Adaptive Software*. Spriger-Verlag, 2000.

23. Howard Shrobe and Jon Doyle. Active trust management for autonomous adaptive survivable systems (atm' for ass's). In Robert Laddaga Paul Robertson and Howard E. Shrobe, editors, *Self-Adaptive Software*. Spriger-Verlag, 2000.

24. G. Steele. *Common Lisp: The Language*. Digital Press, 1984.

Active Software

Robert Laddaga

MIT AI Lab

Introduction

The chief problems that software engineering will face over at least the next two decades are increasing application complexity, and the need for autonomy and serious application robustness. In other words, how do we actually get to declare success when trying to build applications one or two orders of magnitude more complex than today's applications? And, having declared success when building, how do we keep them from absorbing all our productivity to keep them patched together and running with more than just a vague semblance of doing what we want? The sources of increasing application complexity are:

1. simple growth in problem size, as a result of success at previous problem sizes and increased hardware capacity;
2. the fact that many applications are now more closely tethered to the real world, actively utilizing sensors and actuators, or being required to respond in real-time;
3. the enmeshed nature of today's applications – such as enterprise requirements to link all the elements of business process where it is useful to do so.

There has always been a significant difficulty with software robustness, for which the chief causes were high part counts, insufficient natural constraints, and requirements of interpretation of results; all of which make software innately difficult to make robust. In addition to these problems, further causes of insufficient robustness in the future will be:

1. The increase in software complexity that we discussed above;
2. The difficulty in getting modules built by one individual or team to interface with others, not quite so organically connected during the development cycle; and
3. Requirements change - the fact that as we use software, we discover that it can "almost" do more than we originally thought, or that we didn't quite understand precisely what we wanted the software for.

These dramatic problems, new at least in scale for the upcoming decades, require changes in our approach to software engineering. The old approaches to these problems: object oriented programming, client-server architectures, middleware architectures, distributed computation, verification, and exhaustive or statistical testing, etc. are all clearly insufficient to the task. While significant improvements to all these technologies are possible and also highly desirable, those improvements themselves won't be sufficient to the task.

P. Robertson, H. Shrobe, and R. Laddaga (Eds.): IWSAS 2000, LNCS 1936, pp. 11-26, 2000.
© Springer-Verlag Berlin Heidelberg 2000

We are proposing a collection of novel approaches that are informed by a single theme: that software must take active responsibility for its own robustness, and the management of its own complexity.

Naturally software can only do this if the software designer is able to program the software to take on these meta-tasks, and to supply the program with appropriate meta information: designs, alternative computations, goals and world state. This can only be done when we supply the designer with new tools, architectures, and patterns. Among these technologies, I want to mention the following four: tolerant software; self-adaptive software; physically grounded software and negotiated coordination.

Problems with Software

There are three principal interrelated problems facing the software industry. These are escalating complexity of application functionality, insufficient robustness of applications, and the need for autonomy. These are the problems that must be addressed if we are to continue to meet the software challenges of the future. These problems are interrelated because in general, greater robustness is necessary but not sufficient to deal with more complex operations, and autonomy generally increases complexity, and requires great robustness. Before considering how best to deal with these problems, we first consider how they arise and interrelate.

Lack of inherent limits on software functionality, combined with current successful applications, creates a demand for ever increasing software functionality, and without significant additional effort, this increased functionality will come with increased complexity. The decreasing cost of computational hardware, as compared to mechanical hardware and personnel costs, and the non-recurring nature of software development expense, provide economic incentives for software to assume more functional burden, and hence more complexity. Networking and communication between processing nodes also increases software complexity.

A second, and significantly more important source of complexity is an increasing emphasis on embedded software. It has been true for some time that 98% of the processors produced each year are utilized in embedded applications. The vast majority of those applications use less sophisticated and powerful processors, but use of more powerful processors and memory in embedded applications is growing even more quickly than that of less powerful processors. The physical reality of sensors and effectors guarantees that there will be cross cutting constraints that complicate tasks, violate modularity boundaries, and in general, make software more difficult to write, read, and update. Most microcontrollers have been used in point solutions, controlling a single device or sensor. Networking of controllers, and sharing information and coordinating control of complex assemblies of sensors and effectors, is happening rapidly today. For example, today cars mostly use microcontrollers to deploy a single airbag, or modulate a single brake. Tomorrow's cars will provide generalized traction control, using engine, transmission, and breaks and generalized accident response, coordinating multiple airbags, engine response, and notification to emergency channels. This type of networked, coordinated control will bring significant additional complexity to embedded applications.

It is also the number, breadth and pervasiveness of embedded applications that drive the requirement of autonomy. As embedded applications deal with both more data, and more data sources, it becomes more difficult to count on human beings to directly manage systems. Even in situations where a human being will exercise significant control, it is essential for the embedded system to be capable of autonomous operation, in order for it to have sufficient capability of informing, supporting and guiding the human controller.

In assessing the degree of functional complexity, physically embedding, and autonomy we are likely to see in the near future, let's consider the emerging computational infrastructure in general. We will see variations of several orders of magnitude in communication bandwidth, further chaotic, emergent and unreliable behavior from networks, huge numbers, great heterogeneity and unreliability of host nodes, no possibility of centralized control, and serious concerns about deliberate attempts to compromise systems. Data sets and work loads can be expected to be extremely dynamic, and control functions will also be dynamic and situation dependent. We can also expect weak theories of system behavior, for perception and sensing in particular, and weak knowledge about the degree of trust we can have in operability and intentions of system components – hardware and software.

In the area of robustness, there is a significant irony. We mentioned above that the malleability and unlimited quality of software contribute to software taking on more of the functional burden in systems. Despite the enormous malleability of software *itself*, software *applications* are incredibly brittle. They tend to work only in a narrow domain of utilization, and exclusively in a predetermined subset of that domain. Outside the intended use of its creators, software applications fail miserably. They also evidence lack of robustness over time. As functional and performance changes are required, software applications are difficult to maintain, difficult to pass from one programming team to another, and difficult to update, preserving correctness, performance, and maintainability.

The inherent complexity of software systems makes testing and proving correctness each suffer from combinatorial overload. Imagine the complexity of an automobile engine, if we built it atom by atom. Our "character set" would consist of a subset of the elements, and the number of possible combinations would be staggeringly huge. Despite larger numbers of such character-atoms, there is considerably less freedom in combining the mechanical atoms, than in combining characters into programs. The complexity induced conceptual overload means that testing and verification are even more limited than the domain of applicability, and increasing that domain exacerbates the testing and verification problems. In a sense, we are deliberately reducing robustness, in the form of ability to accommodate a wide range of domain conditions, in order to make the program more understandable. However, what we chiefly understand about such programs is that they are brittle and fragile.

Are Current Methods Enough?

One might, however, stipulate that everything discussed above is true, but that current methods and technology of software development will continue to be adequate to the tasks ahead. We make the strong claim that this is not so. Instead we believe that two features create, exacerbate and interrelate the problems mentioned above: meeting the needs of embedded systems, and software development technology that provides insufficient support for modifiability of software applications. Further, the lack in current development technology to support both highly modifiable and physically grounded software systems, will ensure that the challenges indicated above will not be met by current technology. Physical interactions of embedded systems violate functional modularity, and hence make systems more complex, less robust, and more difficult to operate autonomously. Systems that are built using tools that are oriented to building things once, and right, make it difficult to add complex functionality incrementally, which in turn makes it difficult to build in sufficient robustness and autonomy.

To see why this is so, first consider how we currently manage complexity. The chief tool we have for dealing with computational complexity is an abstraction mechanism: functional decomposition. Functional decomposition includes breaking problems down into functional components, recursively. These components can be individually programmed, and then combined in relatively simple ways. The principle that makes functional decomposition generally work is that we can limit the complexity of interactions among functional units.

For non-embedded applications, it is relatively easy to limit interaction complexity to clean interfaces between functional modules. Even these non-embedded applications have real world context that adds interaction complexity, such as deadlines, and resource scarcity, such as memory, processors, communication bandwidth, OS process time slots, and other similar resources. We typically handle these issues via Operating System policies of sharing, priority and fairness, and by depending on the programmer to build in sufficient capacity.

With embedded applications, it is impossible to prevent pervasive intrusion of real world concerns. This intrusion increases complexity and results in tighter constraints on the computational resources, which we deal with by using explicit resource control, or using special real-time capable Operating Systems. In highly connected and decentralized embedded systems, higher level general resource managers may not always be a workable option. Even when there is some approach to dealing with resource allocation issues, the remaining interaction constraints are still the individual responsibility of the programmer, adding to his conceptual burden. Therefore, the cleanliness and value of functional decomposition is dramatically reduced. Also, resource conflicts are a chief source of interaction complexity themselves, which necessarily violates modularity based principally on functional decomposition. Since we generally handle resource management implicitly, we don't replace the violated functional modularity with any other form of modularity.

Even worse than the modularity violations, the implicit management of resources is handled statically, rather than dynamically. It is clearly advantageous to late bind the decisions about resource management and conflict resolution, since the exact nature of these conflicts is highly context dependent. In order to late bind resource conflict resolution policy implementations, we must explicitly represent and reason about such resource management issues.

There are some excellent evolutionary programming methodologies, that make it relatively easy to modify software over time. We might speculate that if we simply shifted to more use of those technologies, we could converge to sufficiently robust applications. However we modify our software, returning the software/system to the shop to redesign, reimplement and retest involves a very large response time delay. That delay is often critical, and in general it means that we run software "open loop". Of course, it is much more desirable to run software "closed loop", in which evaluation and adjustment happens in real time.

Software is the most malleable part of most systems that we build, but the software applications themselves, once built, are remarkably rigid and fragile. They only work for the set of originally envisioned cases, which is often only a proper subset of the cases we need to have the software handle. Traditional approaches to enhancing the robustness of software have depended on making all the abstractions (requirements, specifications, designs, and interfaces) more mathematically precise. Given such precision we could attempt to prove assertions about the attributes of the resulting artifacts. Then, whether precisely specified or not, the software systems would be extensively tested. For complex software artifacts, operating in complex environments, extensive testing is never exhaustive, leaving room for failure, and even catastrophic failure. Also, often, the precision of specification works against producing systems that reliably provide service which good enough, delivered soon enough. However, there is significant distinction between engineered tolerance and simple sloppiness. Much software is today is built on the assumption that software will have bugs and that systems will simply crash for that reason. The further assumption is that regardless of how much testing is done "in the factory", the bulk of the "testing" will happen while the software is in service, and all repairs will happen "in the shop". We mean something very different by software tolerance.

A New Approach to Software

We have claimed that problems with future software development efforts center around handling increased functional complexity, providing substantially increased robustness, and providing autonomy. These problems are all exacerbated by increasing emphasis on embedded systems, and by a "do it once, right" engineering approach. What we are proposing is a radically new form of abstraction, that we call *Active Software*. The overarching themes of the Active Software approach are that ***software must take active responsibility for its own robustness, and the management*** *of its own complexity*; and that to do so, *software must incorporate representations of its goals, methods, alternatives, and environment.*

Research can provide us with software systems are active in several senses. They will be composed of modules that are nomadic, going where network connectivity permits. They will be able to register their capabilities, announce their needs for additional, perhaps temporary capability, evaluate their own progress, and find and install improvements and corrections as needed and as available anywhere in the network. They will manage their interfaces with other modules, by negotiation and by implementing flexible interfaces. Thus active software is nomadic, self-regulating, self-correcting, and self aware. In order to accomplish these purposes, the underlying environments and system software must support these capabilities.

We do not as yet have a clear and unambiguous understanding of this new approach. What we do have is a collection of technologies that can be viewed as component technologies under Active Software. By discussing and comparing the component technologies, we will attempt to get a clearer picture of the Active Software concept. In fact, the concept of Active Software derives from some common aspects of the component technologies.

The component technologies are self adaptive software, negotiated coordination, tolerant software and physically grounded software. Self adaptive software evaluates its behavior and environment against its goals, and revises behavior in response to the evaluation. Negotiated coordination is the coordination of independent software entities via mutual rational agreement on exchange conditions. Tolerant software is software that can accommodate any alternatives within a given region. Physically grounded software is software that takes explicit account of spatio-temporal coordinates and other physical factors in the context of embedded systems.

The four listed technologies are not a partition of the concept of Active Software. It would probably be useful to have a partition of the concept, but the current four components are certainly not exclusive, and they are probably not exhaustive either. For example, negotiation of interfaces can provide tolerant interfaces, but there are certainly other ways to get tolerance. Also, physically grounded software is necessary for self adaptive embedded systems, but physically grounded software need not be self adaptive. Neither is active software the only new approach to building software able to address the challenges we have discussed. Aspect oriented programming is an extremely interesting alternative, and complementary approach [7].

Self Adaptive Software

Software design consists in large part in analyzing the cases the software will be presented with, and ensuring that requirements are met for those cases. It is always difficult to get good coverage of cases, and impossible to assure that coverage is complete. If program behaviors are determined in advance, the exact runtime inputs and conditions are not used in deciding what the software will do. The state of the art in software development is to adapt to new conditions via off-line maintenance. The required human intervention delays change. The premise of **self adaptive software** is that the need for change should be detected, and the required change effected, *while the program is running* (at run-time).

The goal of self adaptive software is the creation of technology to enable programs to understand, monitor and modify themselves. Self adaptive software understands: *what it does; how it does it; how to evaluate its own performance; and thus how to respond to changing conditions.* We believe that self adaptive software will identify, promote and evaluate new models of code design and run-time support. These new models will allow software to modify its own behavior in order to adapt, at runtime, when exact conditions and inputs are known, to discovered changes in requirements, inputs, and internal and external conditions.

A definition of self adaptive software was provided in a DARPA Broad Agency Announcement on Self-adaptive Software [2]:

> Self-adaptive software evaluates its own behavior and changes behavior when the evaluation indicates that it is not accomplishing what the software is intended to do, or when better functionality or performance is possible.

> …This implies that the software has multiple ways of accomplishing its purpose, and has enough knowledge of its construction to make effective changes at runtime. Such software should include functionality for evaluating its behavior and performance, as well as the ability to replan and reconfigure its operations in order to improve its operation. Self adaptive software should also include a set of components for each major function, along with descriptions of the components, so that components of systems can be selected and scheduled at runtime, in response to the evaluators. It also requires the ability to impedance match input/output of sequenced components, and the ability to generate some of this code from specifications. In addition, DARPA seek this new basis of adaptation to be applied at runtime, as opposed to development/design time, or as a maintenance activity.

Self adaptive software constantly evaluates its own performance, and when that performance is below criteria, changes its behavior. To accomplish this, the runtime code includes the following things not currently included in shipped software:

1. descriptions of software intentions (i.e. goals and designs) and of program structure;
2. a collection of alternative implementations and algorithms (sometimes called a reuse asset base).

Three metaphors have been useful to early researchers on self adaptive software: coding an application as a dynamic planning system, or coding an application as a control system, or coding a self aware system, [9]. The first two are operational metaphors, and the third deals with the information content and operational data of the program.

In programming as planning, the application doesn't simply execute specific algorithms, but instead plans its actions. That plan is available for inspection, evaluation, and modification. Replanning occurs at runtime in response to a negative evaluation of the effectiveness of the plan, or its execution. The plan treats computational resources such as hardware, communication capacity, and code objects (components) as resources that the plan can schedule and configure. See [1], [6], [11], and [16].

In program as control system, the runtime software behaves like a factory, with inputs and outputs, and a monitoring and control unit that manages the factory. Evaluation, measurement and control systems are layered on top of the application, and manage reconfiguration of the system. Explicit models of the operation, purpose and structure of the application regulate the system's behavior. This approach is more complex than most control systems, because the effects of small changes are highly variable, and because complex filtering and diagnosis of results is required, before they can serve as feedback or feed-forward mechanisms. Despite the difficulties of applying control theory to such highly non-linear systems, there are valuable insights to be drawn from control theory, and also hybrid control theory, including for example the concept of stability. See [6], [8], and [13].

The key factor in a self aware program is having a self-modeling approach. Evaluation, revision and reconfiguration are driven by models of the operation of the software that are themselves contained in the running software. Essentially, the applications are built to contain knowledge of their operation, and they use that knowledge to evaluate performance, to reconfigure and to adapt to changing circumstances (see [9], [17], and [14]). The representation and meta-operation issues make this approach to software engineering also intriguing as an approach to creation of artificial intelligence.

Problems, Future Issues:

The hardest and most important problem for self adaptive software is evaluation. There is great variability in the ease with which evaluation can be accomplished. The hardest case, where we have an analytic problem without ground truth available, may require us to use probabilistic reasoning to evaluate performance at runtime. There is still much work to be done in determining what classes of application require what forms of evaluation, which tools will provide better evaluation capability, and to what extent such tools will need to be specific to particular application domains.

Because self-adaptive software is software that adapts and reconfigures at runtime., there are crucial issues of dynamism and software architecture representation to be addressed in building development tools. Any piece of software that is revised on the basis of problems found in the field can be thought of as adaptive, but with human intervention and very high latency. Thus, we can think of these problems as generally when and how we implement the functions of evaluating program performance, diagnosing program problems and opportunities, revising the program in response to problems/opportunities, and assuring that desirable program properties are preserved, and who implements these functions. The single large step of changing the binding time for these functions can provide a tremendous amount of help with these problems. If we evaluate and diagnose performance immediately, at run time, and if further we can revise the program in response to diagnostics, then we can build a significantly adaptive functionality.   In such a system, immediate evaluation, diagnosis and repair can play an enormous role in testing behavior and assuring the preservation of desirable features.   It is much easier to introduce this kind of late binding in dynamic languages and environments that already support significant late binding.   Similar concerns relate to explicit rendering of software structure or architecture: reconfiguration causes one to pay close attention to modularity, and to the unit of code that is considered configurable or replaceable. However, current dynamic languages aren't sufficient to the task, without the following improvements:

1. More introspective languages, and better understanding of how to use introspection;
2. Improving the debug-ability of embedded, very high level, domain specific languages;
3. Better process description – including better event handling and description, and explicit consideration of real time;
4. Better structural descriptions – inclusion of architecture description languages in programming languages (see [3], [4], [10], [11], and [12].

We will also have problems with runtime performance. It takes time to evaluate outcomes of computations and determine if expectations are being met. Most often, expectations will be met, and checking seems like pure overhead in those cases. On the other hand, comprehensively evaluating what algorithms and implementations will be used is an advantage if it means that we can select the optimal or near optimal algorithm for the input and state context we have at runtime, rather than a preselected design time compromise. Additionally, hardware performance keeps increasing, but perceived software robustness does not. Even so, effort will need to go into finding ways to optimize evaluation cycles, and develop hierarchical systems with escalating amounts of evaluation as needed for a particular problem.

Performance is also a problem at software creation time. The kind of programming that delivers code able to evaluate and reconfigure itself is difficult to build by hand. We would therefore prefer automated code generation technology. Specifically, we like approaches that generate evaluators from specifications of program requirements and detailed designs.

Advances in computer hardware provide challenging opportunities. Self adaptive software runtime support also exploits opportunities identified by evaluators and replanning operations to restore/improve functionality or performance. It is clear that reconfigurable software could provide a useful top level application programming level for reconfigurable hardware.   In such a system, the hardware configuration would simply be another resource to be scheduled and planned.   Another opportunity lies in helping to address the increasing mismatch between processor speed and memory access speeds. One of the approaches being taken is to move portions of processing out to memory modules, to reduce the requirement to move all data to main microprocessor. Self adaptive and reconfigurable software can play a role in dynamically determining the distribution of components in such highly parallel architectures.

Negotiation

One of the ancillary problems to be addressed in any software system, (and the primary problem of some systems), is resource allocation and resolution of resource contention. The principal tool humans use for these problems is negotiation, and active software aims at the same goal. The advantages of negotiation are that it is inherently distributed, inherently multi-dimensional, and robust against changes in circumstances. Although centralized, one dimensional (e.g. price) negotiation is possible, it is neither necessary nor natural. Negotiated settlements need not themselves be robust against changed circumstances, but then the answer is to simply renegotiate, so no special exception handling is required.

Commercial business processes, logistics systems, and DoD weapon and C3 systems, all have hierarchical control, gatekeeping barriers, and incur delays based on unnecessary human interaction. The hierarchical control induces a command fan-out and data fan-in problem that seriously limits the ability of such systems to scale with the problems they are designed to solve. In many cases we improve our ability to manage such systems by distributing computing resources, but without making the crucial application changes needed to make these applications genuinely distributed in nature. Organization with compartmented groups inhibits the flow of information and commands needed to rapidly respond to crises and an adversary's moves. In addition, passing data and commands across these organizational barriers includes further delay as items are added to input queues of human action processors.

Logistics provides paradigm examples of systems that cannot afford centralized control and decision making, nor afford artificial limits on scalability. Weapon systems that must respond to attacks automatically, such as Aegis or Electronic Countermeasures (ECM), are extreme examples that add a requirement of hard real-time response. What is needed are locally competent and efficient mechanisms for assessing situations and taking actions, which percolate information and intelligence up to higher levels, I.e. a *bottom-up* approach to system operation. The bottom-up approach emphasizes peer-to-peer communication, and *negotiation* as a technique for resolving ambiguities and conflicts. This entails a fundamentally new approach to how we build the complex systems of the future, (see [21]).

The new approach promises multiple benefits:
- Near linear scalable systems
- Highly modular, recombinant systems with distributed problem solving
- Removal of middle-man organizations in logistics and planning

The goal of Negotiation Software Agents (NSA) is to autonomously negotiate the assignment and customization of dynamic resources to dynamic tasks. To do this we must enable designers to build systems that operate effectively in highly decentralized environments, making maximum use of local information, providing solutions that are both good enough, and soon enough. These systems will have components that communicate effectively with local peers, and also with information and command concentrators at higher levels of situation abstraction. They will explicitly represent goals, values, and assessments of likelihood and assurance, and reason about those quantities and qualities in order to accomplish their task.

Negotiation systems will scale to much larger problem sizes by making maximum use of localized, rather than global information, and by explicitly making decision theoretic trade-offs with explicit time-bounds on calculation of actions. This new technology will enable us to build systems that are designed to utilize, *at the application level*, all the distributed, networked computational resources (hardware, operating systems, and communication) that have been developed over the past two decades. These advantages will be especially effective in cooperative action, since the process of matching tasks and resources is naturally decentralized in the NSA approach.

The first NSA task is development of the basic framework for bottom-up organization. This includes three subtasks, the first of which is discovery of peer NSAs, and their capabilities, tasks and roles. Second, NSAs must be able to determine how to get access to data, information and authorizations, and they must have secure authorization procedures. Finally, there must also be processes for coordination and information sharing at levels above the peer NSAs.

The second NSA task is reasoning based negotiation. Its subtasks are: handling alternatives, tradeoffs, and uncertainty, including noting when new circumstances conflict with current plans; enabling speedy, optimized and time-bounded reasoning processes to allow for real-time response; and procedures for assuring that goals are met.

A promising approach to reasoning under uncertainty is to use explicit decision theoretic methods, and develop heuristics and approximate decision theoretic approaches. Use of market based trading ([18], [19] and [20]), and qualitative probabilities are alternative approximate approaches. Satisficing and anytime algorithms will also be useful.

Tolerant Software and Interfaces

As an alternative to the approach of increasing precision to make applications "bullet-proof", we envision that reliability will result from an ability to tolerate non-critical variations from nominal specification. The concept of software tolerance derives from a consideration of the concept of mechanically interchangeable parts, and the role they played in the industrial revolution. In order for parts to be interchangeable (and hence significantly speedup the assembly of mechanical devices) there had to be a match between the ability to produce similar parts, and the ability of the overall design to accommodate whatever differences remained among the similar parts. Software systems today have highly intolerant designs, requiring components that exactly match rigid requirements. While this mechanical view of tolerance is useful, and has a direct analog in the area of component technology and software reuse, there are other significant aspects to tolerance. For example, we often don't need mathematically exact answers to questions for which such answers are possible. We often don't need exhaustive searches when those are conceptually possible but impractical. Tolerance involves a critical examination of acceptable variation, and engineering methods and technology in support of building systems with appropriate tolerance.

Tolerant software covers three related concepts:

1. Applications that don't have to be 100% correct – these include algorithms that are inherently probabilistic, applications where the answer is always checked by humans, queries that are inherently inexact (e.g. "Show me a selection of restaurants in Oxford.")
2. Lower level software that is checked by higher level applications and system software – examples are disk controllers, memory subsystems, UDP network protocol (checked by TCP layer or application software).
3. Analogy of mechanical tolerance, and interchangeable parts – this in particular includes software interfaces, word processor input formats, and middleware (RPC,RMI,CORBA [15]) information exchange, for example.

Other examples include:

*   a web search engine, in which 24 by 7 availability is more important than being able to access the full database on every query;
*   mailer software advertising a conference, or new product - not every potential recipient needs to receive it;
*   object oriented programming systems, which often have highly specific code dispatched for arguments of specific types, and a more general (and less optimal) code for dealing with the remainder of cases.

Tolerant Interfaces

We said the concept of interface tolerance derives from a consideration of the concept of mechanically interchangeable parts, and the role they played in the industrial revolution. The place where this analogy comes closest in software systems is in the interfaces between software modules or components, which play the role of mechanical parts. Unlike the case of mechanical tolerances, based on standards and static design principles, tolerant interfaces are active interfaces. Tolerant interfaces know how they interface with other modules, know or can find out how other modules handle their own side of interfacing, and can modify their own interface behavior to meet the requirements of interfacing with other modules. Thus tolerant interfaces can actively modify their interface behavior to meet interface requirements. They may also need to be able to negotiate interface responsibilities with other modules, in much the same way that modems today negotiate over the protocol they will use during data communication.

Clearly, to have these capabilities, the code will need to contain and operate on explicit descriptions of intent, specifications, design, program structure and mapping of tasks to functions. Also, the code will need to contain a large number of alternative interface implementations, or have access to such alternatives over network connections.

Another important concept for tolerant interfaces is that of wrapped data (objects, agents or smart data). Consider, for example, self-extracting compressed archives of programs. The file contains the software needed to decompress, and install the program at your site. Even now such installation programs accept some parameters from the user, but more could be done in this regard. This type of approach is useful in situations where you have data exchange where provider and consumer share responsibility or capability to operate on the data.

Imagine a sensor-actuator application, in which image data is gathered by a sensor, and delivered to a consumer that controls actuators. The sensor module sends data wrapped/prefixed with code for interpretation of the data. The consumer needs to change some operators or filters, in the context of the sensor's interpretation code. The sensor and consumer code cooperatively arrange interfaces and a configuration suitable for the appropriate sharing of processing tasks and algorithms.

Tolerant software requires research on:
- Automated analysis and implementation of interface requirements
- data wrapping/prefixing
- calculation and mitigation of risks and consequences of software breakdown
- assurance/validity checking for tolerant combinations
- performance optimization

We mentioned earlier that the relationships of these components of active software are not simple. Negotiation technology can clearly be used to help build active tolerant interfaces, and tolerant interfaces are necessary for self adaptive software.

Physically Grounded Software

The most challenging software to write, debug, and maintain is software for embedded systems. Traditionally, we produce such software by writing relatively low level code, and counting cycles and memory usage in order to ensure real time requirements. Behavioral assurance is very hard to obtain, requiring combinations of difficult verification technology and exhausting (but not exhaustive) testing. This approach to embedded software will not continue to work as systems get more complex, more connected and require more functionality. In place of traditional approaches, we are advocating Physically Grounded Software (PGS). PGS is software that is thoroughly model based. It incorporates models of its environment, of its operational theory, of its behavior and of crucial physical quantities, including time, space, information and computational requirements. Those models will drive the design of systems, generation of code, refinement and maintenance of systems, and evaluation of behavior and behavioral guarantees.

We argue that computational power for embedded systems is becoming abundant. We should use this power to ease the design problem of embedded systems. This will require development of model driven simulations, for both design and runtime, development of language support for computations about time, space and other physical quantities, and special support for composition of such modules with behavioral guarantees, which we are calling a framework.

The age of shoehorning complex embedded systems into feeble processors is coming to an end. In avionics, for example, today's embedded software systems are the glue which integrate the entire platform, presenting high level situation awareness to the pilot. But since these systems must evolve constantly; our traditional approaches of entangling concerns in order to meet space and time constraints has led to unmaintainable software systems which are inconsistent with the goal of evolution.

Embedded systems that attempt to use software to integrate collections of systems, such as integrated avionics, require a model-based approach to be comprehensible, maintainable and evolvable.   Model based approaches must further tie together standard operational control and failure recovery via models that relate layered systems dealing with behavior at different levels of generality and abstraction. In particular, an overall mission oriented model, with goals and plans is required to generate recovery actions. Subgoals and subtasks must recurse through the layers of the embedded systems to assist in tying the relevant behavior models together.

PGS is a prerequisite for successful autonomous systems.   The goals of autonomous systems are reliable, safe, and cooperative operation of free-ranging systems in the world. There are numerous examples of autonomous systems: agent-based software that ranges over cyberspace performing information services including retrieval and delivery of information [5]; autonomous air, land, or sea vehicles; autonomous mobile robots in physical proximity to humans; automated plants and factories; and automated maintenance and repair systems. Such systems need to cooperate with each other and with humans.

Autonomous systems must also be reliable and robust enough to serve in real world, changing environments. A gross metric for the safety and reliability of such systems is that they be safe and reliable enough to actually be deployed and used where unsafe, unreliable operation would cause physical or economic harm. Reliability implies an element of goal driven operation, which requires the ability to dynamically structure and utilize resources to achieve a desired external state change, and the ability to handle uncertainty, and unpredicted situations. Robustness means that a desired behavior or functionality is maintained under changing external and internal conditions.   Reliability and robustness assumes dynamic internal organization, integrated self-monitoring, diagnostics and control, and fully integrated design of the physical processes and information processing that forms the autonomous system. An increasingly important requirement for autonomous systems is cooperation. Cooperation is an ability to participate in the dynamic distribution of goals (and tasks) and in the coordinated execution of required behaviors.

Embedded software should be developed against the backdrop of model based frameworks, each tailored to a single (or a small set of) issues. A framework, as we use the term, includes:

- a set of properties with which the framework is concerned,
- a formal ontology of the domain,
- an axiomatization of the core domain theory,
- analytic (and/or proof) techniques tailored to these properties and their domain theory,
- a runtime infrastructure providing a rich set of services, and
- an embedded language for describing how a specific application couples into the framework.

A framework thus reifies a model in code, API, and in the constraints and guarantees the model provides. Frameworks should be developed with a principled relation to the underlying model, and preferably generated from a specification of the model. The specification of the model should be expressed in terms of an embedded language that captures the terms and concepts used by application domain experts.

The ontology of each framework constitutes a component of a semantically rich meta-language in which to state annotations of the program (e.g. declarations, assertions, requirements). Such annotations inform program analysis. They also facilitate the writing of high level generators which produce the actual wrapper methods constituting the code of a particular aspect.

Corresponding to each framework are analytic (or proof) tools that can be used to examine the code which couples to this framework. Each such analytic framework can show that a set of properties in its area of concern is guaranteed to hold as long as the remaining code satisfies a set of constraints. The analysis of the overall behavior of the system is, therefore, decomposed.

References

[1]   I. Ben-Shaul, A. Cohen, O. Holder, and B. Lavva, ``HADAS: A network-centric system for interoperability programming,'' International Journal of Cooperative Information Systems (IJCIS),vol. 6, no. 3&4, pp. 293--314, 1997.
[2]   ``Self adaptive software,'' December, 1997. DARPA, BAA 98-12, Proposer Information Pamphlet, www.darpa.mil/ito/Solicitations/ PIP_9812.html.
[3]   Garlan, David & Shaw, Mary. "An Introduction to Software Architecture," 1-39. Advances in Software Engineering and Knowledge Engineering Volume 2. New York, NY: World Scientific Press, 1993.

[4]   Garlan, D.; Allen, R.; & Ockerbloom, J. "Exploiting Style in Architectural Design Environments." SIGSOFT Software Engineering Notes 19, 5 (December 1994): 175-188.

[5]   Jennings, K. Sycara, and M. Wooldridge A Roadmap of Agent Research and Development. In Autonomous Agents and Multi-Agent Systems, Vol. 1, No. 1, July, 1998, pp. 7 - 38.

[6]   G. Karsai and J. Sztipanovits. A model-based approch to self-adaptive software. IEEE Intelligent Systems,May/June 1999:46{53,1999.

[7]   Kiczales G., Lamping J., Mendhekar A. et al. *Aspect-Oriented Programming.* In proc. European Conference on Object-Oriented Programming, Finland, 1997.

[8]   M. M. Kokar, K. Baclawski, and Y. Eracar. Control theory-based foundations of self-controlling software . IEEE Intelligent Systems,May/June 1999:37{45,1999.

[9]   R. Laddaga. Creating robust software through self-adaptation. IEEE Intelligent Systems, May/June 1999:26{29,1999.

[10]   Luckham, David C., et al. "Specification and Analysis of System Architecture Using Rapide." IEEE Transactions on Software Engineering 21, 6 (April 1995): 336-355.

[11]   Nenad Medvidovic, Alex Quilici, David S. Rosenblum, and Alexander L. Wolf. An Architecture-Based Approach to Self-Adaptive Software. IEEE Intelligent Systems and Their Applications, vol. 14, no. 3, pp. 54-62 (May/June 1999).

[12]   Nenad Medvidovic and Richard N. Taylor. Exploiting Architectural Style to Develop a Family of Applications. IEE Proceedings Software Engineering, vol. 144, no. 5-6, pp. 237-248 (October-December 1997).

[13]   D. J. Musliner, R. P.Goldman,M.J.Pelican, and K. D. Krebsbach, ``Self-Adaptive Software for Hard Real-Time Environments," IEEE Intelligent Systems,vol. 14, no. 4, pp. 23--29, July/August 1999.

[14]   G. Nordstrom, J. Sztipanovits, G. Karsai, A. Ledeczi: "Metamodeling - Rapid Design and Evolution of Domain-Specific Modeling Environments", Proceedings of the IEEE Conference and Workshop on Engineering of Computer Based Systems, April, 1999.

[15]   Object Management Group, The Common Object Request Broker: Architecture and Specification. Revision 2.2,February 1998. Available at: http://www.omg.org/corba/corbaiiop.html.

[16]   P. Robertson and J. M. Brady. Adaptive image analysis for aerial surveillance. IEEE Intelligent Systems,May/June 1999:30{36,1999.

[17]   J. Sztipanovits, G. Karsai: "Model-Integrated Computing", IEEE Computer, April, 1997

[18]   CA Waldspurger, T Hogg, B Huberman, JO Kephart, and WS Stornetta: Spawn: A Distributed Computational Economy.   IEEE Transactions on Software Engineering 18:103-117.

[19]   Wellman, M: "Market-oriented programming: Some early lessons." In Market-Based Control: A Paradigm for Distributed Resource Allocation (S Clearwater, ed.). World Scientific, 1996.

[20]   Wellman, M: A market-oriented programming environment and its application to distributed multicommodity flow problems. Journal of Artificial Intelligence Research, 1:1-23, 1993.

[21]   ``Autonomous Negotiating Teams," October, 1998. DARPA, BAA 99-05, Proposer Information Pamphlet, www.darpa.mil/ito/Solicitations/ PIP_9905.html.

Continuous Self-Evaluation for the Self-Improvement of Software

Leon J. Osterweil and Lori A. Clarke

Department of Computer Science, University of Massachusetts,
Amherst, MA 01003 USA

1 Introduction

Software systems are increasingly essential to the operation of all aspects of our society. Clearly the operation of these systems has profound effects on society. Less recognized, but no less important, is the effect that societal activity has on software, placing continual pressure upon software systems to improve. In that software systems function as societal change agents, it follows naturally that the changes wrought by software systems rebound back as pressures for these systems themselves to improve in order to meet more closely the changing requirements of society. These pressures are felt as growing gaps between societal requirements and operational profiles. These gaps serve both as measures of required improvement and as vectors that should be used to direct improvement efforts and measure their success.

Evaluation of operational profiles is thus clearly central to all software improvement efforts. We are interested in self-improving software systems, namely those incorporating mechanisms for the automation of the improvement process. In this paper we suggest one such mechanism, namely the automation of the process of continuous self-evaluation. This process should be designed to continuously measure the gap between software system operation and requirements, thereby providing a basis for self improvement efforts, and a yardstick by which the success of these efforts can be measured.

In a manual, or human-driven, software improvement process humans take the lead in carrying out the testing and evaluation of software, humans infer the changes that need to be made, humans effect the changes, and humans reinstall the modified software, at which point the improvement cycle begins again. Software self-improvement suggests that some or all of these activities are to be assisted, or entirely carried out, autonomously by the software itself, rather than being done solely by humans. Self-improvement also suggests that the impetus for improvement can come from observations that the system makes upon itself, rather than from human initiative. Thus a self-improving system might be expected to be improving continuously, rather than only when humans elect to attempt improvements. In this paper we describe how we propose to transition much of the responsibility for testing and evaluation of software from humans and onto automated tools and processes. We indicate where there is interesting research required in order to reduce the dependence upon humans in improvement activities.

P. Robertson, H. Shrobe, and R. Laddaga (Eds.): IWSAS 2000, LNCS 1936, pp. 27–39, 2000.

The essence of our idea is that deployed software should be under continuous testing, analysis, and evaluation, drawing heavily upon the computational resources and actual utilization patterns found in the deployment environment. As the amount and nature of possible testing and analysis are virtually limitless, there is value in continuing these activities perpetually. It is important, however, that the activities not be unfocussed or undirected. We propose that the process of perpetual testing and analysis be guided by incremental results and findings so as to produce increasingly sharp and definitive results. It is suggested that these results will inevitably lead to increasingly well-informed suggestions about what modifications to the software seem most likely to lead to real improvements. Thus, our perpetual testing and analysis proposal is aimed not only at reducing the need for human involvement in evaluation, but also at assisting human effort in proposing improvements.

There are substantial technical challenges in doing this. We propose that both dynamic testing and static analysis go on essentially endlessly, but that results from each of these activities be used to focus and sharpen the other's activity. Research into how best to make these two complementary evaluation approaches most synergistic is needed. We envision orchestrating this synergy through the use of precisely defined processes, and there is considerable research to be done in this area as well.

2   Approach

While self-modifying code has existed since the earliest days of computing [1], there is ample evidence that it poses clear dangers. Of most concern to us is the fact that self-modifying code is generally difficult or impossible to analyze, and therefore the range of its possible behaviors is difficult or impossible to bound. For this reason we seek a way in which software can modify itself, without necessitating the need for code to modify itself.

Our approach to this problem is to view a software product as an aggregate of diverse types of software artifacts, including such types of components as a requirements specification, an architecture, low level design specifications, code, test cases, and analysis results (eg. see Figure 1). Going further, Figure 1 also suggests that the software product is also characterized by a variety of constraints that specify the way in which the various components should be related to each other. The constraints are particularly important because they are to be used to determine when and how the components of the product need to be modified. Thus, for example, when test results derived through execution of testcases are inconsistent with the requirements to which they should be related, this is a signal that product modification is needed.

The foregoing suggests that a collection of tools should also be considered to be part of the software product. These tools are the devices that are used to help build the components of the product and to determine the degree to which the product is internally consistent. Thus, as is further suggested by Figure 1,

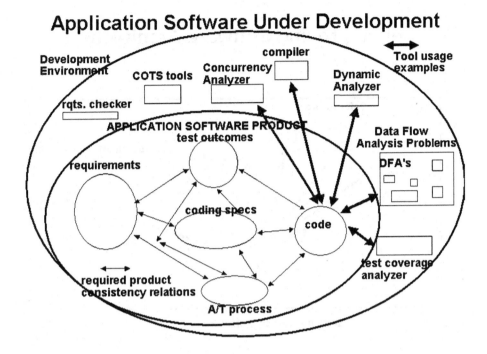

Fig. 1.

compilers, design tools, testcase monitors, and static analyzers are all examples of tools that should be considered to be part of the overall software product.

While we suggest that a complete software product should be viewed as this complex aggregate of artifacts, relations and tools, we also suggest that responsibility for the evaluation and modification of this product reside outside of the software product itself. In Figure 2, we indicate that a complete self-modifying software product also include, in addition to the software product itself, a component that contains the process by which various components of the software product (code, in particular) are to be modified. By doing so we assure that no component of the software product need modify itself. Rather, a separate component, the modification process, is responsible for modifying other components, such as the code.

In classical software development, tools are applied in order to build and test the product and its components right up until deployment. But at deployment the product code is separated from the rest of the components, and from its constraints and tools, and is placed in the deployed environment (see Figure 3). As a consequence the deployed code can no longer be evaluated as thoroughly and easily. Modifications to the deployed code are made without the aid of development tools, and often without being related to non- code artifacts. Ultimately the deployed code takes on an identity of its own, with poorly understood rela-

Self-Improving Software Architecture

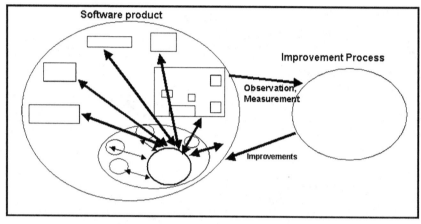

Self-Improving Software Product

Fig. 2.

tions to design, requirements, and even test cases. Thorough evaluation of such code becomes increasingly difficult and the effectiveness of improvement efforts becomes harder to determine.

We propose that deployed software product code remain tethered to the other product components (including the software product modification process), as well as to the constraint and tool sets that comprise a complete product (see Figure 4). By doing this, it becomes possible for powerful development tools to continue to evaluate the consistency of the code with other artifacts and to detemine the effectiveness of improvement efforts. Thus the perpetual testing approach implies that software code be perpetually enhanced by access to an environment that supports its evaluation and improvement (we shall refer to this as the development environment, even though it will persist past initial development), and takes a proactive role in assuring that evaluation continues to make positive contributions to the improvement of the software. Coordination of diverse and numerous types of testing and analysis artifacts that exist in the development and deployed environments is a daunting job that is prohibitively expensive and error-prone if carried out manually. Instead, a highly automated testing and analysis process integrates testing and analysis tools and artifacts, using the available computing resources that can be acquired at any given time.

Deployment: Now

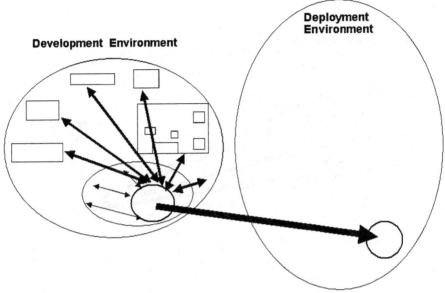

Fig. 3.

Although this process is considered to be an integral part of the product, it is not required to be resident with the code in the deployed environment.

3 Technical and Research Challenges

3.1 Deployment Considerations

It is important to emphasize that the nature of the interconnection and interaction between the development environment and the deployed code that is (presumably) being evaluated perpetually will vary considerably, depending upon the considerable variation in deployment situations. Thus, for example, it may be quite reasonable to expect that non- critical prototype research software deployed, for example, in a university research setting, should be under continuous, thorough, and highly intrusive evaluation, and continual interaction with its development environment. On the other hand, the evaluation of mission critical realtime software code deployed in a military environment may need to be far less thorough and intrusive in order to avoid dangerous degradation of performance. We contend that continuous monitoring and evaluation of all types of software should be the norm. While concerns about degradation of performance of mission critical systems are clearly legitimate, so also must be

Deployment: As it Should Be

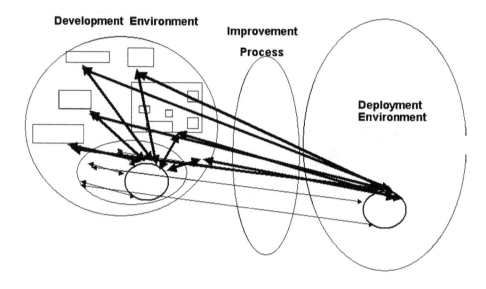

Fig. 4.

concerns about the need to continuously improve such systems. Without continuous monitoring, such improvement efforts can become needlessly expensive and ineffective. Clearly there is a large spectrum of deployment situations between the two extremes just illustrated. It is our belief, however, that we can fashion a corresponding spectrum of approaches to supporting the provision of the benefits of perpetual testing. Certainly the degree to which it is feasible to connect deployed code to the rest of the product will dictate the degree of likely effectiveness of self-evaluation and self-improvement.

Clearly the furnishing of parameterized monitoring capabilities, controls over communication between deployment and development environments, and rehosting of major portions of the development environment can be used to tailor specific perpetual testing implementations. All of these pose significant technical challenges that need to be addressed by research.

3.2   Analysis and Testing Research

Clearly the core of the needed research centers on the area of testing and analysis. In the section we identify the key testing and analysis research issues that must be addressed in order to bring the promise of perpetual testing to fruition

Incremental Retesting and Reanalysis As suggested above, the essence of perpetual testing is to continuously track the widening gap between operational software behaviors and increasing pressures for improvement caused by continuous evolution of requirements. Thus, testing cannot be thought of as a batch process taking place from time to time, and having well-defined starting and ending points. Rather, testing and analysis are ongoing activities that must continuously build upon past results, and continuously produce new incremental results that are themselves to be viewed as the basis for further increments.

This incremental view of testing and analysis is not new, being conceptually quite similar to work done on smart, optimized regression testing [12,20,19,21]. This earlier work has been aimed at determining which sections of an evolved software system have not been altered by the evolution, and then determining which test cases and analyses need not be repeated in order to study the behavior of the evolved system. Sections of the evolved program that implement new and altered behaviors are thus identified as subjects requiring new testing and analysis. Often these new testing and analysis regimes can be evolved from earlier test cases and analysis problems.

Unfortunately, much of this earlier work assumes, usually of necessity, that the evolving software system does not have a requirements specification against which it is to be evaluated. That being the case, the best that can be done is to partition the software into those parts that have not undergone change, and therefore need no reevaluation, and that those have undergone change, and do need reevaluation. In the absence of a requirements specification, however, the nature of the new evaluation of the modified parts must be left ot humans, and cannot benefit substantially from automation.

Our vision of perpetual testing addresses this problem by hypothesizing a rich web of interconnections between the software code and such other key types of artifacts as design elements and requirements specifications. By using this web of interconnections it should be possible to use information about changes in the code and in the requirements to specify not only the code to be retested, but also the sorts of test cases and analysis problems that would be effective.

This discussion suggests some key research issues in this area. One such issue is how to establish a discipline for specifying constraints among the diverse types of artifacts in a software product, and then using these constraints as the basis for synthesizing test cases and analysis problems. Figure 2 indicates general and symbolic types of constraints, but only suggests the specific constraints that function to tie the diverse parts of a software product together. These specific constraints must be the basis for specific testing and analysis regimes. More fundamentally, if there is to be an automatic process for building these test cases and analysis problems, then this process is likely to be most straightforward and tractable if the constraints are all specified using a standard formalism. The nature of that formalism seems to be a basic research issue. The use of such standard mathematical disciplines as predicate logic, set theory, and lambda calculus should be evaluated.

Integration of Techniques A sizeable body of early work in dynamic testing [8,10] has made it very clear that dynamic testing can be highly effective in detecting failures in running software systems, but that this technique is ineffective in demonstrating the absence of faults in such systems. On the other hand it has been demonstrated [16,5] that static analysis systems can demonstrate the absence of faults for many key classes of errors. Early work in formal verification [7,2] showed that it is possible to verify the complete functioning of software systems, but often at very great cost. In still other work [15] it has been shown that these diverse approaches to software evaluation are synergistic in many ways, and that these synergies could be exploited in a Perpetual Testing regime.

Indeed, the vision of Perpetual Testing suggests that different types of evaluation of software systems are likely to be needed at different times, and that different degrees of assurance about software systems are also needed at different times. This suggests that perpetual testing will require diverse analysis and testing techniques to be synergistically integrated and reintegrated dynamically and in diverse ways. Previous research that has described how the different analysis techniques could complement one another [15,22], have proposed fixed integration strategies consistent with the assumption that testing was a phase of fixed duration. These activities have teamed less expensive, but usually less precise, analysis techniques with more expensive, but very precise, techniques, often greatly reducing computation costs and human intervention. For example, static dataflow analysis scans can focus and sharpen dynamic testing regimens, and can be used to iteratively generate and solve successions of dataflow analyses, that iteratively sharpen analytic results. These prototype integrations indicate many opportunities for synergy, and the clear feasibility of effecting new integrations dynamically. Developing such integrations and how to effect them dynamically is clearly a key research issue.

Perpetual testing also entails the need to provide different levels of assurance about software system behavior at different times. Formal verification systems have had an overly simplistic view that a property is either proved (when all relations among its various lemmas and theorems have been proved), or is completely without support. Testing systems have maintained records of thoroughness (various notions of coverage), as well as sets of properties in the form of test oracles, but have not related levels of assurance to particular properties. Static analysis tools have been limited to a distinction between verified properties ("must" results) and inconclusive ("may") results.

Integration of analysis and testing techniques, and particularly integration of post- deployment usage information, provides an opportunity for a far richer set of constraints among properties, techniques, and levels of assurance. For example, a property may be "verified" by a static dataflow analysis that depends upon the absence of an aliasing relation that is monitored in testing. Each asserted property of a software system can be supported by a collection of analyses and assurances of differing strengths, which are propagated through the web of the relations and constraints among the diverse types of software artifacts. Monitoring of deployed software is critical in this regard, and explicit constraint links on patterns monitored in the deployed software provide a way to calibrate and strengthen assurances established in the development environment.

The realization of such sophisticated integrations of tools and technologies, in support of the establishment of such a subtle range of levels of assurance will require a considerable amount of research directed towards determining precisely how the different forms of testing and analysis can support each other.

Specification-based Analysis Testing is currently practiced as a human intensive process. Testers must develop test cases, run the test cases and then evaluate the results. The latter task can be particularly time consuming, tedious, and error prone. Specification-based testing techniques are being developed so that humans no longer have to play the role of oracle [18]. The specification formalisms used should be studies as the basis not only for testing but also for a range of analysis techniques.

Currently different types of analysis are based upon the evaluation of software systems against specifications captured using different formalisms. Thus, for example, some modern dataflow analyzers use a quantified form of regular expressions for expressing properties that are to be validated [13,14,5,6], others use temporal logic specifications[17], while still others use graphical interval logic [3,4]. The different specification formalisms overlap strongly in their expressive power, but also differ to some extent. Thus, different analysis and testing approaches have different ranges of efficacy. If these approaches as to be integrated successfully, the specifications used to drive them must be integrated as well.

Doing so should help the specification base for a software system to grow as a coherent and consistent body of knowledge over time. Over time, as users gain experience with a software product, new specifications will be formulated continuously, some perhaps through the actions of the different analyzers themselves. Faults discovered after deployment are to be captured by new specifications of the intended behavior so that future improvement of the software product can be evaluated against these specifications as well. As the specification base grows, more and more of the reanalysis and retesting should be driven by this base. This should not only improve the quality of the testing and analysis, but should also improve the quality of the software product, and reduce the amount of human intervention required.

Predictive-driven Analysis and Testing A perpetual testing framework provides a unique opportunity to gather metrics about the sequence of modifications to the software product and to use those metrics to predict the most appropriate analysis or testing technique for evaluation of subsequent modifications. For example, a code subcomponent that has a history of containing faults might be given a high priority for reanalysis if it is modified. Information about the kinds of faults that were discovered in the past and metrics about the component itself, such as if it uses concurrency or has complicated data structures, would impact the choice of analysis approach to employ. Also, past execution costs could be used to predict computing resources that would be needed to complete the analysis in a timely fashion. Finally, if one technique proved to require substantial human interaction in the past for problems with a similar metric footprint, then less consumptive techniques would presumably need to be considered.

Recent work on testing and analysis has just started to address using metrics to drive the choice of analysis techniques. With perpetual testing we expect to be able to be more complete and effective in gathering information about the software being evaluated, the kinds of faults discovered (or properties verified) by the analysis and testing techniques, the computing resources used, and the amount of human intervention required. On the basis of this information, we should be able to develop a predictive model of what appears to be the best testing and analysis process. This model would itself be the subject of evaluation and would continue to be modified as we gathered more experimental evidence. This should lead to a predictive meta-model to be incorporated as part of the overall software product. As more information is learned about a particular software product and its modification history, this information would be used by the meta model to evolve a predictive model to drive the testing and analysis process for that software.

3.3   Perpetual Testing Process Development

Analysis and testing activities should be viewed as processes to be developed as software is, from requirements through coding, evaluation, and evolution. This is particularly important for perpetual testing processes. Because they are to be indefinitely ongoing processes, it is essential that clear goals be specified beforehand, so that progress towards those goals be continually monitored, and so that revisions to either goals, of processes, or both can be made continually. Thus, perpetual testing can reasonably be viewed as the integration of sequences of applications of both testing and analysis tools in demonstrable support of precisely articulated analysis and testing goals. Being specific and precise about these goals and requirements seems particularly important.

It also seems particularly important to develop actual executable code for analysis and testing processes. As an example, consider the fact that dynamic regression testing entails iteration that is comfortably expressed with traditional loops. Deciding when and whether to follow coarse-grained, static dataflow analysis with more precise, sharpened dataflow analyses is expressible with traditional case and if-then-else constructs. In both cases, the fine scale detailed specification of exact procedures to carry out in order to obtain the needed analysis products can readily be specified. Doing so in an executable language makes it possible to then used computing power to automate these evaluation processes, thereby moving them towards becoming self-evaluation processes.

Completely automatic testing and analysis processes will require complex control structures. For example, it is often important to program immediate reactive responses to such testing failures as incorrect results and system crashes. Dataflow analysis results may also need to trigger fixed standard subsequent reanalysis. The reporting of analysis results obtained at deployment sites might be triggered by timer events, or by the very action of their being completed. All of these argue for a process language that integrates proactive control constructs with reactive programming constructs.

All of this argues for a powerful and comprehensive language for the specification of actual executable process code to guide the execution of these perpetual testing processes, and therefore the continuous self-evaluation of software products. In our work we have demonstrated such a process programming language [9,11] and we are beginning to use it to program perpetual testing processes. We regard this as promising initial research and suggest the need for more research into process languages and their use to program effective perpetual testing processes.

4   Summary

The perpetual testing and analysis approach promises to enable the continuous self- evaluation of software throughout the sequence of modifications occuring during its entire lifetime, and thereby to enable software self-improvement that can be measured and evaluated. Key to doing this is to perpetually link deployed software code to the rest of the overall software product's components, constraints, tools, and the perpetual testing process itself. This should ultimately increase the confidence that people will have in their software products. As software products become larger and more complex, they will become ever more difficult to evaluate and improve, trust, and predict unless an approach such as perpetual testing is explored.

Acknowledgments

This work is being carried out as a collaboration among: Leon Osterweil, Lori Clarke and George Avrunin at the University of Massachusetts, Debra Richardson at the University of California at Irvine, and Michal Young at the University of Oregon. At the University of Massachusetts, this research was partially supported by the Air Force Research Laboratory/IFTD and the Defense Advanced Research Projects Agency under Contract F30602-97-2-0032. The views and conclusions contained herein are those of the authors and should not be interpreted as necessarily representing the official policies or endorsements, either expressed or implied, of the National Science Foundation, the Defense Advanced Research Projects Agency, the Air Force Research Laboratory/IFTD, or the U.S. Government.

References

1. *IBM 7090 Principles of Operation.*
2. E. W. Dijkstra. *A Discipline of Programming.* Prentice-Hall, Englewood Cliffs N. J., 1976.
3. L. K. Dillon, G. Kutty, L. E. Moser, P. M. Melliar-Smith, and et al. A graphical interval logic for specifying concurrent systems. *ACM Transaction of Software Engineering and Methodology*, 3(2):131–165, 1994.
4. L. K. Dillon and Y. S. Ramakrishna. Generating oracles from your favorite temporal logic specifications. In *Fourth ACM SIGSOFT Symposium on Foundations of Software Engineering*, 1996.
5. M. B. Dwyer and L. A. Clarke. Data flow analysis for verifying properties of concurrent programs. In *Second ACM SIGSOFT Symposium on Foundations of Software Engineering*, pages 62–75, New Orleans, LA, 1994. ACM Press.
6. M. B. Dwyer and L. A. Clarke. Flow analysis for verifying specifications of concurrent and distributed software. Technical Report 99-52, University of Massachusetts, Computer Science Dept., 1999.
7. C. A. R. Hoare. An axiomatic basis of computer programming. *Communications of the ACM*, 12(10):576–583, 1969.
8. W. E. Howden. Functional program testing. *IEEE Transactions on Software Engineering*, SE-6(2):162–169, 1980.
9. S. M. Sutton Jr. and L. J. Osterweil. The design of a next generation process language. In *Joint 6th European Software Engineering Conference and the 5th ACM SIGSOFT Symposium on the Foundations of Software Engineering*, pages 142–158. Springer-Verlag, 1997.
10. R. A. Kemmerer. *Proceedings of the ACM SIGSOFT '89 Third Symposium on Software Testing, Analysis and Verification (TAV3).* 1989.
11. B. S. Lerner, L. J. Osterweil, J. Stanley M. Sutton, and A. Wise. Programming process coordination in little-jil. In *6th European Workshop on Software process Technology (EWSPT '98)*, pages 127–131, Weybridge, UK, 1998. Springer-Verlag.
12. H. K. N. Leung and L. White. A cost model to compare regression at the integration level. In *Conference on Software Maintenance*, pages 201–208, Sorrento, Italy, 1991. IEEE Computer Society Press.
13. K. M. Olender and L. J. Osterweil. Cecil: A sequencing constraint language for automatic static analysis generation. *IEEE Transactions of Software Engineering*, 16(3):268–280, 1992.
14. K. M. Olender and L. J. Osterweil. Interprocedural static analysis of sequencing constraints. *ACM Transactions on Software Engineering and Methodology*, 1(1):21–52, 1992.
15. L. J. Osterweil. Using data flow tools in software engineering. In *Program Flow Analysis: Theory and Application.* Prentice-Hall, Englewood Cliffs N. J., 1981.
16. L. J. Osterweil and L. D. Fosdick. Dave–a validation error detection and documentation system fir fortran programs. *Software Practice and Experience*, 6(4):473–486, 1976.
17. A. Pnueli. The temporal semantics of concurrent programs. In Kahn, editor, *Semantics of Concurrent Computation*, pages 1–20. Springer-Verlag, New York, 1979.
18. D. J. Richardson, S. L. Aha, and T. O. O'Malley. Specification-based test oracles for reactive systems. In *Fourteenth International Conference on Software Engineering*, pages 105–118, Melbourne, Australia, 1992.

19. D. S. Rosenblum, Y. F. Chan, and K. P. Vo. Testtube: A system for selective regression testing. In *Sixteenth International Conference on Software Engineering*, pages 211–220, Sorrento, Italy, 1994.

20. G. Rothermel and M. J. Harrold. A safe efficent algorithm for regression test selection. In *Conference on Software Maintenance*. IEEE Computer Society Press, 1993.

21. G. Rothermel and M. J. Harrold. Selecting regression tests for object-oriented software. In *International Conference on Software Maintenance*, pages 14–25. IEEE Computer Society Press, 1994.

22. M. Young and R. N. Taylor. Combining static concurrency analysis with symbolic execution. *IEEE Transactions on Software Engineering*, 14(10):1499–1511, 1988.

Active Trust Management for Autonomous Adaptive Survivable Systems
(ATM's for AAss's)

Howard Shrobe and Jon Doyle

MIT AI Lab, Cambridge, MA 02139, USA,
hes@ai.mit.edu,
http://www.ai.mit.edu/people/hes/

Abstract. The traditional approaches to building survivable systems assume a framework of absolute trust requiring a provably impenetrable and incorruptible Trusted Computing Base (TCB). Unfortunately, we don't have TCB's, and experience suggests that we never will.

We must instead concentrate on software systems that can provide useful services even when computational resource are compromised. Such a system will 1) Estimate the degree to which a computational resources may be *trusted* using models of possible *compromises*. 2) Recognize that a resource is compromised by relying on a system for long term *monitoring and analysis* of the computational infrastructure. 3) Engage in *self-monitoring, diagnosis and adaptation* to best achieve its purposes within the available infrastructure. All this, in turn, depends on the ability of the application, monitoring, and control systems to engage in *rational decision making* about what resources they should use in order to achieve the best ratio of expected benefit to risk.

1   A Scenario

Within the MIT Artificial Intelligence Laboratory an ensemble of computers runs a Visual Surveillance and Monitoring application. On January 12, 2001 several of the machines experience unusual traffic from outside the lab. Intrusion Detection systems report that several password scans were observed. Fortunately, after about 3 days of varying levels of such activity, things seem to return to normal; for another 3 weeks no unusual activity is noticed. However, at that time, one of the machines (named Harding) which is crucial to the application begins to experience unusually high load averages and the application components which run on this machine begin to receive less than the expected quality of service. The load average, degradation of service, the consumption of disk space and the amount of traffic to and from unknown outside machines continue to increase to annoying levels. Then they level off. On March 2, a second machine in the ensemble (Grant) crashes; fortunately, the application has been written in a way which allows it to adapt to unusual circumstances. The system considers whether it should migrate the computations which would normally have run on Grant to

P. Robertson, H. Shrobe, and R. Laddaga (Eds.): IWSAS 2000, LNCS 1936, pp. 40–49, 2000.

Harding; however, these computations are critical to the application. The system decides that in spite of the odd circumstances noticed on Harding earlier, it is a reasonable choice.

Did the system make a good choice? It turns out it did. The system needed to run those computations somewhere; even though Harding was loaded more heavily than expected, it still represented the best pool of available computational resources, other machines were even more heavily loaded with other critical computations of the application. But what about all the unusual activity that had been noticed on Harding? It turns out that what had, in fact, transpired is that hackers had gained access to Harding by correctly guessing a password; using this they had set up a public FTP site containing among other things pirated software and erotic imagery. They had not, in fact, gained root access. There was, therefore, no worry that the critical computations migrated to Harding would experience any further compromise. (Note: the adaptive system in this story is fictional, the compromised computers reflect an amalgam of several real incidents).

Let's suppose instead that (1) the application was being run to protect a US embassy in Africa during a period of international tension (2) that we had observed a variety of information attacks being aimed at Harding earlier on (3) that at least some of these attacks are of a type known to be occasionally effective in gaining root access to a machine like Harding and that (4) they are followed by a period of no anomalous behavior other than a periodic low volume communication with an unknown outside host. When Grant crashes, should Harding be used as the backup? In this case, the answer might well be the opposite; for it is quite possible that an intruder has gained root access to Harding; it is also possible that the intent of the intrusion is malicious and political. It is less likely, but still possible, that the periodic communication with the unknown outside host is an attempt to contact an outside control source for a "go signal" that will initiate serious spoofing of the application. Under these circumstance, it is wiser to shift the computations to a different machine in the ensemble even though it is considerably more overloaded than Harding.

What can we learn from these examples?

1. It is crucial to estimate to what degree and for what purposes a computer (or other computational resource) may be *trusted*, as this influences decisions about what tasks should be assigned to them, what contingencies should be provided for, and how much effort to spend watching over them.

2. Making this estimate depends in turn on having a model of the possible ways in which a computational resource may be *compromised*.

3. This in turn depends on having in place a system for long term *monitoring and analysis* of the computational infrastructure which can detect patterns of activity such as "a period of attacks followed by quiescence followed by increasing degradation of service". Such a system must be capable of assimilating information from a variety of sources including both self-checking observation points within the application itself and intrusion detection systems.

4. The application itself must be capable of *self-monitoring and diagnosis* and capable of *adaptation* so that it can best achieve its purposes with the available infrastructure.
5. This, in turn, depends on the ability of the application, monitoring, and control systems to engage in *rational decision making* about what resources they should use in order to achieve the best ratio of expected benefit to risk.

Systems that can do the above things can be resilient in the face of concerted information attacks. They can carry on through non-malicious intrusions; that is they can figure out when compromises within the infrastructure can't actually hurt them.

Our claim is simple but revolutionary: "Survivable systems make careful judgments about the trustworthiness of their computational environment and make rational resource allocation decisions accordingly."

The claim is deceptively simple: To make it real one needs to develop serious representations of the types of compromises, of the trustworthiness of a resource, and of the goals and purposes of the computational modules within an application. One also needs to build monitoring, analysis and trend detection tools and adaptive computational architectures. Finally, one needs to find a way to make the required rational decision making computationally tractable. None of this is easy, but we have ideas and ongoing projects addressing each of these issues.

2   Trust in Survivable Systems

Traditional approaches to building survivable systems assume a framework of absolute trust. In this view, survivable systems require a provably impenetrable and incorruptible Trusted Computing Base (TCB). Unfortunately, we don't have TCB's, and experience suggests that we never will.

Instead, we will need to develop systems that can survive in an imperfect environment in which any resource may have been compromised to some extent. We believe that such systems can be built by restructuring the ways in which systems organize and perform computations. The central thrust of this approach is a radically different viewpoint of the trust relationships that a software system must bear to the computational resources it needs.

The traditional TCB-based approach takes a binary view of trust; computational resources either merit trust or not, and non-trusted resources should not be used. The traditional view also considers trustworthiness as a nearly static property of a resource: trust lost is never regained, short of major system reconstruction. Consequently, these systems wire decisions about how and where to perform computations into the code, making these decisions difficult to understand, and preventing the system from adapting to a changing runtime environment.

We agree with this viewpoint on the crucial role of the assessment and management of trust, but reject the assumptions about the binary, static nature of trust relationships as poor approximations to real-life computing situations. We instead base our approach on a different, more realistic set of assumptions:

1. All computational resources must be considered suspect to some degree, but the degree of trust that should be accorded to a computational resource is not static, absolute, or known with full certainty. In particular, the degree of trustworthiness may change with further compromises or efforts at amelioration in ways that can only be estimated on the basis of continuing experience. The system must thus continuously and actively monitor the computational environment at runtime to gather evidence about trustworthiness and to update its trust assessments.
2. Exploiting assessments of trustworthiness requires structuring computations into layers of abstract services, with many distinct instantiations of each service. These specific instantiations of a service may vary in terms of the fidelity of the answers that they provide, the conditions under which they are appropriate, and the computational resources they require. But since the resources required by each possible instantiation have varying degrees of trustworthiness, each different way of rendering the service also has a specific risk associated with it.
3. The best method for exploiting assessments of trustworthiness requires making explicit the information underlying decisions about how (and where) to perform a computation, and on formalizing this information and the method used to make the decision in a decision-theoretic framework. The overall system adapts to the dynamism of the environment and to the changing degrees of compromise in its components by deciding dynamically which approach to rendering a service provides the best likelihood of achieving the greatest benefit for the smallest risk. We do not require that the system uses explicit decision-theoretic calculations of maximal expected utility to make runtime decisions; the system may instead use the decision-theoretic formalizations to decide on policies and policy changes, which then are used to compile new code governing the relevant behaviors.
4. The system must consider selected components to be fallible, even if it currently regards them as trustworthy, and must monitor its own and component behaviors to assure that the goals of computations are reached. In the event of a breakdown, the system must first update its assessments of the trustworthiness of the computational resources employed and then select an alternative approach to achieving the goal.

2.1 How Active Trust Management Can Support Autonomous Adaptive Survivable Systems

These considerations motivate an architecture both for the overall computational environment (Active Trust Management) and for the application systems which run within it (Autonomous Adaptive Survivable Systems). The environment as a whole must constantly collect and analyze data from a broad variety of sources, including the application systems, intrusion detection systems, system logs, network traffic analyzers, etc. The results of these analyses inform a "Trust Model", a probabilistic representation of the trustworthiness of each computational resource in the environment. The application systems use this trust model to help decide which resources should be used to perform each major computational step; in particular, they try to choose that resource which will maximize the ratio of expected benefit to risk. This "rational decision making" facility is provided as a standard utility within the environment. The application systems also monitor the execution of their own major components, checking that expected post-conditions are achieved. If these conditions fail to hold, diagnostic services are invoked to determine the most likely cause of the failures and thereby to determine the most promising way to recover. In addition to localizing the failure, the diagnostic services can also infer that underlying elements of the computational infrastructure are likely to have been compromised and these deductions are forwarded to the monitoring and analysis components of the environment to help inform its assessments of trustworthiness. Finally, having accumulated sufficient evidence, the monitoring and analysis systems may decide that it is likely that some resource has, in fact, been compromised. This will have an immediate impact if the resource is being used to perform a computation which would be damaged by that specific form of compromise; in such cases, the monitoring and analysis components transmit "alarms" into the running application, causing it to abandon its work and to immediately initiate recovery efforts.

Thus the application system forms a tight feedback control loop whose goal is to guarantee the best possible progress towards providing the services the application is intended to provide to its users (i.e. the applications are Autonomous Adaptive Survivable Systems "AASS's"). The computational infrastructure also forms a feedback control loop whose goal is to maintain an accurate assessment of the trustworthiness of the computational resources; this assessment can then inform the application systems' decision making and self-monitoring which in turn helps inform the long-term assessments of trustworthiness (Active Trust Management "ATM").

This vision leads us to focus our efforts in four major areas:

1. Models of Trust and Compromise
2. Perpetual Analytic Monitoring
3. Autonomous Adaptive Survivable Systems
4. Rational Decision Making in a Trust-Driven Environment

3   Models of Trust and Compromise

Making rational decisions about how to use resources in an environment of imperfect trust requires information about what resources can be trusted, and for what purposes. We are developing models of trust states that go beyond mere information about whether or how a system has been subject to attack to represent whether or how different properties of the system have been compromised, and finally to represent whether they can be trusted for a particular purpose even if compromised. We also represent the degree to which these judgments should be suspected or monitored.

These models provide the point of intersection among all the other elements of the proposed approach. Trust plays a central role in resource allocation decisions. All decisions about what to do must be based on beliefs about the situation in which the action is to be taken. We can think of the degree of trust one places in a system as the degree to which one is willing to rely on the proper functioning of the system without also dedicating unusual effort to preparing for the contingency of failure. Since preparations for contingencies consume resources, this makes trust management a central resource allocation issue.

The trust model is organized into three levels above that of raw behavior:

The lowest level of the trust model represents the results of initial interpretations such as *attacks* and *anomalous behavior*. At this level we collect, filter and organize the necessary information so that it can trigger trend templates and feed into Bayesian inference networks. As we saw in our scenarios, we are not primarily interested in what attacks or anomalous behaviors have taken place, but rather in what they imply about what compromises might actually be present.

The middle level of the trust model deals with *compromises*. The attack level only tells us that malicious or anomalous activity has taken place. But what we are interested in is whether someone has actually succeeded in an attack and has used that to exploit or corrupt resources. That such a compromise has occurred can be inferred by matching the temporal patterns of activity to a template for a particular compromise. In the scenario we saw an example of this in which the gaining of unauthorized user level access was indicated by the temporal pattern of password sweeps followed by quiescence followed by increasing resource consumption.

The highest level of the trust model deals with *trustworthiness*. The fact that a resource has been compromised does not in and of itself imply that it is totally unsafe to utilize it. That conclusion depends on the precise way in which the consumer wants to utilize the resource as well as on assessments of the *intention* of the compromiser. In our scenarios, we presented two different examples: in the first the system was compromised by "teenaged hackers" looking for free resources, in the second it was compromised by state-sponsored malicious agents. Clearly, we should generally be more wary of using a resource in the second case than the first; but if we are not very sensitive to quality of service and perhaps only care about the integrity of our data, then the first case is not all that risky.

Knowledge of attack types guides the organization's attempts to defend against future attacks. Knowledge of compromises indicates the threats to operations. Knowledge of trust states guides how the organization carries on in the face of partially-understood compromises. Because intent plays a central role, it too must be modeled throughout the three layers, moving from raw reports about behavior at the base level, to statements about intent in the middle layer and finally entering into assessments of trustworthiness at the highest level.

4   Perpetual Analytic Monitoring Keeps the Trust Model Current by Detecting Trend Patterns Which Are Indicative of Compromise

The Perpetual Analytic Monitoring component of our project is based on the MAITA system which consists of a library of monitoring methods, an architecture for operating networks of monitoring processes, and a flexible, display-oriented control system for quickly constructing, composing, modifying, inspecting, and controlling monitoring networks [3,2,1].

The goal of Perpetual Analytic Monitoring is to assess the trustworthiness of the computational resources in the environment. The scenario illustrates that building a trust model involves more than just detecting an intrusion. Indeed, what was important was a template of activity patterns consisting of several temporal regions: First there was a period of attacks (particularly password scans). Then there was a "quiescent period". Then there was a period of increasing degradation of service. Finally, there was a leveling off of the degradation but at the existing high level. We call such a temporal pattern a "trend template".

A trend template has a temporal component and a value component. The temporal component includes landmark time points and intervals. Landmark points represent significant events in the lifetime of the monitored process. They may be uncertain in time, and so are represented with time ranges. Intervals represent periods of the process that during which constant dynamics obtain. Value changes are described in terms of various standard curves. The value component characterizes constraints on individual data values and specifies constraints that must hold among different data streams. The representation is supported by a temporal utility package (TUP) that propagates temporal bound inferences among related points and intervals [12,11].

The MAITA monitoring method library includes entries at varying levels of computational detail. For example, the most abstract levels speaks of constructing and comparing a set of hypotheses about what is going on, without providing any details about how the hypotheses are constructed or compared. The intermediate level, uses the TrenD$_x$ [8,7,13,10,6] trend monitoring system to recognize trend templates.

Trend templates are necessary, but not sufficient in themselves. We also need to make inferences about the factual situation at hand (e.g., are international tensions rising?) and about the intentions, and states of mind of significant players (e.g., would it be likely that they are trying to attack me?). All of these inferences involve the combining of evidence to provide assessments of the likelihood of certain propositions. Bayesian networks provide a convenient formalism for representing and reasoning with basic probabilistic information.

The principal goal of our Monitoring and Analysis tools is to keep the Trust Model current. However, when these tools have achieved a high degree of confidence that a compromise has occurred, the monitoring and analysis system must generate an alarm asking currently executing application components to rollback and attempt to use alternative strategies and resources.

5 Autonomous Adaptive Survivable Systems Use Trust Models and Self Reflection to Select Computational Strategy and to Recover from Compromise

Autonomous Adaptive Survivable Systems have the goal of adapting to the variations in their environment so as to render useful services under all conditions. In the context of Information Survivability, this means that useful services must be provided even when there have been successful information attacks.

AASS's achieve adaptivity in two ways: First, they include many alternative implementations of the major computational steps, each of which achieves the same goal but in different ways. An AASS is therefore a Domain Architecture; it capitalizes on the "variability within commonality" which is typical of the service layers in any software domain. Each service is annotated with specifications and is provided with multiple instantiations optimized for different purposes.

AASS's are implemented in a *Dynamic* Domain Architecture: all the alternative instantiations of each service, plus the annotations describing them are present in the run-time environment; the decision of which alternative instantiation of a service to employ is made dynamically and as late as necessary. Before each step is actually initiated, the system first assesses which of these is most appropriate in light of what the trust model tells it about compromises and trustability. We may view this as an extremely dynamic and information rich version of Object-Oriented Programming in which method invocation is done in decision-theoretic terms, i.e., we invoke that method most likely to succeed given the current trust state.

The second way in which AASS's achieve adaptivity is by noticing when a component fails to achieve the conditions relied on by other modules, initiating diagnostic, rollback and recovery services. This depends on effective monitoring of system performance and trustworthiness which in turn requires a structured view of the system as decomposed into modules, together with teleological annotations that identify prerequisites, post-conditions and invariant conditions of the modules. These teleological models also include links describing how the post-conditions of the modules interact to achieve the goals of the main system and the prerequisites of modules further downstream. Tools in the development environment use these representations to generate run-time monitors that invoke error-handling services if the conditions fail to be true. The exception-management service is informed by the Dynamic Domain Architecture's models of the executing software system and by a catalog of breakdown conditions and their repairs; using these it diagnoses the breakdown, determines an appropriate scope of repair; possibly selects an alternative to that invoked already and then restarts the computation.

Thus, we remove exception handling from the purview of the programmer, instead treating the management of exceptional conditions as a special service provided by cooperating services in both the run-time and development environments. Model-based diagnostic services [4,9,5,14] play a key role in an AASS's ability to recover from a failure. This is done by providing models not only of the intended behavior of a component but also of its likely failure modes. These application-layer models are linked to models of the behavior of the computational infrastructure on which the application components execute. Again these include models both of expected and compromised behavior. The diagnostic task then is to identify the most likely set of such models which is consistent with the observed behavior. This helps the application decide how to recover from the failure and restore normal functioning. It also provides evidence to the overall monitoring environment about the trustworthiness of the underlying computational resources, particularly when the most likely diagnosis is that one of the resources has been compromised.

In summary, a dynamic domain architecture provides the following services that enable Autonomy, Adaptivity and Survivability in the applicatino System:

1. Synthesis of code that selects which variant of an abstract operator is appropriate in light of run-time conditions.
2. Synthesis of monitors that check whether conditions expected to be true at various points in the execution of a computation are in fact true.
3. Diagnosis and isolation services that locate the cause of an exceptional condition, and characterize the form of the breakdown which has transpired.
4. Selection of alternative methods that achieve the goal of the failed computation using different means (either by trying repairs or by trying alternative implementations, or both).
5. Rollback and recovery services that establish a consistent state of the computation from which to attempt the alternative strategy.
6. Reallocation and re-optimization of resource allocations in light of the resources remaining after the breakdown and the priorities obtaining at that point. These services may optimize the system in a new way in light of the new allocations and priorities.

6 Rational Decision Making Uses Decision-Theoretic Models and the Trust Model to Control Decisions about Component Selection and Resource Allocation

We assess system trustworthiness and performance according to the trust and teleological models in order to make decisions about how to allocate computational resources. To ensure that these decisions represent a good basis for system operation, we are developing detailed decision-theoretic models of trustworthiness, suspicion, and related concepts as applied to information systems and their components. These models will relate notions such as attractiveness of a system as a target, likelihood of being attacked, likelihood of being compromised by an attack, riskiness of use of the system, importance or criticality of the system for different purposes, etc.

The models will also relate estimates of system properties to an adaptive system of decision-theoretic preferences that express the values guiding the operation of both system modules and the system as a whole. We are develop mechanisms that use these elements to allocate system resources optimally given task demands, trustworthiness judgments, and the resources available.

We believe that the combination of these ideas will lead to systems that can adapt to and survive infomation attacks.

References

1. C. Cao, J. Doyle, I. Kohane, W. Long, and P. Szolovits. The MAITA monitoring library and language. In preparation, 1998.
2. C. Cao, J. Doyle, I. Kohane, W. Long, and P. Szolovits. The MAITA monitoring network architecture. In preparation, 1998.
3. C. Cao, J. Doyle, I. Kohane, W. Long, and P. Szolovits. The MAITA system: an overview. In preparation, 1998.
4. R. Davis, H. Shrobe, W. Hamscher, K. Wieckert, M Shirley, S. Polit
Diagnosis Based on Descriptions of Structure and Function
AAAI, National Conference on Artificial Intelligence Pittsburgh, PA., 1992 pp 137-142.
5. J. deKleer and B. Williams
Reasoning About Multiple Faults
AAAI, National Conference on Artificial Intelligence, Philadelphia, Pa., 1986, pp 132-139.
6. J. Fackler, I. J. Haimowitz, and I. S. Kohane. Knowledge-based data display using trendx. In *AAAI Spring Symposium: Interpreting Clinical Data*, Palo Alto, 1994. AAAI Press.
7. I. J. Haimowitz and I. S. Kohane. Automated trend detection with alternate temporal hypotheses. In *Proceedings of the Thirteenth International Joint Conference on Artificial Intelligence*, pages 146–151, Chambery, France, 1993.
8. I. J. Haimowitz and I. S. Kohane. An epistemology for clinically significant trends. In *Proceedings of the Eleventh National Conference on Artificial Intelligence*, pages 176–181, Washington, DC, 1993.
9. W. Hamscher. Modeling digital circuits for troubleshooting. *Artificial Intelligence*, 51:223–227, 1991.
10. I. Kohane and I. Haimowitz. Hypothesis-driven data abstraction. In *Symposium on Computer Applications in Medical Care*, Washington, DC, 1993.
11. I. S. Kohane. Temporal reasoning in medical expert systems. In R. Salamon, B. Blum, and M. Jørgensen, editors, *MEDINFO 86: Proceedings of the Fifth Conference on Medical Informatics*, pages 170–174, Washington, Oct. 1986. North-Holland.
12. I. S. Kohane. Temporal reasoning in medical expert systems. TR 389, Massachusetts Institute of Technology, Laboratory for Computer Science, 545 Technology Square, Cambridge, MA, 02139, Apr. 1987.
13. I. S. Kohane and I. J. Haimowitz. Encoding patterns of growth to automate detection and diagnosis of abnormal growth patterns. *Pediatric Research*, 33:119A, 1993.
14. B. Williams and J. deKleer. Diagnosis with Behavior Modes. In *Proceedings of the 11th Joint Conference on Artificial Intelligence*, IJCAI-89, pages 1324–1330, Detroit MI, 1989 .

Towards Semantics of Self-Adaptive Software

Duško Pavlović

Kestrel Institute, Palo Alto, USA
dusko@kestrel.edu

Abstract. When people perform computations, they routinely monitor their results, and try to adapt and improve their algorithms when a need arises. The idea of self-adaptive software is to implement this common facility of human mind within the framework of the standard logical methods of software engineering. The ubiquitous practice of testing, debugging and improving programs at the design time should be automated, and established as a continuing *run time* routine.

Technically, the task thus requires combining functionalities of automated software development tools and of runtime environments. Such combinations lead not just to challenging engineering problems, but also to novel theoretical questions. Formal methods are needed, and the standard techniques do not suffice.

As a first contribution in this direction, we present a basic mathematical framework suitable for describing self-adaptive software at a high level of semantical abstraction. A static view leads to a structure akin to the Chu construction. An dynamic view is given by a coalgebraic presentation of adaptive transducers.

1 Introduction: Specification Carrying Code

One idea towards self-adaptive software is, very roughly, to introduce some kind of "formalized comments", or Floyd-Hoare style annotations as first class citizens of programs. Together with the executable statements, they should be made available to a generalized, *adaptive* interpreter, extended by an automated specification engine (e.g., SPECWARE™-style), supported by theorem provers and code generators. This adaptive interpreter would not only evaluate the executable statements, but also systematically test how their results and behaviour satisfy the requirements specified in the formal annotations. Such testing data could then be used for generating improved code, better adapted to the specifications, often on the fly. On the other hand, the formal specifications could often also be refined, i.e. adapted to the empiric data obtained from testing a particular implementation.

1.1 Automated Testing and Adaptation

Coupling programs with their specifications in a uniform, automatically supported framework would, at the very least, allow monitoring correctness, reliability,

P. Robertson, H. Shrobe, and R. Laddaga (Eds.): IWSAS 2000, LNCS 1936, pp. 50–64, 2000.

safety and liveness properties of programs, with respect to the specified requirements, as well as the particular distribution of the input data, and any other aspects of the execution environment that may become available at run time.

In some cases, one could hope for more than mere monitoring of the relationship between an abstract specification and its implementation. Indeed, software can often be improved and adapted to its specifications in a predictable fashion, once its running behaviour can be observed on concrete inputs. This is, for instance, usually possible in the cases when the correctness criteria are not absolute, *viz* when the software only approximates its specification. Software that models physical systems, or stochastic processes, or even just computes genuine real numbers or functions, is usually of this kind: the infinitary nature of the output data precludes the exact solutions, which can only be approximated. But the approximations can, in principle, always be improved, on an additional cost. Comparing the actual runs of such software with its abstract specifications may suggest optimizing this cost, say, by adjusting the coefficients in the numeric formulas to the observed distribution of the input data. In some cases, different distributions may even justify applying different algorithms, which can be abstractly classified in advance, so that the adapted code can be synthesized on the fly.

Self-adaptive software can perhaps be compared with an engineer monitoring the results of his computations, updating the methods and refining the model. The point is here that a part of this process of adaptation can and needs to be automated.

1.2 Dynamic Assembly and Reconfiguration

Furthermore, in a complex software system, the adaptation cycle of a software component can take into account not only the run time behaviour of the component itself, but also the behaviour of the other components, and the changes in the environment at large.

In order to be combined, software modules must contain sufficient information about their structure and behavior. Conventional *application programming interfaces*, APIs, are intended to carry such information but APIs are usually under-specified (they contain just signature/type information), are often based on unfulfilled assumptions, and are prone to change. Conventional APIs are thus insufficient for the task of assured composition.

Ideally, APIs would completely capture all assumptions that influence behavior. However, formally verifying such completeness is usually infeasible — some degree of API partiality is inevitable in practical software development. Nevertheless, in dynamically adaptable software, API partiality should continually *decrease* as the interfaces evolve during the lifetime of a system, together with the specifications and implementations of its components and perhaps even its architecture.

We believe that the requirement of dynamically adaptable software naturally leads to the idea of specification-carrying code: an adaptable program must carry a current specification of its functionality, an adaptable specification must come with a partial implementation. Adaptability requires a simultaneous and interactive development of the logical structure and the operational behavior.

Moreover, specification-carrying code is the way to accommodate and support, rather than limit and avoid, the rich dynamics of *ever changing interfaces*, so often experienced in large software systems, with the unpredictable interactions arising from the ever changing environments. The fact that specifications, implementations, interfaces and architectures in principle *never stop changing* during their lifetime, should not be taken as a nuisance, but recognized as the essence of the game of software, built into its semantical foundation, and implemented as a design, and when possible a runtime routine.

Of course, adjusting the behaviour of autonomous software components to each other, tuning them in on the basis of their behaviour, or getting them to interact in a desired way, can be a very hard task. But if their abstract specifications in a generic language are maintained on a suitable formal platform, and kept available at run time, their possible interactions and joint consistency can be analyzed abstactly, e.g. using theorem provers, and their implementations can be modified towards a desired joint behaviour. This may involve reimplementing, i.e. synthesizing new code on the fly, and is certainly not a straightforward task. However, it seems unavoidable for the independently implemented components, necessary for the compositional development of systems — and we believe that it is also within the reach of the current software synthesis technologies.[1]

In any case, a software system that needs to adapt its code and behaviour the run time data, or to the changes of the environment, while maintaining its essential functionality, will surely need to carry and maintain a specification of this functionality in some form, perhaps including a history record, and a current correctness certificate. Since this task, and the structures involved, clearly go beyond the existing software methodologies, a careful analysis of the semantical repercussions seems necessary. Building the suitable design and development environments for the specification carrying self-adaptive software will require a mathematical framework with some nonstandard features. In the present paper, a crude, initial picture of some of these features is outlined. Section 2 describes the structure and the intended interpretation of an abstract category of specification carrying modules. This can be viewed as a first attempt at denotational semantics of such bipartite modules, involving a structural and a behavioral component. Section 3 briefly outlines the structures needed for a dynamic view of the adaptation process, and the way to adjoin them in the described semantical framework.

---

[1] The idea of adding abstract logical annotations to code can be seen as a generalization of Necula and Lee's [12] combination of *proof-carrying-code* and *certifying compilers*. While mainly concerned with the security properties of mobile code, many of the ideas that arose in that work do seem to apply in general, and provide evidence for the imminent realizability of the present ideas.

2   Category of Specification Carrying Programs

As the name suggests, a specification carrying program consists of a program P, a specification S, and a satisfaction, or model relation $\models$ which tells how they "carry" each other, i.e. establishes the sense in which P satisfies S. Formally, a specification carrying program is thus a triple $\langle P, \models, S \rangle$.

But what precisely are P, $\models$, and S? In principle, a formal specification S is a logical theory in a generic specification language (e.g., the higher-order predicate logic). A program P, on the other hand, here means a description of a computational behaviour in one of the available formalisms: it can be a transition system, an automaton, or simply a piece of code in a sufficiently general programming language. Finally, the satisfaction relation $q \models \psi$ tells which of the formulas ψ of S are satisfied at each of the states q of P.

Although diverse formalisms can be used for the particular presentations of P and S, they can always be uniformly represented as categories. The classifying categories $\mathbb{P}$ and $\mathbb{S}$ are derived respectively from the program P and the specification S using the known procedures of operational semantics and categorical model theory. The satisfaction relation $\models$ then becomes a functor from $\mathbb{P} \times \mathbb{S}$.

But we shall not attempt to present this abstract framework directly, but rather begin by motivating its main features and the underlying ideas, especially as they arise in extant frameworks. Some of the underlying mathematics will be outlined, but the details are beyond the scope of this presentation.

2.1   Contracts: The Game of Refinement and Adaptation

Intuitively, an adaptive module $\langle P, \models, S \rangle$ can be thought of as a *contract* between a programmer and a client: the client specifies the requirements in S, and the programmer provides the program P in response. This intuition yields a conceptual basis for the discipline and theory of software *refinement* [1,11].

The process of software adaptation can now be viewed as a *game* played between the client and the programmer: the former refines the specification S, say to S', and the latter tries to respond accordingly by adapting the program P to P' accordingly, i.e. in such a way that the satisfaction $\models$ is preserved. This means that a predicate φ from S should be satisfied in a state q of P if and only if the translation φ' of φ to S' is satisfied in all states q' of P' that simulate the state q.

In summary, an adaptation transformation of $\langle P, \models, S \rangle$ into $\langle P', \models', S' \rangle$ consists of

- a simulation $P \xleftarrow{f_P} P'$, and
- an interpretation $S \xrightarrow{f_S} S'$,

such that for all predicates φ in S and all states q' in P' holds

$$q' \models' f_S(\varphi) \iff f_P(q') \models \varphi \tag{1}$$

The pair $f = \langle f_P, f_S \rangle$, satisfying (1), is an *adaptation* morphism

$$\langle P, \models, S \rangle \xrightarrow{f} \langle P', \models', S' \rangle$$

An abstract semantical framework for software adaptation is thus given by the category $\mathcal{C}$ of specification carrying programs, viewed as contracts $C = \langle P_C, \models_C, S_C \rangle$, with the adaptation morphisms between them.

Contracts as intervals. Note that the morphism $f : \langle P, \models, S \rangle \longrightarrow \langle P', \models', S' \rangle$ is running concurrently with the specification refinement $f_S : S \longrightarrow S'$, but in the *opposite* direction from the simulation $f_P : P' \longrightarrow P$. An imprecise, yet instructive analogy is that a contract $\langle P, \models, S \rangle$ can be thought of as a real interval $[p, s]$. The desired software functionality, that S and P are approximating in their different ways, then corresponds to a point, or an infinitely small interval contained between p and s. The refinement/adaptation game of the client and the programmer now becomes an interactive search for greater lower bounds p, and smaller upper bounds s, i.e. for smaller and smaller intervals, nested in each other, all containing the desired point. This process brings the programs and their specifications closer and closer together, so that they better approximate the desired functionality from both sides, i.e. in terms of the behavior and the structure. Viewed in this way, an adaptation morphism becomes like a formal witness of the interval containment

$$[p, s] \supseteq [p', s'] \iff p \leq p' \wedge s' \leq s$$

The morphism $\langle P, \models, S \rangle \longrightarrow \langle P', \models', S' \rangle$ thus corresponds to the containment $[p, s] \supseteq [p', s']$, the interpretation $S \longrightarrow S'$ to the relation $s \geq s'$, and the simulation $P' \longrightarrow P$ to $p' \geq p$.

Of course, the analogy breaks down on the fact that a specification S and a program P are objects of different types. Nevertheless, the satisfaction relation $\models$ measures "the distance" between P and S, and the mathematical structures arising from refinement/adaptation remain similar to those encountered in approximating numbers by intervals. In spite of its imprecision, the metaphor remains instructive. Moreover, the view of S and P as the approximations of an ideal point where the program is optimally adapted to the specification, does seem conceptually correct. To better approximate this point, S prescribes a minimum of structure necessary for expressing some part of the desired functionality, whereas P provides the simplest behaviour sufficient for implementing it. The client's strategy is to refine S to S' along $f_S : S \longrightarrow S'$, to constrain the input/output requirements more, and make programmer's task harder. The programmer, on the other hand, must enrich the behaviour P to P', in order to better fit the task. This means that P' must at least be able to simulate P, along $f_P : P' \longrightarrow P$.

In any case, the client provides the input/output requirements S, whereas the programmer supplies in P the computation steps transforming the inputs to the outputs. Semantically speaking, the structural, "upper bound" descriptions of software are thus driven by its denotational aspects, *viz* the structure of the datatypes and the functions that need to be refined and implemented. This is summarized in a spec S. On the other hand, a "lower bound" description of a desired piece of software is driven by its operational aspects, and in our particular case by the behaviour of a given implementation P, that needs to be adapted, or optimized for better performance. While conceptually different, the structural/denotational and the behavioural/operational aspects can be captured in a uniform setting [22], which would perhaps make the idea of contracts as intervals more convincing for some readers, or at least give the "intervals" a more familiar appearance. However, as they stand, specification carrying programs can be represented and implemented using mostly the readily available semantical frameworks, on the basis of the extant specification and programming environments.

2.2   Example: Adaptive Sorting

To give the reader an idea of what a concrete specification carrying module looks like, and how it adaptats on the fly, we sketch an (over)simplified example, based on the material from [23,24]. We describe how a sorting module can be automatically reconfigured in response, say, to the observed distributions of the input data.

Suppose that sorting is done by a Divide-and-Conquer algorithm, e.g. Quicksort, or Mergesort. The idea of the Divide-and-Conquer sorting is, of course, to decompose ("divide") the input data, sort the parts separately, and then compuse ("conquer") them into a sorted string. The abstract scheme is:

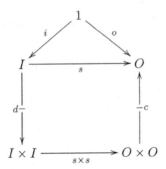

In words, there are two sorts, I for the inputs and O for the outputs, and the desired sorting function s maps one to the other. In principle, I should be the type of bags (multisets) over a linear order, whereas O are the ordered sequences, with respect to the same order. The constants $i : I$ and $o : O$ are used to denote a particular input and the induced output. The bars over the arrows for d and c mean that they are relations, rather than functions. They should satisfy the requirements that

- if $d(x, y, z)$, then $x = y + z$, and
- if $c(x, y, z)$, then $|x| + |y| = |z|$

where $+$ is the union of bags, and $|-|$ maps sequences to the underlying bags. Although they are not functional, these relations are directed by the data flow. That is why they are denoted by the arrows.

The formal specification S_{DC} of the divide-and-conquer algorithms will thus look something like

```
spec Divide-and-Conquer[(S,<): Linear-Order]

    imports
        bag(S),
        ordered-seq(S)

    sorts
        I = bag(S),
        O = oredered-seq(S)

    operations
        s:I->O,
        d:I,I,I -> Bool,
        c:O,O,O -> Bool

    axioms
        d(x,y,z) => x = y + z,
        c(x,y,z) => |x| + |y| = |z|,
        d(x,y,z) /\ c(s(y),s(z),w) => s(x) = w
endspec
```

An abstract program P_{DC}, partially implementing S_{DC} can now be represented as the transition system

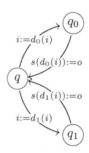

where $d_0(x)$ and $d_1(x)$ denote any bags satisfying $d(x, d_0(x), d_1(x))$. In a way, the state q hides the implementation of d and c, whereas q_0 and q_1 hide the implementation of the sorting of the parts.

The theorems of S_{DC} are satisfied at all states: they are the invariants of the computation. The transitions from state to state induce the interpretations of the specification S_{DC} in itself, mapping e.g. $i \mapsto d_0(i)$ in one case, or $s(d_0(i)) \mapsto o$ in another. They all preserve the invariants, *viz* the theorems of S_{DC}, of course. The satisfaction relation $\models_{DC}$ tells, moreover, for each particular state, which additional predicates, besides the theorems of S_{DC}, have been made true by the executed computational steps, *viz* the substitutions in S_{DC}.

The suitable refinements of S_{DC} yield the specifications S_{QS} of Quicksort and S_{MS} of Mergesort. As explained in [23,24],

- taking $d(x, y, z) \iff x = y + z$ implies that $c(x, y, z)$ must mean that z is a merge of x and y — which yields Mergesort, whereas
- taking $c(x, y, z) \iff x @ y = z$ implies that $d(x, y, z)$ must mean that y and z are a partition of x, such that all elements of y are smaller than every element of z — which yields Quicksort.

Implementing S_{QS} and S_{MS}, one can synthesize executable programs P_{QS} and P_{MS}. While the specifications come with the interpretations $S_{DC} \longrightarrow S_{QS}$ and $S_{DC} \longrightarrow S_{MS}$, the programs come with the simulations $P_{QS} \longrightarrow P_{DC}$ and $P_{MS} \longrightarrow P_{DC}$, showing how the implementations hidden in P_{DC} have been realized.

All together, we now have three contracts, DC, QS and MS, with two adaptation morphisms between them.

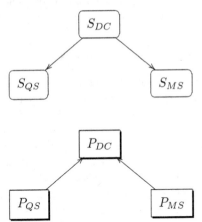

This sorting module can thus run in one of the two modes: Quicksort or Mergesort, and adapt, when needed, between one and the other. At each point of time, though, only one of them needs to be present, since the other can be automatically generated when needed. The module can be set up to monitor its performance, and reconfigure when it falls below some treshold.

Suppose that the module is running as Quicksort, and the input data are coming in almost sorted, which brings it close to the worst-case behavior. The adaptive interpreter aligns P_{QS} and S_{QS}, observes that 98% of the computation time is spent on the divide routine d, and decides to simplify it. It generalizes from S_{QS} to S_{DC}, and chooses the simplest possible d, namely

$$d(x, y, z) \iff x = y + z$$

The theorem prover can now derive that c must be merge, and thus automatically refines S_{DC} to S_{MS}. Since S_{MS} completely determines the algorithm, the code generator can now synthesize P_{MS} in a chosen language. The adaptation path was thus

$$P_{QS} \longrightarrow S_{QS} \longrightarrow S_{DC} \longrightarrow S_{MS} \longrightarrow P_{MS}$$

Of course, in this simple case, the reconfiguration between the two modes could be achieved within a program, with a Quicksort and a Mergesort block. One could build in a performance monitor into the program, maintain its statistics, and then, depending on it, branch to one of the sorting blocks, more suitable for the observed input distributions.

However, the real-life examples, that genuinely require self-adaptation [21], often involve choice between modules too large to be loaded together. One can, furthermore, easily envisage situations when modules couldn't even be stored together, either because of their sizes, or because of their large numbers. With the advent of the agent technologies, there are already situations when there are *infinitely* many logically possible modes of operation, among which one might profitably choose on the fly. With the current level of the program synthesis techniques, of course, this approach would be very hard to realize. Conceptually, however, it seems to be well within reach, and developing the techniques needed for realizing it is a very attractive challenge.

2.3   Institutions, and Satisfaction as Payoff

The bipartite setting of specifications coupled with programs via a satisfaction relation will probably not appear unfamiliar to the categorically minded members of the software specification community. They will recognize the category $\mathcal{C}$ of contracts as conceptually related to *institutions*, although not in all details.

An institution is a very general model theoretic framework. introduced by Goguen and Burstall in [3], and pursued by many others in several different forms. Its main purpose was to fill a conceptual gap in semantics of software. While the formal methods of software engineering are in principle based on universal algebra and model theory, with specifications *statically* describing some computational structures, programs at large are *dynamic* objects, they change state, and behave differently in different states. And while the mathematical theories completely determine the classes of their static models, as well as the notion of homomorphism between them, the software specifications do not pin down the programs that realize them[2]. In model theory, the Tarskian satisfaction relation $\models$ is a fixed, primitive concept; in theory of software specifications, on the other hand, there are many degrees of freedom in deciding what does it mean for a program to satisfy a specification, in particular with respect to its operational behaviour. It is then reasonable to display an abstract satisfaction

---

[2] Not in the sense that all programs implementing a specification can be effectively derived from the specification, like all mathematical models of a theory, and indeed the whole model category, are effectively determined by the theory.

relation $\models$ as a structural part of an institution, that can be varied together with theories and models, while stipulating which models satisfy which theories.[3]

Following this conceptual lead, the satisfaction relation can be generalized from an ordinary relation, where $q \models \psi$ is evaluated as true or false, to an M-valued relation, where $q \models \psi$ can be any element of a distributive lattice, or a suitable category, say M, measuring the degree to which the condition ψ is satisfied at the state q.

In standard game theoretic terms, the relation $\models$ now becomes the payoff matrix, displaying the value of each programmer's response to each client's call. Indeed, if the formulas of S are understood as the set of moves (or strategies[4]) available to the client, and the moves available to the programmer are identified with the states of P, then the satisfaction $\models$ becomes an $P \times S$-matrix of the elements of M, i.e. a map

$$\models : P \times S \longrightarrow M \tag{2}$$

assigning the payoff to each pair $\langle q, \psi \rangle$. It can be understood, say, as displaying programmer's gains for each combination of the moves, and the game acquires the usual von Neumann-Morgenstern form, with the client trying to minimize and the programmer to maximize this gain. The intuitive and logical meaning of the pairs of arrows in opposite directions, like in the adaptation morphisms, has been analyzed in this context in [6], connecting games, linear logic and the Chu construction.

In any case, semantics of specification carrying programs must draw ideas and structures from sources as varied as institutions and game theory, although the goals and methods in each case differ essentially. On the level of abstract categories, both institutions and specification carrying programs can be analyzed along the lines of the mentioned Chu construction [2,14,19]. The lax version [13] is also interesting, capturing the situation when adaptation may not just preserve, but also *improve* the satisfaction relation between the program and the specification. This corresponds to relaxing in (1) the equivalence $\Longleftrightarrow$ to the implication $\Longleftarrow$. If $\models$ and $\models'$ are taken to be general M-valued relations, or payoff matrices, as in (2), a morphism $f : \langle P, \models, S \rangle \longrightarrow \langle P', \models, S' \rangle$ improving satisfaction will be a triple $f = \langle f_P, f_\models, f_S \rangle$, consisting of

- a simulation $P \xleftarrow{f_P} P'$,
- an interpretation $S \xrightarrow{f_S} S'$, and
- for each $q' \in P'$ and $\psi \in S$ an arrow

$$(f_P(q') \models \psi) \xrightarrow{f_\models} (q' \models' f_S(\psi)) \tag{3}$$

in M, with the suitable naturality condition.

---

[3] Institutions thus bridge the gap between static theories and dynamic models by allowing the abstract satisfaction relation to vary. Another way to bridge this gap is to introduce dynamics into theories. This is one of the ideas behind Gurevich's Abstract State Machines (formerly known as evolving algebras) [4].

[4] the distinction is of no consequence here

2.4   Towards Functorial Semantics of Contracts

In order to express the above naturality condition, or work out a generic representation of the category $\mathcal{C}$ of contracts, one needs to present the specifications, and the programs in terms of their respective classifying categories.

Given a specification S, say as a theory in a predicate logic, the objects of the induced classifying category $\mathbb{S}$ will be the well-formed formulas of S, modulo the renaming of variables (α-conversion). The arrows are the functional relations definable in S, modulo the provability. For instance, take formulas $\alpha(\boldsymbol{x})$ and $\beta(\boldsymbol{y})$ in S, as the representatives of objects in $\mathbb{S}$. By renaming, we can achieve that their arguments $\boldsymbol{x}$ and $\boldsymbol{y}$ are disjoint. An $\mathbb{S}$-arrow from $\alpha(\boldsymbol{x})$ to $\beta(\boldsymbol{y})$ will be a predicate $\vartheta(\boldsymbol{x}, \boldsymbol{y})$, such that

$$\vartheta(\boldsymbol{x}, \boldsymbol{y}) \vdash \alpha(\boldsymbol{x}) \wedge \beta(\boldsymbol{y})$$
$$\alpha(\boldsymbol{x}) \vdash \exists \boldsymbol{y}.\ \vartheta(\boldsymbol{x}, \boldsymbol{y})$$
$$\vartheta(\boldsymbol{x}, \boldsymbol{y}') \wedge \vartheta(\boldsymbol{x}, \boldsymbol{y}'') \vdash \boldsymbol{y}' = \boldsymbol{y}''$$

can be proved in S. The arrows of $\mathbb{S}$ thus capture the theorems of S, whereas the objects capture the language. More details can be found in [17].

The point of presenting a theory S as a category $\mathbb{S}$ is that the models of $\mathbb{S}$ can be obtained as the functors $\mathbb{S} \longrightarrow \mathsf{Set}$, preserving the logical structure. This is the essence of functorial semantics [7], and the foundation of categorical model theory [8,9]. The applications to software engineering are discussed in [17].

Related, more direct, but less uniform procedures allow deriving categories from programs. They usually go under the name of operational semantics [18, 25], and come in too many varieties to justify going into any detail here.

Assuming that a specification S and a program P have been brought into a categorical form, and presented as classifying categories $\mathbb{S}$ and $\mathbb{P}$, the satisfaction relation $\models: \mathbb{S} \times \mathbb{P} \longrightarrow \mathbb{M}$ will transpose to a structure preserving functor $\mathbb{S} \longrightarrow \mathbb{M}^{\mathbb{P}}$. When the category $\mathbb{M}$, measuring satisfaction, is taken to be the category Set of sets and functions, $\models$ will thus amount to a *model* of $\mathbb{S}$ in the universe $\mathsf{Set}^{\mathbb{P}}$ of sets varying from state to state in $\mathbb{P}$. A logically inclined reader may be amused to spend a moment unfolding the definition of adaptation morphisms in this model theoretic context, and confincing herself that such morphisms indeed preserve the given sense in which a program satisfies specification, or improve it along the suitable homomorphisms of models.

In any case, the naturality condition on the third component of the adaptation morphisms as defined the preceding section can now be expressed precisely, on the diagram displaying the involved composite functors.

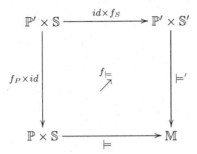

3   Adaptive Interpreter as Coalgebra

While the described category of contracts, implemented and supported by suitable tools, provides the structural framework for software adaptation, it still does not provide a special handle for automated, on-the-fly adaptation and reconfiguration. The dynamics of self-adaptive software requires an additional dimension, to be added to in the actual implementation of the specification carrying modules. The main issue thus remains: *how to implement an adaptive interpreter, able to compute with self-adaptive, specification carrying modules?*

Given a contract $\langle P, \models, S \rangle$, the adaptive interpreter should be able to:

- evaluate P,
- test whether the results satisfy S,
- adapt P, or assist program transformation $P \longleftarrow P'$,
- support refinement $S \longrightarrow S'$.

In a standard setting, the denotation of a program P is a function $p : A \longrightarrow B$, where A and B are the types of the input and the output data, respectively. An adapted program P' will yield a function $p' : A \longrightarrow B$ (where we are ignoring, for simplicity, the fact that the data types A and B can be refined). If adaptation is viewed as a computational *process*, all the instances of an adapted function that may arise can be captured in the form

$$\widetilde{p} : \Sigma \times A \longrightarrow B$$

where Σ is the carrier of adaptation, probably a monoid, or a partial order. The *stages* of the adaptation $\sigma, \sigma' \ldots \in \Sigma$ can be associated with the successive refinements $S, S' \ldots$ of the specification of the adaptive program, and will be derived from them by one of the model theoretic methods developed for this purpose (i.e. as the "worlds", or the forcing conditions induced by the refinement).[5]

---

[5] The stages of adaptation should not be confused with the computational states, through which the execution of a program leads. The execution runs of a program from state to state are, in a sense, orthogonal to its adaptation steps from stage to stage.

All the instances $p, p' \ldots : A \longrightarrow B$ of the adaptive function will now arise by evaluating $\widetilde{p}$ at the corresponding stages $\sigma, \sigma' \ldots \in \Sigma$, *viz*

$$p(x) = \widetilde{p}(\sigma, x)$$
$$p'(x) = \widetilde{p}(\sigma', x)$$
$$\ldots$$

In this way, the process of adaptation is thus beginning to look like a rudimentary dynamic system. The process of *self*-adaptation will, of course, be a system with the feedback

$$\widehat{p} : \Sigma \times A \longrightarrow B \times \Sigma$$

computing at each stage $\sigma \in \Sigma$, and for each input $x \in A$ not only the output $y = \widehat{p}_0(\sigma, x) \in B$, but also the next stage $\sigma' = \widehat{p}_1(\sigma, x) \in \Sigma$, with a better adapted function $p'(x) = \widehat{p}(\sigma', x)$. Extended in this way along the coordinate of adaptation, the specification carrying programs viewed as contracts come in the form

$$\widehat{\models} : \Sigma \times \mathbb{S} \times \mathbb{P} \longrightarrow \mathbb{M} \times \Sigma$$

The predictable adaptation stages are structured in Σ and controlled by the resumption component of $\widehat{\models}$. Alternatively, automated adaptation steps can be encapsulated in specifications and programs themselves, by individually extending the particular functions from stage to stage.

Independently on the level on which it may be captured, the denotation of a self-adaptive function will in any case be a transducer $\widehat{p}$. Transposing it into a *coalgebra*

$$\widehat{p} : \Sigma \longrightarrow (B \times \Sigma)^A$$

brings with it the advantage that the behaviour preserving maps now arise automatically, as coalgebra homomorphisms. (Instructive examples and explanations of this phenomenon can be found, e.g. in [20].) But even more importantly, it allows a considerably more realistic the picture, since it also allows introducing various *computational monads* T on the scene. A coalgebra in the form

$$\widehat{p}_T : \Sigma \longrightarrow (T(B \times \Sigma))^A$$

captures an adaptive family of computations involving any of the wide range of features (nondeterminism, exceptions, continuations ...) expressible by monads [10].

In any case, combining monads and coalgebra will ensure a solid semantical foundation not just for adaptive interpreters, but also for implementing the design environments for self-adaptive software. Explaining either of these theories is far beyond our scope here, but monads seem to have been established as a part of the standard toolkit of functional programmers, and the material about them abounds. Some coalgebraic techniques for implementing processes have been presented in [5,15,16].

References

1. R.-J. Back and J. Von Wright, *The Refinement Calculus: A Systematic Introduction.* (Springer 1998)
2. M. Barr, *∗-Autonomous Categories.* Lecture Notes in Mathematics 752 (Springer, 1979)
3. J.A. Goguen and R.M. Burstall, Institutions: abstract model theory for specifications and programming. *J. of the A.C.M.* 39(1992) 95–146
4. Y. Gurevich, Evolving algebras 1993: Lipari guide. In: *Specification and Validation Methods*, ed. E. Börger, (Claredon Press 1995) 9–37
5. B. Jacobs, Coalgebraic specifications and models of deterministic hybrid systems. In: *Proc. AMAST*, ed. M. Nivat, Springer Lect. Notes in Comp. Sci. 1101(1996) 520–535
6. Y. Lafont and T. Streicher, Games semantics for linear logic. *Proc 6*th *LICS Conf.* (IEEE 1991) 43–49
7. F.W. Lawvere, *Functorial Semantics of Algebraic Theories.* Thesis (Columbia University, 1963)
8. M. Makkai and R. Paré, *Accessible Categories: The Foundations of Categorical Model Theory.* Contemporary Mathematics 104 (AMS 1989)
9. M. Makkai and G. Reyes, *First Order Categorical Logic.* Lecture Notes in Mathematics 611 (Springer 1977)
10. E. Moggi, Notions of computation and monads. *Information and Computation* 1993
11. C. Morgan, *Programming from Specifications.* (Prentice-Hall 1990)
12. G.C. Necula, *Compiling with Proofs.* Thesis (CMU 1998)
13. V.C.V. de Paiva, The Dialectica categories. In: *Categories in Computer Science and Logic*, J. Gray and A. Scedrov, eds., *Contemp. Math.* 92 (Amer. Math. Soc., 1989) 47–62
14. D. Pavlovic, Chu I: cofree equivalences, dualities and ∗-autonomous categories. *Math. Structures in Comp. Sci.* 7(1997) 49–73
15. D. Pavlovic, Guarded induction on final coalgebras. *E. Notes in Theor. Comp. Sci.* 11(1998) 143–160
16. D. Pavlovic and M. Escardo, Calulus in coinductive form. *Proc 13*th *LICS Conf.* (IEEE 1998) 408–417
17. D. Pavlovic, Semantics of first order parametric specifications. in: *Formal Methods '99*, J. Woodcock and J. Wing, eds., Springer Lect. Notes in Comp. Sci. 1708(1999) 155–172
18. G. Plotkin, *Structural Operational Semantics.* Lecture Notes DAIMI-FN 19(1981)
19. V. Pratt, Chu spaces and their interpretation as concurrent objects. In: *Computer Science Today: Recent Trends and Developments*, ed. J. van Leeuwen, Springer Lect. Notes in Comp. Sci. 1000(1995)
20. J.J.M.M. Rutten, Universal coalgebra: a theory of systems. To appear in *Theoret. Comput. Sci.*
21. J. Sztipanivits, G. Karsai and T. Bapty, Self-adaptive software for signal processing. *Comm. of the ACM* 41/5(1998) 66–73
22. D. Turi and G.D. Plotkin, Towards a mathematical operational semantics. In: *Proc. 12*th *LICS Conf.* (IEEE 1997) 280–291
23. D.R. Smith, Derivation of parallel sorting algorithms. In: *Parallel Algorithm Derivation and Program Transformation*, eds. R. Paige et al. (Kluwer 1993) 55–69

24. D.R. Smith, Towards a classification approach to design. In: *Proc.* 5th *AMAST*, Springer Lect. Notes in Comp. Sci. 1101(1996) 62–84

25. G. Winskel and M. Nielsen, Presheaves as transition systems. In: *Proc. of POMIV 96, DIMACS Series in Discrete Mathematics and Theoretical Computer Science* (AMS 1997) 129–140

On Evaluating Self-Adaptive Software

Alex C. Meng

The MITRE Corp.
1820 Dolley Madison Blvd. McLean VA 22102
meng@mitre.org

Abstract. This article attempts to address the issues of evaluating self-adaptive software systems, an emerging discipline. Since the field is in its early phase and has not produced enough mature systems for consideration, we try to approach the evaluation issue by considering a *descriptive* model of self-adaptive software based on control systems. Taking inspirations and using the vocabularies from the *feedforward* and *feedback* control paradigms, this article will illustrate the analogous properties in self-adaptive software and its evaluation consideration such as *stability* and *robustness*. Existing approaches to self-adaptive software take different aspects, ranging from viewing it as new *programming paradigm*, new *architecture style*, new *modeling paradigm* to a new *software engineering principle*. This article tries to elicit the evaluation consideration from these different aspects.

Introduction

Since the publication of D. Knuth's classics "the Art of Computer Programming"[1], building software system has been increasingly an engineering task rather than art. One of the flourishing developments in software design is that of applying formal methods in the specification of software and its architecture. Mature engineering disciplines such as control systems offer robust ways to design systems operating in dynamic environments. Control systems embody many desirable features such as robustness, predictable properties such as stability, quality of service and rigorous analysis. The methodology of building self-adaptive software is such an attempt to take the inspiration of control system as the building principle for software. It will take extensive experiences of building real life self-adaptive systems in order to reach a level of maturity, to which we're just beginning to explore. This paper attempts to give a descriptive model of what a self-adaptive system should consist of and how to evaluate them.

We will describe self-adaptive software from different *aspects*: we can view it as a new *programming paradigm*, a new *architecture style*, and from the problem-solving aspect, we can view it as a new *modeling paradigm*, and as a *software engineering principle* to construct software systems. This paper tries to develop guidelines and questions regarding how to evaluate self-adaptive software systems based on these different aspects. Even though it is an emerging field and there are few real-life

P. Robertson, H. Shrobe, and R. Laddaga (Eds.): IWSAS 2000, LNCS 1936, pp. 65-73, 2000.
© Springer-Verlag Berlin Heidelberg 2000

systems other than prototypes in research laboratories, there are examples of software systems that exhibit similar capabilities of what the self-adaptive software should have:

- Buffer allocation algorithms in DBMS that adjusts the size and allocation strategy of buffers dynamically depending on the system load.
- Network routing algorithm, which modify the routing tables and adjust the routing path dynamically based on the load of network traffic and configuration changes.
- Load balancing algorithms in distributed systems to optimize the system utilization.
- Use of different caching algorithms for memory management in operating systems, depending on the status of memory usage.
- Online learning algorithms.

While these algorithms exhibit adaptive behavior in their own ways, the field is seeking to develop general principles of building self-adaptive software. Due to the lack of self-adaptive systems in practice for evaluation consideration, in this paper, we take the approach of evaluating self-adaptive software from a generic, descriptive model of what self-adaptive software should be. Since the fundamental insight of building self-adaptive software comes from *control theory*, it is natural to think that the evaluation criteria for control systems naturally are applicable to self-adaptive software in a general sense. In this paper, we outline the mapping from the evaluation metrics in control theory to evaluation metrics for software. We discuss the metrics in different aspects of the self-adaptive software listed above.

A Descriptive Model of Self-Adaptive Software

In the recent special issue of IEEE magazine of Intelligent Systems on Self-Adaptive Software we have a glimpse of representative views on many aspects of the self-adaptive software. Fundamentally the aim of software adaptation is *robustness*: a self-adaptive software system can modify its behavior at runtime to accommodate changes in the environment to achieve its design goal. In some sense, autonomous robots offer a concrete example of the same challenges the software designers are facing. Namely, the algorithms that make decisions in the robot need to adapt to unknown situations based on what was known in its knowledge of the environment before and what it discovered now with its sensors. By analogy to software's point of view, the *design specification* will be the static world we know before while the *run-time context* of the environment is what the current situation is. The interactions between these two components form a closely integrated loop for systems to adapt to its challenges. To generalize the concept in a simple diagram, from an architectural standpoint, the vocabulary from control systems such as the *feedback* and *feedforward* control regimes offer concrete models of computation self-adaptive software requires. The following descriptions of the models are taken from [2] from a point of view in process control; a similar concept is also illustrated in [3].

Feedback Control Model

The following figure illustrates the feedback control in a process control setting. Process variables represent the properties of the process that can be measured, while controlled variables are subset of process variables that the system is intended to control. The desired values for the controlled variables are called the set points. Input variables represent the inputs to the process. The purpose of a control system is to maintain specified properties of the outputs of the process with a sufficient range of values to the set points (e.g. *stability*).

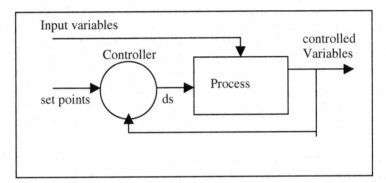

Fig. 1. Feedback control model

The feedback of the values of the controlled variables to the controller at runtime, which computes the delta *ds* between them and the set points, generates control actions to maintain the system in a stable state.

Feedforward Control Model

The other model of control, feedforward, is illustrated in Fig.2.

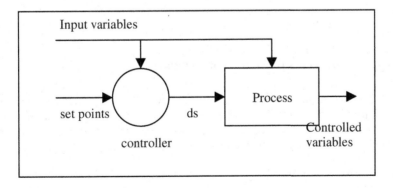

Fig. 2. Feedforward control model

In feedforward model, values of the controlled variables are measured from other process variables given as inputs to the controller. It then computes the delta *ds* between them and the set points at run time for controlling the process.

The feedback and feedforward control models offer a set of vocabularies to describe analogous runtime behavior in self-adaptive software systems. In the literature, it has used the terms such as *reactive* and *deliberative* components describing the feedback and feedforward control models respectively [4]. Using this paradigm, ordinary software systems except with a few exceptions as mentioned before, can be thought of as behaving like actuators or processes, which need to be controlled. In a general sense, the feedforward (deliberative) component prescribes the predicted behavior of the system that guarantees the consistency over a longer period of time, while the feedback (reactive) component adapts to local changes in its environment, both within the run time context. Therefore, the design challenge for self-adaptive software systems is to develop disciplined ways to combine the feedforward and feedback components of the system, and integrate them in a tightly coupled fashion.

Ideally, the self-adaptive software should consist of both components integrated as illustrated in Fig.3.

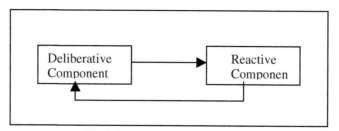

Fig. 3. Integrated architecture

Evaluation Metrics for Control Systems

To consider the evaluation issues for self-adaptive software, which is a difficult task as explained in [5], we take the approach of examining the evaluation metrics in control systems, which gives us insights into the measurement of self-adaptive software. The following set of metrics provides a general guideline for measuring a control system:

- Stability

It is the most important metrics in control. It measures the responsiveness of a system; that is, a system is said stable if its response to a bounded input is itself bounded by a desirable range. In the process model as illustrated before, the system is stable if the controlled variables are within allowable range to the set points.

- Robustness

It is a metrics on the controller. For control systems it may not be sufficient to be nominally stable. They have to remain stable even if the plant or the process is different from the intended plant or process in some measured ways.

There are other metrics such as settling time and transient time. The settling time measures the amount of time it takes for a system to achieve a state in which the value of the control variable is within a desirable bound, while the transient time measures the transient response: the behavior of the system transits from a stable state to another. The focus is to determine if this set of metrics is relevant to measuring self-adaptive software systems. The issues on evaluating self-adaptive software are then equivalent to mapping the evaluation metrics from control systems to the appropriate metrics on the self-adaptive software systems. As illustrated in [5], robustness is the key measurement that the self-adaptive software is about.

There are some metrics that are particularly relevant to evaluating self-adaptive software such as *case coverage*: it refers to the applicable range of the system, per variable of a set of variables; and *monotonicity*, these metrics measures a system's ability to increase its case coverage over time monotonically.

Evaluation Considerations for Self-Adaptive Software

As we proceed to consider the issues of evaluation metrics for self-adaptive software, mapping the key metrics of stability and robustness from control systems to software domain, we consider the evaluation from different aspects of self-adaptive software.

As a New Programming Paradigm

In the context of programming languages and environment, writing self-adaptive software requires facilities that enable a software construct to model its own behavior, the self-knowledge as it is called. At runtime, its semantic context is available for introspection, and modification. Of the existing programming techniques, *reflection* [6] is close to such a facility. With reflection, programs can modify themselves at run time and change their behaviors presumably. But the essential issue of using the reflective programming utility is to determine when and what the program needs to modify itself towards its design goals. That's the issue of runtime evaluation (or monitoring). Once we have an evaluator that tells the "goodness" of the state of the program with some measure, we then have a control issue. Given that goodness measure, the control regime computes the delta (the distance between current state and its goal state) and maintains its stability.

An example of using "reflection + monitoring + control" as the basic paradigm for self-adaptive software and its implementation in an application of image analysis is in [7]. The runtime evaluator in this context is the feedback component while the control provides the feedforward component. In a sense the reflection programming facility provides sensors and actuators in the robotics context to provide the inspection and action that change its environment.

We consider the metrics of stability and robustness mapped from control systems to the reflective programming paradigm.

- Stability

Thinking in the context of feedback control model, concerning its runtime behavior, can the reflection facility provide adequate information about the construct to generate evaluators at run time to check the deviation (or a measure of goodness) and to monitor the condition of the construct? (In this case, the evaluator acts as a sensor providing the feedback in a sense.)

- Robustness

Using reflection, the software can examine its own definition and inspect its values in runtime. Does reflection provide the software specification adequately to model its behavior?

As a New Architecture Style

In the previous section, the feedback and feedforward concepts are briefly illustrated using simplified models in process control [2]. There are formal models and specification languages available to specify architectures such as pipe-and-filter system, event-driven implicit invocation system, object-oriented systems etc. The challenge of specifying an architecture style for self-adaptive software is to formalize the concepts of feedforward and feedback components, and using them as part of the vocabulary used in an architecture description language (ACL) [2]. It needs to specify the interactions between these two components in well-defined ways. Since the architecture elicits the structural aspect of a system, a configuration usually refers to a particular composition of its structural components. One of the key architectural concepts for self-adaptive software is *reconfiguration,* a term when it is used in adaptive control, refers to the system that switches the control regime based on the runtime situation. To map this concept to software, we can think of "*algorithm selection*" [8] as a form of reconfiguration. In this case, a set of algorithms is available for selection at run time and the control issues refer to when and what algorithm to choose at a given time.

While 'configuration" or "controller" are part of typical vocabulary of architecture description, it does not imply the similar semantics self-adaptive software uses. For example, feedback is an essential *interaction* between the controller and evaluator components, which the current architecture language is unable to characterize. We need to develop a richer concept of interaction between components. When the system decides to transit from one configuration to another, the issues of stability and settling time are clearly relevant metrics.

For example, in a pipe-and-filter system, a pipe will connect and a filter will process streamed data in a fixed order. Feedback and feedforward are *process* concepts that require nonlinear order of processing, which is difficult to map to static view of the software architecture. To consider the metrics:

- Stability

Thinking of reconfiguration as the control regime for the architecture, what is the stability analysis? What is its goal state? In some sense, the architecture needs to be evaluated within its embedded problem-solving context and the current trend of domain specific architecture may offer one step toward this direction.

- Robustness

Switching algorithm at runtime changes a system's behavior. When the system transits from one algorithm to another, what guarantee does it have regarding to case coverage in order that previously solved case by one algorithm will continue on the new algorithm?

As a New Modeling Paradigm

Model-based approach to software construction provides a good example of the "feedforward" component for self-adaptive software; namely, a complete specification of the model, together with the synthesizing processes (the interpreters) will enable the system to generate executable code for the target environment. However, to achieve the possibility of runtime behavior modification, the approach requires the controller component to provide environment feedback. In the paper [10], the controller component is realized in a *reconfiguration* mechanism: it evaluates the performance of the system and provides the means of re-synthesizing the dataflow and control construct in a safe and consistent manner at runtime. As a modeling paradigm, this approach provides two interactions; namely, the feedfoward process, from model to the executable, the synthesis, and the feedback process, from execution to reconfiguration, the runtime re-synthesis.

- Stability

Model based approach provides a disciplined way to generate provable correct software according to its model. The issue of stability in this case is to avoid the *thrashing* behavior. That is, the system continuously re-synthesizes upon small change in its runtime context. To achieve feedback, the concept of reconfiguration provides an on-the-fly synthesizing capability. Another issue of stability becomes relevant: how would the reconfiguration component determine that the system is or isn't approaching to its target state after re-synthesizing?

- Robustness

The modeling paradigm requires a complete specification of the behavior of the software system, which may not be feasible in specifying a highly dynamic and unknown environment. Presumably monitors can be generated based on the specification to guard the runtime conditions that need to be maintained. In a dynamic environment, it is difficult to specify system behavior. Also, it takes time and system resource to re-synthesis a system. How would the reconfiguration mechanism take into account for performance and resource contention?

As a Software Engineering Principle

This aspect takes the view of treating building software system as equivalent to building a control system. This approach views the software itself as the *plant* (or the process to be controlled) and the feedback control architecture is the software architecture. As illustrated in [9], besides the feedback loop, it incorporates the adaptation and reconfiguration based on adaptive control theory. We can generalize the control model as the concept of *algorithm selection* in software engineering as its adaptive control in the sense that the system will switch to a different algorithm on the fly when the environment changes. In this case, the software designer will write a repertoire of applicable algorithms instead of just one and the key challenge in software adaptation is on choosing the right algorithm for the right environment. The evaluation issues then becomes the recasting of the metrics on control system to the software area.

- Stability

Using algorithm selection as the adaptive control, we have the same issue of thrashing, that is, the mechanism will keep switching algorithms due to small change of the evaluation. It creates instability.

- Robustness

To provide a rigorous formulation of the software process as in the mathematical formulation of control system, it may limit the scope of the applicability of the methodology to the software system that lends itself to formal analysis.

Summary

Self-adaptive software is a rapidly emerging discipline and there are many aspects to the fundamental concept, namely, software system modifies its runtime behavior to adapt to the environmental changes. To facilitate such an ability we propose that self-adaptive software should consist of two components: the feedforward component that provides specification of the software and its predictability and the feedback component to take the runtime feedback from the environment. However, the general model of self-adaptive can be viewed from many different aspects such as a new programming and modeling paradigm, a new architecture style or a software engineering principle. Due to lack of experience from mature systems, it is a difficult task to lay down the evaluation metrics. However, this article takes views from control system and tries to elicit evaluation considerations for different aspects.

Acknowledgement

The author would like to thank for the workshop organizers for constructive criticisms to make the paper readable and improve the technical quality.

Reference

1. Knuth, Donald E.: The Art of Computer Programming, Addison-Wesley, Reading, Massachusetts, 1973.
2. Shaw, M., Garlan, D.: Software Architecture, Prentice Hall, Upper Saddle River, New Jersey, 1996. Chapter 2.
3. Dean T., Wellman, M.: Planning and Control, Morgan Kaufmann Publishers, San Mateo, California, 1991. Chapter 8.
4. Arkin, R.: Behavior-Based Robotics, The MIT Press, Cambridge, Massachusetts, 1998. Chapter 6.
5. Laddaga, R.: Creating Robust Software through Self-Adaptation, IEEE Intelligent Systems, May-June (1999) 26-29.
6. Smith, B.: Reflection and Semantics in a Procedural Language, Tech. Report 272, MIT Library for Computing Science, Cambridge, Massachusetts, 1982.
7. Robertson, P., Brady M.:Adaptive Image Analysis for Aerial Surveillance, IEEE Intelligent Systems, May-June (1999) 30-36.
8. Oreizy, P., Gorlick, M, Taylor, R., Heimbigner, D., Johnson, G., Medvidovic, N., Quilici, A., Rosenblum, D., Wolf, A.: An Architecture-Based Approach to Self-Adaptive Software, IEEE Intelligent Systems, May-June (1999) 54-62.
9. Kokar, M., Baclawski, K., Eracar, A.: Control Theory-Based Foundations of Self-Controlling Software, IEEE Intelligent Systems, May-June (1999) 37-45.

Mapping an Application to a Control Architecture: Specification of the Problem

Mieczyslaw M. Kokar[1], Kevin M. Passino[2], Kenneth Baclawski[1], and Jeffrey E. Smith[3]

[1] Northeastern University, Boston, Massachusetts, USA
kokar@coe.neu.edu
kenb@ccs.neu.edu
[2] Ohio State University, Columbus, Ohio, USA,
passino@ee.eng.ohio-state.edu
[3] Sanders, A Lockheed Company, Nashua, New Hampshire, USA
jeffrey.e.smith@lmco.com

Abstract. This paper deals with self-adapting software that is structured according to a control theory architecture. Such software contains, in addition to its main function, two components - a Controller and a Quality-of-Service module. We show an example of an application and analyze the mapping of this application onto various control theory-based architectures. The application is a radar-based target tracking system. We show how architectural constraints are propagated through the mapping. We also analyze various architectural solutions with respect to stability and time complexity.

1 Introduction

Recently, it has been recognized that change in requirements over the life time of a piece of software is inevitable. This recognition has resulted in the emergence of such research areas as software architectures, software development frameworks, self-adapting software [2,4,7], and others. One of the directions in this research (cf. [3]) has been to follow the control metaphor in software development, i.e., to treat the basic software functionality as a *plant* and then add some *redundancy* to control this plant. The redundant software is called the *controller*. The controller is designed to monitor changes in requirements, determine when the software is not meeting those requirements, and make changes to the software (plant) to make sure that it is continually updated so that the requirements are met.

There are various architectures known in the control community. If one wants to follow the control paradigm of engineering software, one needs to know how to map a specific problem onto one of the control architectures. In this paper we consider an example software system and analyze various control architecture realizations of this functionality. In this process, we show how to rationalize some of the architectural decisions.

P. Robertson, H. Shrobe, and R. Laddaga (Eds.): IWSAS 2000, LNCS 1936, pp. 75–89, 2000.

2   System and Problem Specification

As a case study we have chosen software that implements a resource scheduler for a multiple target tracking domain. The goal of the system is to track multiple targets, i.e., estimate their states (e.g., position, velocity), with satisfactory precision, given the resources (in this case it is one radar). The task must be performed within given time bounds. This kind of a problem has been captured as the following metaphor:

> *Make resource allocation such that it is good enough and it is made soon enough (cf.* Broad Agency Announcement on Autonomous Negotiating Teams, BAA-99-05, DARPA, November 1998*).*

In order to perform its task, the system must allocate resources so that a measure of accuracy of tracking is high ("good enough"). This accuracy depends on the time when the resource (the radar) is given to a specific target (*revisit time*) and the length of the time interval that the radar is measuring that target (*dwell time*). The tracking and the radar allocation functions must be computed within the time constraints dictated by the revisit time of the radar. Moreover, the time for switching the radar among the targets imposes additional constraints on the system. This constitutes the "soon enough" constraint.

According to the approach we are using to specify the architecture, first, we need to view the system in the environment. This is represented in Figure 1. In this figure, the radar measures targets and sends measurements to the tracker, which in turn, controls the radar. The tracker interacts with the (human) operator.

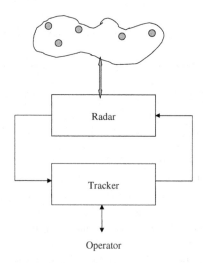

Fig. 1. The Tracking System

2.1   Target Environment Model

The target environment in Figure 1 has N mobile targets (i.e., we assume that the number of targets in the environment is fixed). Suppose that the dynamics of the ith target is given by

$$x^i(k+1) = f^i(x^i(k), u^i(k)) + \Gamma w^i(k) \tag{1}$$
$$y^i(k+1) = g^i(x^i(k+1), u^i(k+1)) + v^i(k+1) \tag{2}$$

for $i = 1, 2, \ldots, N$, where k is the time index and we assume that there is a sampling period of T (hence $x(k)$ represents $x(kT)$, the state at time $t = kT$). Here, $x^i \in \Re^n$ is the state vector of the ith mobile target (e.g., its elements typically contain position and velocity), $u^i \in \Re^p$ is its input (e.g., a steering command), and $y^i \in \Re^m$ is the output (e.g., the output of the radar that senses the position of target i). The nonlinear dynamics are specified via f^i and g^i. These could be developed using first principles of physics to form a continuous time model that is transformed (e.g., using Euler's approximation) to the above discrete time representation. The term $w^i(k)$ in Equation 1 represents "process noise" and Γ describes how this noise is distributed to the states. Typically, $w^i(k)$ is assumed to be zero mean white Gaussian noise with a fixed variance. The "output channel" is given in Equation 2 and there is a "measurement noise" $v^i(k+1)$ given there that represents the lack of accuracy of our sensor (e.g., the inaccuracy of a radar to measure the position of a target). Typically, it is assumed that v^i is zero mean white Gaussian noise with a fixed variance and that v^i and w^i are independent noise sequences. We assume this here also.

The model tells us certain important facts about the environment that impact our ability to track targets. First, note that the number of outputs (measurements) m is typically less than n which represents that we cannot measure the full state of the ith mobile target. Moreover, even if we can measure a component of the state of the target (e.g., position) the measurement is corrupted by the noise v^i, and the problem of estimating the state of the mobile target (which would tell us its position, velocity, and perhaps acceleration) is further complicated by the process noise w^i.

2.2   Tracker Methods and Model

The typical approach to solve the state estimation problem is to use (extended) Kalman filters, one for each of the N targets. In such an approach, the radar is focused on one target at a time so that only one of the N Kalman filters updates its estimate using a measurement, while the others continue estimating the state using only prediction based on the model of the mobile target[1]. It is important to note that, even with the complications mentioned above, the estimate $\hat{x}^i(k)$

---

[1] Assuming the measurement-to-track association problem is solved

of $x^i(k)$ that the Kalman filters produce can typically be made to be reasonably reliable. It is for this reason that in this paper we will assume that

$$\hat{x}^i(k) \approx x^i(k), k = 0, 1, 2, \ldots$$

for $i = 1, 2, \ldots, N$ so that we can reliably estimate the state of each of the N targets so we know where they are at. We also make this assumption since our focus is not on Kalman filter development, but on the management of the radar to track multiple targets, and in particular on software architectures for how to structure the system that manages the radar.

Besides producing estimates of the state of the mobile targets, the Kalman filters (or other processing algorithms) can provide a characterization of the uncertainty in the estimate (e.g., via the covariance matrix of the innovations process of the Kalman filter). To maintain our focus on the management of the radar, rather than Kalman filtering, we model the uncertainty in the estimate of the state vector of the ith mobile target (when the radar is not focused on the ith target) with

$$\theta_i(t) = p_i t \tag{3}$$

so that we assume that the uncertainty in the state grows linearly with time $t \geq 0$. In discrete time we have $\theta_i(k) = p_i kT$. Later, we will allow p_i to evolve dynamically over time so that the uncertainty in the estimate may be state dependent. For now, we assume that p_i, $i = 1, 2, \ldots, N$, are known constants. We think of p_i as being the rate of uncertainty increase in the information we have about the ith target.

2.3   Scheduler

The task of the scheduler is to manage (point) the radar so as to maintain as much certainty about the locations of the mobile targets as possible. In the above framework it points the radar by picking which of the N Kalman filters in the tracker will be able to use a measurement update to produce its estimate (again, assuming the measurement-to-track association problem is solved). Hence, if it directs the radar at the ith mobile target, it is then directing it so as to reduce uncertainty $\theta_i(t)$ in the estimate for the ith target. Normally, there is a "dwell time" for the radar and, as it is focused on a target for a longer time, it gets more accurate information about that target; however, this is constrained since obtaining perfect information is not possible due to process and sensor noise (and other characteristics). For now, assume that when a radar is focused on the ith target, it reduces the uncertainty about its state estimate at a rate of r_i, $i = 1, 2, \ldots, N$. Hence, pointing the radar at a target for only a very brief time does not result in immediate gain of all possible information (up to the measurement and process noise). Later, we will consider the case where the r_i are not constants, but evolve according to some dynamics.

To summarize how the scheduler interacts with the tracker, note that the model of our process is now given by

$$\theta_1(t) = p_1 t$$
$$\theta_2(t) = p_2 t$$
$$\vdots$$
$$\theta_{i*}(t) = p_{i*} t - r_{i*} t \tag{4}$$
$$\vdots$$
$$\theta_N(t) = p_N t$$

for the case where the radar is focused on target i∗ so that it is reducing the uncertainty associated with the estimate of that target's location. It is the task of the scheduler to select $i*$ at each time instant. Inspecting Equation 4 it is clear that the task of the scheduler is to try to maintain bounded values for the θ_i, i.e., it wants

$$\sum_{i=1}^{N} |\theta_i(t)| \leq B \tag{5}$$

for all $i = 1, 2, \ldots, N$ for as small of a value of the bound B as possible (since low values of B provide a characterization of high certainty about the information about the *entire* target environment).

The scheduling problem is complicated by the fact that the radar can only be switched from focusing on one target to another in a finite time so that there is a "delay" $\delta_{i,j}$ in switching from the ith target to the jth target. Clearly, during this delay time the radar is useless and the uncertainties for all the targets goes up. Hence, if the policy for the scheduler switches too often, then it wastes all its time performing the switching. However, if it does not switch often enough, some uncertainty will rise too high. In such a case, during the period of time $\delta_{i,j}$, for all i

$$\theta_i(t) = p_i t \tag{6}$$

There are certain properties of the underlying scheduling problem that are independent of how we specify the scheduler. For instance, there is the concept of the "capacity" of the radar resource. Mathematically, we will not be able to achieve boundedness for Equation 4 if we do not have

$$\sum_{i=1}^{N} \frac{p_i}{r_i} < 1 \tag{7}$$

Additionally, the radar cannot be pointing to more than one direction (target) at a time. Also, the amount of time the radar is pointing to the various targets cannot exceed the time period of one radar sweep, T_r. To express this constraint we need to introduce the variables describing the dwell times for particular targets, τ_i. The constraint then is

$$\sum_{i=1}^{N} \tau_i \leq T_r \tag{8}$$

We will refer to these two inequalities as the "capacity conditions" for the radar resource. It characterizes a necessary condition to be able to achieve boundedness, no matter what scheduling policy we choose.

3   Architectures

This problem can be mapped to various architectures:

1. Centralized One-Module architecture (where one function collects inputs about all the targets and makes radar scheduling decisions as well as computes estimates),
2. Centralized Two-Module (where there are two functions, one for tracking and one for radar scheduling),
3. Decentralized (n functions are allocated to track targets - one function per target - based on the radar measurements, and one function is allocated to schedule the radar)
4. Others, e.g., Decentralized Negotiation (where each of the targets is represented by an agent whose responsibility is to negotiate (with the radar agent) for the radar resource).

The criteria that can guide the architecture selection process are:

1. Overall performance of the system (in this case the level of uncertainty about the states of the targets),
2. Computational complexity (time performance of the system),
3. Controllability (is the goal of the system achievable given the decomposition of the functionality?)
4. Observability (is the state of the system computable given a finite sequence of outputs?)
5. Stability (can the system be organized so that orderly behavior will result?)
6. Scalability (can the system be easily adapted to handle larger amounts of input?)
7. Versatility (includes modularity; relevant for adaptability, i.e., for the ability to adjust to changing situations, e.g., changing number of targets, or changing target dynamics)

In this paper we are focusing only on the issues of stability and computational complexity.

3.1   Stability

A system (e.g., Equation 4) is said to be "stable in the sense of Lagrange" [6] if for every initial condition (e.g., in Equation 4 the $\theta_i(0)$) such that the initial condition lies within a certain bound (e.g., $\sum_{i=1}^{N} \theta_i(0) \leq \alpha$) there exists a bound B such that Equation 5 is satisfied (note that B may depend on α). Clearly, stability in the sense of Lagrange is simply a type of boundedness property. Typically, in practical applications, we would like B to be as small as possible.

Lagrange stability only says that *there exists* a bound for the uncertainty trajectories. A slightly stronger stability condition is that of *uniform ultimate boundedness* (UUB), where for every initial condition the trajectories are bounded, and as time goes to infinity, they will all approach a B-neighborhood of the origin where we know the bound B (e.g., it typically depends on the parameters of the problem - in this case the rates p_i and r_i.

Note that if the scheduler has chosen a specific $i*$ for a long enough time it may be possible to reduce θ_{i*} to near zero. When this happens it normally does not make sense to keep the radar focused on that target (however, if it is a very high priority target then we may want to maintain as much information about it as possible). It is clear that to be able to achieve boundedness, the scheduler cannot ignore any one target for too long (i.e., the "revisit time" for any one target cannot be too long) or its corresponding uncertainty will rise to a high value.

3.2   Complexity

While there are many concepts of computational complexity, the focus of this paper is on time complexity as a function of the number N of targets during a single sampling period. This corresponds to the "soon enough" requirement discussed in Section 2.

In the rest of the paper, we first describe what we mean by "architecture." Then we outline the mapping of our problem to a number of control-based architectures. Finally, we discuss the issues of complexity and stability associated with some of these architectures.

4   What Is "Architecture"?

The term "architecture" is often used to represent various meanings - from the specification of a structure of the system to be built, through the design of the system, to the global properties of a system. We follow the definition used by the IEEE Working Group on the IEEE P1471 standard [1,5]. According to this conceptualization, architecture is defined by an *architectural description*. An architectural description must conform to a number of requirements, e.g., it must identify the *stakeholders* and their *concerns*. An architectural description consists of a number of *views* developed according to *viewpoints*. The IEEE P1471 does not specify any specific views, leaving it up to the architect. But it requires that if there are multiple views, they must identify *inter-view consistency*, i.e., it has to identify consistency constraints and, possibly, any inconsistencies, if they exist. Concerns are specified in *models*. Models can use various representation languages.

In this paper we focus on two views: *user's view* and *structural view*. The user's view captures the requirements on the external interactions between the system under development and its environment. Among others, it captures the user's concern, which in this particular case is the accuracy ("good enough") and the timeliness ("soon enough") of the tracking function. The structural view should include at least three parts: *components, relations* and *consistency constraints*. Accordingly, to map a specific solution to a control architecture, we need to define these three parts.

4.1   System Architecture

First, we specify the architecture of a tracking system without a control loop. Such a system does not have any built-in mechanisms for compensating for disturbances.

We specify this architecture as consisting of three components - the tracker, the radar and the operator, with relations as shown in Figure 1. The constraint is that the tracker knows the states of the targets "good enough", as specified by Equation 5. To specify that the tracker knows the states of the targets "soon enough", we must introduce one more variable, T_c, representing the computation time of the algorithm (i.e., the time needed to perform both the computation of the state estimates and the schedule) and the time to switch the radar from one target to another. In the rest of the paper we do not take into consideration the radar switch time, i.e., we assume that $\delta_{i,j} = 0$. The constraint is then represented by the inequality

$$T_c < T_r \tag{9}$$

It states that the length of the computation is bounded by the radar sweep period T_r. Note that this constraint makes a direct connection to the complexity of the computation. Two more constraints that participate in the specification of this architecture are given by Equations 7 and 8.

4.2   Feedback Based Control Architecture

The Closed Loop (Feedback) Model presented in [3] is shown in Figure 2. We present this architecture here simply to show that, in the following subsections, we will be using this structure as a recurring pattern for various architectural solutions.

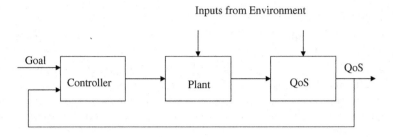

Fig. 2. Conventional Feedback Control Architecture

5 Mapping to Feedback Control Architectures

5.1 One-Module Feedback Based Control Architecture for Tracker

The resulting control-based architecture would include the plant, consisting of two main functions (*track* and *schedule*), the *QoS* module, the *controller* and the *feedback loop*, as shown in Figure 3. We have already discussed the *track*, *schedule* and *QoS* functions. The *controller* for this system would be useful when the parameters p_i, r_i are unknown and thus need to be estimated. Using the control paradigm we would then estimate these parameters incrementally with the amount of increment in each iteration controlled by the *controller* module.

The *Goal* (also called *set point* in the control literature) is expressed here as a value of the constant B (see Equation 5). The constraints are:

$$QoS = \Theta \leq B \tag{10}$$

$$T_c = \sum_{s=1}^{3} T_s \leq T_r \tag{11}$$

where s enumerates computational modules. Equation 11 states the "soon enough" constraint, i.e., that the computation time for all the three modules does not add up to more than the allowed time bound T_r.

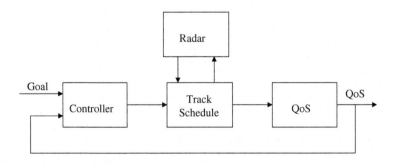

Fig. 3. One-Module Tracker Control Architecture

5.2   Two-Module Architecture

The basic system architecture, as specified above, involves two functions, *track* and *schedule*, both being part of the same plant. This mapping is not natural from the point of view of control theory. In control theory, the plant is considered as a black box that takes inputs and generates outputs. In other words, the plant should be represented by only one function. In order to satisfy this requirement, the plant would need to be split into two, one for *track* and one for *schedule*, as shown if Figure 4.

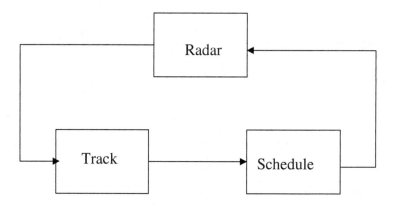

Fig. 4. First Decomposition of Tracker

The control-based architecture would add two controllers, one for each of the two modules, as shown in Figure 5. In general, it also might add two *Goals* and two *QoS* modules. In other words, the overall goal might need to be decomposed. However, for this particular case, we use the same goal, i.e., the goal is still to reduce the uncertainty of the state of the tracked objects. Consequently, we also use the same *QoS* as feedback. The "good enough" constraint would need to bound the computation of all five modules by the allowed time T_c. The constraints are:

$$QoS = \Theta \leq B \tag{12}$$

$$T_c = \sum_{s=1}^{5} T_s \leq T_r \tag{13}$$

Equation 12 represents the "good enough" constraint and 13 represents the "soon enough" constraint.

5.3   Decentralized Architecture

Instead of having one function to track all the targets, we can have a copy of the tracking function instantiated for each target. The system architecture is shown

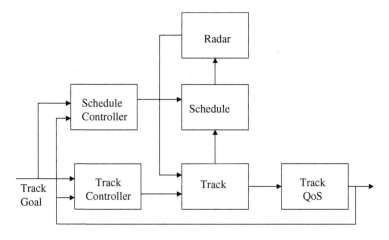

Fig. 5. Control Architecture for the First Decomposition

in Figure 6. This architecture can be mapped onto the control architecture by adding a controller, a QoS module and a feedback loop for each of the trackers and for the scheduler. Additionally, we would need to define *Goal* for both the schedule controller and for each of the tracker's controllers. One possibility is to define bounds B_i on the *QoS* of each tracker and use them as goals. The goal of the scheduler though must account for all targets. We can use the global bound B in Equation 5 for this purpose. This means that we would need a *QoS* module to implement this equation. We do not show a drawing of such an architecture since such a figure would be too complicated.

The constraints for this architecture are stated below.

$$QoS_i = \Theta_i \leq B_i, \ i = 1, \ldots, n \tag{14}$$

$$T_c = \sum_{s=1}^{3(n+1)} T_s \leq T_r \tag{15}$$

Additionally, Equation 5 defines the global constraint on the *QoS* of the scheduler.

6 Comparing Various Architectures

6.1 Stability

Stability is a binary concept; a system can be either stable or not. Typically, we are interested in designs of systems that guarantee stability. Moreover, we may design a system in such a way that it operates in a region that is bounded by a "safety zone" from an unstable behavior. We made such an assumption in the problem specification (see Equation 5). Moreover, we assumed that the problem

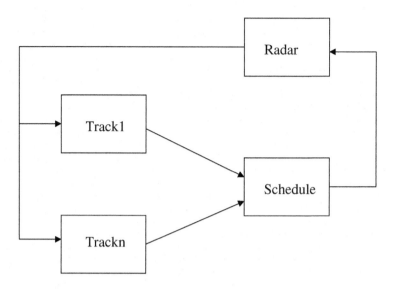

Fig. 6. Decentralized System Architecture

specification constraints should be preserved in the target control theory based architectures. This assumption is represented as a mapping rule

$$\text{refined\_constraints} \implies \text{problem\_constraints} \qquad (16)$$

Following this rule, we performed the mapping of the problem onto various control theory based architectures so that the resulting architectures guarantee stability.

As a consequence of this assumption, the stability constraint is not a discriminant characteristic that could be used for comparing the architectures. However, when performing this mapping, we realized that we can satisfy the stability constraint in many different ways. In other words, we could use different types of constraints (Equations 10 through 15), all of which would satisfy the rule given by Equation 16.

The architectural constraints, however, induce a different classification. Note that they constrain the algorithms with respect to both the accuracy of tracking and the time of computation. For instance, in the one-module architecture (where there is no explicit partition between tracking and scheduling), the system designer has a lot of flexibility in how to satisfy the "soon enough" architectural constraint. The designer is (theoretically) free to choose either a shorter computation for tracking or for scheduling, as long as their sum does not exceed T_r. Or the designer may choose an algorithm that would make a decision on where to spend more time (in tracking or scheduling) at run time, as long as the overall computation time is within the required limits. In the two-module architecture, on the other hand, since the architectural constraints are fixed for each of the modules by the architect, the designer is more constrained in the design choices.

Similarly, for the "good enough" constraint, the one-module control based architecture requires the satisfaction of the accuracy constraint by one module. In the two-module architecture, on the other hand, both tracking subsystem and the scheduling subsystem must satisfy the same constraint, and thus the designer has less flexibility in the solution space. The distributed architecture imposes n constraints, i.e., one for each target. This architecture is thus even less flexible from this point of view. Trade-offs between time spent on computation for particular targets must be made under any architecture, however in the one-module architecture the trade-off may be made at the design or the run time, while in the distributed architecture (at least in the approach described in this paper) the trade-off is made at the architecture design time.

6.2   Complexity

The computational tasks involve tracking, scheduling, QoS and control. The complexity of the computation depends on many parameters, such as the precise algorithms used for control and tracking. In this discussion, we focus on the how the complexity increases as the number of targets (N) increases, i.e., how he system scales up.

Consider first the simplest control architecture in which there is just one QoS module and one control module. The QoS and control functions are performed independently for each target, so the time complexity of these tasks are both $O(N)$. Furthermore, this independence property implies that one can perform these two computational tasks on a distributed system. In particular, if there are $\Omega(N)$ processors available, then the time complexity of these two tasks can be reduced to $O(1)$.

The tracking function uses a processing algorithm such as a Kalman filter, as noted in Section 2.2, for each target. Unlike the QoS and control functions, the targets are not necessarily independent. When two targets visually coincide or nearly coincide, it is necessary to disambiguate the two signals. Except for this situation, the time complexity of tracking is $O(N)$. If n targets nearly coincide with one another, the time complexity of disambiguation is $O(n^2)$ for these n targets. Under mild assumptions, such as no more than $\sqrt{N}$ targets may come close to coinciding, the time complexity of tracking remains $O(N)$. As with the QoS and control functions, the basic tracking computation may be distributed. In addition, groups of nearly coincident targets need to be disambiguated, which can also be distributed as long as different groups are not too close.

The last function to consider is the scheduling function. This function is responsible for allocating the radar resource to the targets. Scheduling involves interactions between targets so it cannot be done for each target in parallel. Although resource allocation problems are typically NP-complete, the assumptions embodied in Equation 4 and the assumption that $\delta_{i,j}$ are all equal to 0 imply that this particular resource allocation problem is tractable.

The simplest scheduling algorithm is the one that simply chooses the target with the largest uncertainty, with the dwell time equal to the maximum period of time during which it is possible to reduce the uncertainty for this target. This function can be performed by computing a maximum. The time complexity for this computation is $O(N)$. Unlike the other functions, this computation cannot be performed in time $O(1)$ on a distributed system. By decomposing the computation hierarchically, it can be performed in time $O(\log(N))$ by $\Omega(N)$ processors.

Taken together, the total time complexity is $O(N)$ on a single processor, and the total time complexity is $O(\log(N))$ on $\Omega(N)$ processors. This is the time complexity to compute a single dwell on a single target. For this to be "soon enough", it must not exceed the current dwell time.

More complex scheduling algorithms perform some amount of advance planning to improve performance. This is especially important when the $\delta_{i,j}$ are not zero. The simple scheduling algorithm above will still work when $\delta_{i,j}$ is nonzero, and one can bound its performance. However, the simple scheduling algorithm is not optimal. In fact, computing the optimum is equivalent to the traveling salesman problem, so it is an NP-complete problem. Nevertheless, small amounts of planning can improve performance without requiring exponential time complexity.

Advance planning takes place during a longer period of time than a single dwell, and it can be as large as the radar sweep time, T_r. In this case, the total complexity T_c must not exceed T_r (Equation 9). Using the simple scheduling algorithm above, the time complexity of scheduling for a radar sweep is $O(N^2)$ on a single processor, and $O(N \log(N))$ when distributed on $\Omega(N)$ processors. Therefore, the "soon enough" constraint for this algorithm is that the time complexity not exceed T_r.

7   Conclusions

In this paper we discussed the problem of mapping an application to a control theory-based architecture. The mapping process consisted of two main steps - first, developing a *basic architecture* of the system without any control loop, and then mapping such an architecture to a control-based architecture. The mapping involves adding a controller and a QoS module to each component of the basic architecture, specification of control goals for each of the controllers, and specification of constraints.

As our case study we have chosen one kind of control theory-based architecture – the feedback control architecture. We considered three basic architectures: one-module, two-module, and distributed ($n + 1$-module).

Often the selection of an architecture is considered as a selection of the structure of the system, i.e., showing a data flow diagram of the system. Clearly, as is shown in this paper, this is not sufficient. The mapping must also include the propagation of the constraints from the basic system to the control theory-based system. This step may be achieved in many different ways. The requirement that we followed in our process was that the satisfaction of the constraints in the control-based system must imply the satisfaction of the system level architectural constraints. It seems natural that the architect should try not to overconstrain the system since such a system would have a narrower domain of applicability (less versatility). Also, the selection of the constraints impacts the complexity of the algorithms that need to be used to implement a given architecture. It is the architect's job to define the constraints wisely so that the impacts are balanced.

In this paper we focused only on two kinds of criteria by which one can compare various architectural solutions: stability and complexity. We formulated constraints in such a way as to guarantee the stability of each of the systems. Therefore, the comparison of architectures by the stability measure does not classify the systems into stable and unstable, since all of them are stable, but into more constrained and less constrained.

Acknowledgments

This research was partially supported by a grant from the Defense Advanced Research Projects Agency.

References

1. R. Hilliard. Using UML for architectural description. *Lecture Notes in Computer Science: Proceedings of UML'99*, pages –, 1999.
2. G. Karsai and J. Sztipanovits. A model-based approch to self-adaptive software. *IEEE Intelligent Systems*, May/June 1999:46–53, 1999.
3. M. M. Kokar, K. Baclawski, and Y. Eracar. Control theory-based foundations of self-controlling software. *IEEE Intelligent Systems*, May/June 1999:37–45, 1999.
4. R. Laddaga. Creating robust software through self-adaptation. *IEEE Intelligent Systems*, May/June 1999:26–29, 1999.
5. Institute of Electrical and Electronics Engineers. Draft recommended practice for architectural description: Ieee p1471/d5.2. Piscataway, NJ, December 1999.
6. K. M. Passino and K. L. Burgess. *Stability Analysis of Discrete Event Systems*. John Wiley, 1998.
7. P. Robertson and J. M. Brady. Adaptive image analysis for aerial surveillance. *IEEE Intelligent Systems*, May/June 1999:30–36, 1999.

Transient Management in Reconfigurable Systems

Gyula Simon, Tamás Kovácsházy, and Gábor Péceli

Department of Measurement and Information Systems,
Technical University of Budapest, Hungary
e-mail:{simon, khazy, peceli}@mit.bme.hu

Abstract. Self-adaptive systems reconfigure themselves to improve their operation when changes in the environment imply to do so. Reconfiguration usually means the replacement or modification of some functional components so that the new components provide better performance, more robust operation, or better functionality. Such a reconfiguration, however, may cause undesirable transient effects, which may (temporarily) degrade the performance of the overall system. This paper investigates two important aspects of transient management: (1) the proper choice of the structure that has advantageous transient properties (to be chosen in design-time); and (2) the proper run-time transient management.

1 Introduction

The study of reconfigurable systems is a very attractive area of research related mainly to larger scale, distributed intelligence monitoring and control systems [1], [2], [3]. Nowadays, the design and implementation of such systems is solved using the so-called model-based approach. In model based systems a priori knowledge is directly represented as a built in model, which must be able to follow changes in the environment for optimal performance.

To provide a realization framework for reconfigurable model based systems, the concept of System with Modes of Operation (SMO) has been proposed [1], see Fig. 1 for a conceptual SMO. In an SMO, the model changes are represented as transitions between modes. Modes and possible transitions are set up during the design phase or inserted at run-time. Some modes are classified as operational mode, other modes are failure modes corresponding to failure conditions in the system or in the environment. Generally, mode transitions are considered being bi-directional, i.e., mode transition can occur in both directions. For every mode there exists at least one configuration, which defines all the necessary realization details.

Transitions between different configurations may cause undesirable transient effects, which must be kept as low as possible to avoid system degradation. In our understanding, transient management can be divided into two main fields: design-time and run-time management. The proper system structure must be chosen in design-time (either for modes known exactly in design-time, when matched structures can be applied; or for modes composed in run-time, when structures with 'general good properties' should be chosen).

P. Robertson, H. Shrobe, and R. Laddaga (Eds.): IWSAS 2000, LNCS 1936, pp. 90-98, 2000.

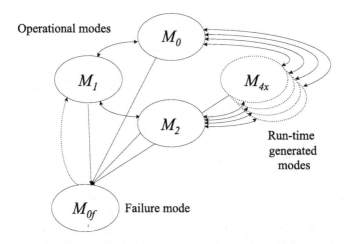

Fig. 1. System with modes of operation. Example with four operational modes and one failure mode (Modes M_0 to M_{4x} are operational modes, where M_{4x} is generated run-time; M_{0f} is a failure mode with autonomous repair to M_1)

This paper highlights the importance of transient management, and examines the two main aspects of the problem: the proper choice of the structure, and the run-time management of the transients.

The reconfiguration methods are presented in Section 2, which is followed by a short introduction to reconfiguration transients in Section 3. In Section 4 the structural dependence of the transients will be examined, while Section 5 compares different transient management techniques.

2   Reconfiguration Methods

There are various methods proposed in the literature to realize the run-time configuration changes due to mode transitions (see [1] for an overview). Generally, the task of the reconfiguration method is to transform the system to a new configuration corresponding to a new mode. A straightforward and redundant way of reconfiguration is shown in Fig. 2. The so-called *output switching method* operates more systems in parallel, and in case of reconfiguration the output of the proper system is selected. The parallel implementations are operated through the whole lifetime of the system, therefore the computational cost is multiplied roughly by the number of existing modes.

The output switching method can be used only in systems, in which the modes are known in design time. A more serious drawback of this method is that the reconfigured part cannot be in a feedback loop. Thus, for all practical cases other methods must be used.

The *one-step reconfiguration method* removes the old system and inserts the new one into operation in one step (possibly in one sampling interval), similarly to the output switching method; but the new system is *not* operated before the removal of

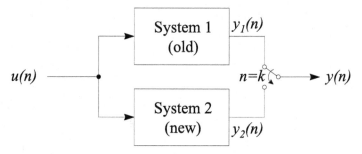

Fig. 2. Output switching method

the old system, so it has no information on the past life-period of the environment. So in parallel with the configuration change, different transient management techniques should be applied that properly initialize the new system's state variables. The optional state variable update tries to compensate the absent memory of the new system in a way that the new system 'feels like' operating there for a long time. In this paper this method will be used, and all transient management techniques will be discussed in this framework.

3   Reconfiguration Transients

The run-time reconfiguration brings up several open questions both in the field of realization and system design. The reconfiguration transients originate from the different behavior of the system before and after the reconfiguration. Reconfiguration transients may not be tolerated because of their possibly high amplitude and extreme dynamics [4], [5]. For example, these transients manifest themselves in control systems as wide deviations from the expected controlled variables, saturation, and even system component failures due to overload [1]. In audio signal processing the transients are heard as disturbing clicks and pops in the audio signal [5].

The optimal transition of a reconfigured system is highly environment and system dependent, therefore various transient definitions and transient measures exist. A straightforward practical definition of such transients is the difference between the measured value in the reconfigured system, and the ideal value in a reference system. The reference system is a hypothetical system, which operates in the new mode for a long time. In this paper this definition is used.

4   Structure Dependence of Reconfiguration Transients

In many cases the required functionality can be realized by different structures. In reconfigurable systems one can utilize the fact that the possible implementations have very different secondary properties, which enables the optimization of the transients in design time. In [6] and [7] it was shown that the proper selection of the signal processing structure leads to dramatic improvement of the reconfiguration transient

Table 1. Parameters (gain and time-constants) of the plant in different operating modes. MODE1 is slow (the dominant time constant T_1=10 s) with low gain (1). MODE2 is faster (T_1=5s), and the gain is higher (2).

System parameters	MODE 1	MODE 2
Gain	1	2
T_1	10s	5s
T_2	4s	2s
T_3	1s	1s

Table 2. Controller transfer functions for MODE1, and MODE2

Controllers	MODE 1	MODE 2
$H(z)$	$\dfrac{8.6130 - 17.1960z^{-1} + 8.5829z^{-2}}{1.0000 - 1.9885z^{-1} + 0.9885z^{-2}}$	$\dfrac{2.3884 - 4.7601z^{-1} + 2.3717z^{-2}}{1.0000 - 1.9590z^{-1} + 0.9590\,z^{-2}}$

behavior of (open-loop) discrete-time linear filters. Here the properties of the one step reconfiguration method will be analyzed in simple (closed loop) control systems.

The experimental system consists of a continuous-time plant with one input and one output, controlled by a discrete-time PID controller. The plant has two operating modes. The first mode is a low-gain and slow system, the second one is a higher gain and faster system, see Table 1 for system parameters. Two matched discrete-time PID controllers were designed to appropriately control the plant in both modes (resulting critically damped closed-loop systems). The transfer functions of the controllers are shown in Table 2. If the plant is in MODE 1 and it is controlled by a controller in MODE 2, the closed-loop system is slower than it is expected. On the other hand, if the plant is in MODE 2 and the controller is in MODE 1, the closed loop system is under-damped. Both scenarios require the reconfiguration of the controller to achieve optimal performance.

Here it is not considered how and why mode changes occur in the plant; neither considered how the mode changes are identified and decision is made to reconfigure the controller. It is assumed that originally the plant is controlled by a PID controller *not* designed for that particular plant, and then the controller is reconfigured to a more appropriate one. The reconfiguration is done using the one-step reconfiguration method. To ease the comparison of the structures, in the following examples no sophisticated state update mechanisms were used, the new controller simply preserves the states of the old one (since the order of the controllers were the same, it can easily be done, see TM 2 in Section 5).

The transient caused by the reconfiguration is analyzed for two different realizations of the controller: the transposed direct structure II (see Fig. 3.a) and the scaled parallel structure (Fig. 3.b) realizations. Note that both structures provide exactly the same transfer function with an appropriate choice of parameters, apart from negligible differences due to computational precision. However, their behavior is completely different during the reconfiguration.

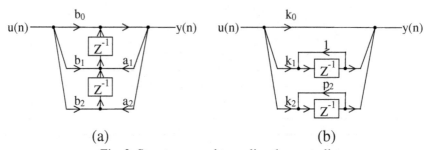

(a)   (b)

Fig. 3. Structures used to realize the controller.
(a) transposed direct structure II, (b) scaled parallel structure.

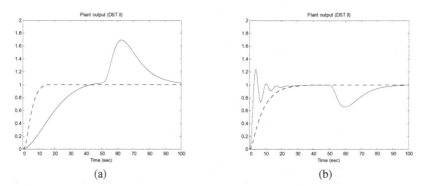

(a)   (b)

Fig. 4. Step responses of the closed loop control systems. The controller was implemented using the transposed direct structure II of Figure 3.a. The reconfiguration was done by the one-step reconfiguration method at time instant 50s. (a) The plant is in MODE2. Solid line: controller reconfiguration MODE1→MODE2, dotted line (for reference): controller in MODE2, no reconfiguration. (b) The plant is in MODE1. Solid line: controller reconfiguration MODE2→MODE1, dotted line (reference): controller in MODE1, no reconfiguration

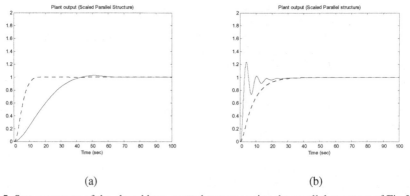

(a)   (b)

Fig. 5. Step responses of the closed loop control systems using the parallel structure of Fig 3.b. See Fig. 4 for explanation

The step responses of the closed loop systems, reconfigured at time instant 50s by the one-step reconfiguration method, are shown on Fig. 4 and Fig. 5 for the transposed direct structure II and for the scaled parallel controller realizations, respectively. It is clearly visible that in the example the scaled parallel realization produced much less transients.

Unfortunately, it cannot be stated that for all possible controller parameter sets the parallel realization performs better. However, it is true that the scaled parallel structure has certain advantageous properties, which makes it more suitable for most applications. The detailed analysis of the structure for special input signals in an open-loop scenario can be found in [7].

5   Run-Time Transient Management Techniques

The following example illustrates the importance of the run-time transient management through an example with a complex nonlinear system in a feedback loop. Some possible transient management techniques are also compared.

A simulated two-link planar robot arm (see Fig. 6), which is a strongly nonlinear mechanical system, is controlled by simple digital controllers. Two separate controllers were used, one on each joint. The robot arm is controlled so that the end position of the second arm (where the tool is applied) moves on a triangle. To illustrate the reconfiguration effects, two modes are present in the system. When the modes change, the joint controllers are reconfigured. In the example, MODE 1 is the lower part of the triangle, and MODE 2 is the upper part (see the upper right plot of Fig. 7). In MODE 1 controller set 1, while in MODE 2 controller set 2 is used.

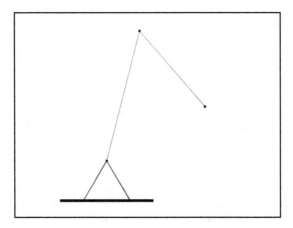

Fig. 6. The simulated two-link planar robot used in the example. The links are 0.6m and 0.8 m long, their mass is 1kg and 0.5 kg (concentrated in the joints), and the friction coefficients are 3 kgm^2/s.

The joints are controlled by simple digital PID controllers. The input of each controller is the joint appropriate position error e_k (the difference between the desired and measured joint angle). The simple control algorithm is the following:

$$x_1(k) = x_1(k-1) + T_S \cdot e(k-1), \tag{1}$$

$$x_2(k) = e(k-1), \tag{2}$$

$$y(k) = P \cdot e(k) + I \cdot x_1(k) + D \cdot (e(k) - x_2(k)) / T_S, \tag{3}$$

where P, I, and D are the parameters of the controller, T_S is the sampling interval, and $x(k)$ is the two-element parameter vector of the controller. The structure of the controller is a parallel representation, as can be seen in equations (1)-(3). In order to make the effects more eye-catching, the structure is not scaled.

The change of modes, thus the reconfiguration is made in time instant 10s (MODE 1 $\rightarrow$ MODE 2) and in time instant 14s (MODE 2 $\rightarrow$ MODE 1). Four different transient management (TM) techniques were used to conduct system transitions:

TM 1: (State zeroing method) The state variables are set to zero when the controller's parameters are changed. In this case the new controller always starts from a zero-energy state, so its behavior is predictable, and moreover, the transients are independent of the realization's structure. As the second row of Fig. 7 clearly shows, the reconfiguration caused large transients in the joint angles, thus producing large tool position errors, too.

TM 2: (State preserving method) The state variables of the new controller are initialized to the values of the old ones. This solution may be useful when the successive parameter sets are similar. A drawback of this solution is that the transient behavior of the new controller strongly depends on the last state of the old controller. In the example, the reconfiguration causes large transients (because the controllers are quite different), as shown in the third row of Fig. 7.

The idea of the next reconfiguration strategies is to force the new controller to continue the operation of the old one as smoothly as possible.

TM 3: The state variables are initialized so that the new controller's output and it's first derivative be the same as those of the old controller's. It is clear, that having two free parameters (the initial state vector), it can easily be done by solving a linear equation with two variables. The transients caused by the reconfiguration can be seen in the fourth row of Fig. 7.

The idea can naturally be extended to fit more derivatives if there are more state variables in the system. This mathematical approach, however, neglects the physical background. Analyzing the realized structure's physical background a hybrid-solution can be constructed, which gives the best solution:

TM 4: The second state variable (x_2) keeps the value of that of the old controller, while the first one (x_1) is used to fit the output trajectory of the controllers. Having one degree of freedom the derivatives are not fitted in this case, but the results are very nice: the transient effects are low as shown in the last row of Figure 7. The explanation is that although the new controller in TM 3 will smoothly continue the old controller's trajectory in the first sample, the state variable may contain such 'strange'

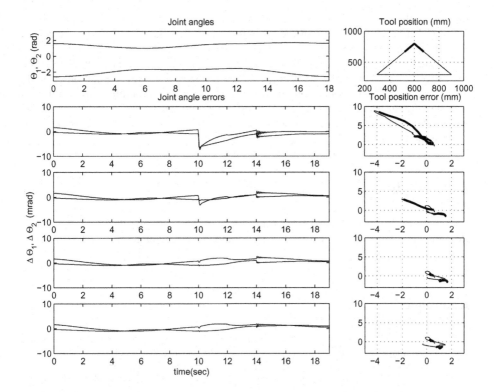

Fig. 7. Reconfiguration transients of the two-joint planar robot arm. The reconfiguration of the joint controllers was done in time instants 10s and 14s. *1ˢᵗ row*: ideal joint angles (left), and tool trajectory (right), where mode one and mode two are indicated by thin and thick lines, respectively. *2ⁿᵈ row- 4ᵗʰ row*: joint angle errors and tool position error trajectories using different reconfiguration strategies. On the tool position error trajectories thick lines show the effect of the reconfiguration transients.

values, which would never occur in normal operation. These 'strange' values change, of course, and thus transients are produced at the output.

6 Conclusions

In this paper two aspects of the reconfigurable systems' transient effects were examined. It was shown that the transients originating from the change of certain system blocks or parameters, strongly depend on the processing structure. Thus in the design-time the proper choice of the system representation can highly improve the overall performance. Examples were shown to illustrate the phenomenon in simple control systems.

It was also illustrated that the reconfiguration transients can be managed in run-time. In addition to the evident and often-used state zeroing and state preserving methods, other methods were suggested, which show much better transient properties. It must also be emphasized that the reconfiguration management has to be aware of the structure of the system to be reconfigured, in order to reach optimal results.

Although there are no comprehensive theoretical results yet, it is clear that certain structures have superior transient properties, and using these representations usually has no significant additional computational cost. In a quite complex environment it was shown that transient management is possible, and the system's performance can be much higher than that of without transient management, at a price of a small computational overhead.

Acknowledgement

The research described here was sponsored, in part, by the Defense Advanced Research Projects Agency (DARPA) (US) under agreement number F33615-99-C-3611.

References

1 Sztipanovits, J., Wilkes, D. M., Karsai, G., Biegl, C., Lynd, L. E.: The Multigraph and structural adaptivity. IEEE Transactions on Signal Processing, Vol. 41 (1993) 2695-2716
2 Barford, L., Manders, E. J., Biswas, G., Mosterman, P. J., Ram, V., Barnett, J.: Derivative estimation for diagnosis. In Proceedings of the 1999 IEEE International Workshop on Emerging Technologies, Venice, Italy (1999) 9-15
3 Moore, M. S.: Model-Integrated Program Synthesis for Real-Time Image Processing. PhD thesis, Vanderbilt University, Nashville, Tennessee (1997)
4 Kovácsházy, T., Péceli, G.: Transients in adaptive and reconfigurable measuring channels. In Proceedings of the International Symposium on Measurement Technology and Intelligent Instruments ISMTII'98, Miskolc, Hungary (1998) 247-252
5 Valimaki, V., Laakso, T. I.: Suppression of transients in variable recursive digital filters with a novel and efficient cancellation method. IEEE Transactions on Signal Processing, Vol. 46 (1998) 3408-3414
6 Péceli, G., Kovácsházy, T.: Transients in Reconfigurable DSP systems. IEEE Transactions on Instrumentation and Measurement, Vol. 48 (1999) 986-989
7 Kovácsházy, T, Péceli, G.: Scaling strategies for reconfigurable digital signal processing systems. . In Proceedings of the Workshop on Intelligent Signal Processing WISP'99, Budapest, Hungary (1999) 215-220

Model-Integrated Embedded Systems

Akos Ledeczi, Arpad Bakay, and Miklos Maroti

Institute for Software Integrated Systems
Vanderbilt University, Nashville, TN 37235
{akos,bakaya,mmaroti}@isis.vanderbilt.edu

Abstract. Model-Integrated Computing is a proven technology for designing and implementing complex software systems. Making the design-time models available at run-time benefits the development of dynamic embedded systems. This paper describes a paradigm-independent, general infrastructure for the design and implementation of model-integrated embedded systems that is highly applicable to self-adaptive systems.

1   Introduction

Model-Integrated Computing (MIC) is a proven technology for designing and implementing complex software systems [1]. Research at the Institute for Software Integrated Systems at Vanderbilt University has clearly shown the advantages of the model-based approach in a wide range of industrial, engineering and scientific applications. The greatest advantages of this technology can be achieved in application domains with these specific characteristics:

1. The specification calls for or allows hierarchical decomposition, either from a single aspect or from multiple aspects: for example tasks/subtasks, spatial/physical/hardware segmentation, units of commanding or supervision responsibility, etc.
2. The complexity of the system precludes the success of any ad-hoc approach, while careful analysis can identify relationships inside the computing environment, along which a sensible modularization is feasible.
3. The computing system is required to change frequently, because of successive refinements of the algorithms applied (application prototyping phase), because of changes in the computing infrastructure (e.g. hardware) or due to continuous changes in the specification, as a consequence of the evolution of the environment under control.

Remarkably, most embedded software development projects also feature one or more of the above characteristics. Whether we consider the domain of consumer electronics, telecommunications or military applications, they all face the challenging problem of quickly, safely, and efficiently producing software for changing requirements and computing infrastructure. Decomposition is a common technique here as well, while—due to the complexity and real-time nature of the applications and the limited resources of the underlying infrastructure—multiple

P. Robertson, H. Shrobe, and R. Laddaga (Eds.): IWSAS 2000, LNCS 1936, pp. 99–115, 2000.

aspects and a complex set of relations with different characteristics must also be taken into consideration.

A significant part of embedded systems are also required to be fault-tolerant, manageable, or even externally serviceable, both in the hardware and the software sense. The model-based approach is definitely helpful in providing these features, since the decomposition boundaries usually also identify standardized access points for those operations.

As models are good tools for humans in understanding and creating complex structures, they also have definite advantages if the system itself is expected to be *reflective*, i.e. to be able to supervise its own operation. Eventually this facilitates the creation of self-adaptive computing architectures, where automatic adaptation itself is based and carried out on the well-understood models of the embedded system.

The use of models or similar concepts for embedded, adaptive computing has been investigated by other research groups as well [6]. Research at ISIS is aimed at leveraging our experience in model integrated computing to create a model-based embedded system infrastructure which is efficient in both its run-time characteristics and the human effort required for development, verification and systems management during the entire life cycle of the system [7]. Partly to accomplish these and also because of additional requirements, design goals also include platform and language independence, standards compliance, support for multiple forms of networking capabilities, and extensibility for unforeseen applications and requirements.

While most of the above requirements support each other in the sense that conforming to one often helps to meet the others, one of them, probably the most important one, run-time efficiency, tends to conflict with the others. Indeed this constitutes the most challenging part of our research: finding optimal compromises while porting elegant high-level programming concepts to an environment, where efficiency and economical resource utilization remain the primary issues.

The research presented here was made possible by the generous sponsorship of the Defense Administration Research Projects Agency (DARPA) under contract (F30602-96-2-0227), and by the Boeing Company.

2   Model-Integrated Computing

Model-Integrated Computing (MIC) employs domain-specific models to represent the software, its environment, and their relationship. With Model-Integrated Program Synthesis (MIPS), these models are then used to automatically synthesize the embedded applications and to generate inputs to COTS analysis tools [11]. This approach speeds up the design cycle, facilitates the evolution of the application and helps system maintenance, dramatically reducing costs during the lifecycle of the system.

Creating domain-specific visual model building, constraint management, and automatic program synthesis components for a MIPS environment for each new domain would be cost-prohibitive for most domains. Applying a generic environment with generic modeling concepts and components would eliminate one of the biggest advantages of MIC—the dedicated support for widely different application domains. An alternative solution is to use a configurable environment that makes it possible to customize the MIPS components for a given domain.

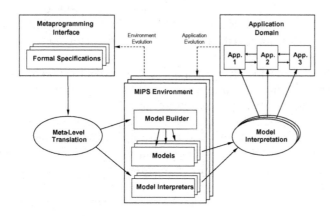

Fig. 1. The Multigraph Architecture

The Multigraph Architecture (MGA) is a toolkit for creating domain-specific MIPS environments. The MGA is illustrated in Fig. 1. The metaprogramming interface is used to specify the modeling paradigm of the application domain. The modeling paradigm is the modeling language of the domain specifying the objects and their relationships. In addition to syntactic rules, semantic information can also be described as a set of constraints. The Unified Modeling Language (UML) and the Object Constraint Language (OCL), respectively, are used for these purposes in the MGA. These specifications, called metamodels, are used to automatically generate the MIPS environment for the domain. An interesting aspect of this approach is that a MIPS environment itself is used to build the metamodels [2].

The generated domain-specific MIPS environment is used to build domain models that are stored in a model database. These models are used to automatically generate the applications or to synthesize input to different COTS analysis tools. This translation process is called model interpretation.

3   Models in Embedded Systems

Modeling concepts available in the MultiGraph Architecture are suitable for modeling real-time embedded systems. The principal aspect of these models is the one describing the computational modules (tasks, objects) and the communication paths between them. This aspect is usually hierarchical by nature, where leaf nodes of the hierarchy correspond to simple functional modules executed under the kernel's command. If the computing environment includes specialized processing units, or soft-hardware components, those functions are also represented as nodes in this hierarchy [5].

Most modern kernels [8,9] provide a wide range of inter-module communication links: messaging, shared memory, high-speed direct interconnections or network connections. Likewise, the type of information transferred may also vary in volume, priority, real-time characteristics (e.g. high/low volume, raw/buffered, control/data etc.). Components may even have functional interconnections without actually being connected directly at the lowest level.

The ability of the MultiGraph models to represent different aspects of the same objects and different kinds of associations in each aspect makes it possible to cope with these modeling issues. However, functional models are only part of representing an embedded system. Other typical aspects may include modeling a multi-processor and multi-node hardware infrastructure and the assignment of functionality to the nodes. Modeling constraints can be of particular value in these models for representing and managing resource limitations (e.g. power, memory, bandwidth).

Other possible aspects to be modeled include persistent data object management, timing relations, user interface elements (menus, screens), or state transition diagrams if applicable. Whether any of these modeling aspects should really be used, depends on whether the kernel layer is able to use them or pass them on to the functional layer. However, representing certain aspects can be still useful without kernel support if they provide information to an external management/supervisory application or to the evaluator component of a self-adaptive system.

4   General Structure of Embedded Model-Integrated Systems

The basic structure of the proposed embedded model-integrated system is illustrated in Fig. 2. The Embedded Modeling Infrastructure (EMI) can be best viewed as a high-level layer at the top of the architecture, while a classical embedded system kernel (e.g. a real-time kernel like [9]) is located at the bottom. The component that connects these two layers is the translator that we call the *embedded interpreter*. The embedded model provides a simple, uniform, paradigm-independent and extensible API (EMI API) to this interpreter.

Besides the kernel, the modeling system (to be detailed later) and the embedded interpreter, the fourth major component of the computing system is the set of software modules that perform the actual task of the embedded system. These are objects executable by the kernel and responsible for the core functionality of the system. The modeling system is not only able to instruct the kernel to instantiate and execute a set of modules, but it also has means to describe operational parameters for them.

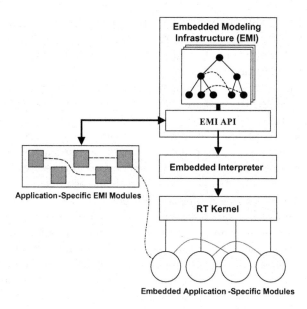

Fig. 2. Embedded Model-Integrated System

These software modules are application-specific, and, since they constitute the most computationally intensive part, performance is given a top priority here. This priority is expected to dominate the selection of the programming language used, so the embedded modeling system does not make any presumptions about it: these modules are just native binary program modules with certain documented characteristics.

While we find it inevitable to implement the core functionality as performance optimized native application-specific modules, our purpose was to avoid application-specific code in the Embedded Modeling Interpreter so that this part would be readily reusable for new applications domains as well. However, as discussed later (see Sect. "Self-adaptive EMI configurations"), practical experience has shown that while data structures carried by the models in the system are able to represent the bulk of the application logic and other relevant information, implementing certain parts (most notably the evaluator) in an application-independent way yields only limited and/or problematical functionality. Consequently, it is preferable to implement these portions in an application specific way.

5 Generative Modeling and Run-Time Modifications

In "traditional" model-integrated computing models are created at design time. They describe a particular solution to a particular problem in the given engineering domain. Being able to work only with a fixed model configuration burned into the system or loaded at boot-up would be a strict limitation on the power of model-integrated computing. The EMI offers two techniques that allow models to evolve during execution.

One is to represent dynamic architectures in a generative manner. Here, the components of the architecture are prepared, but their number and connectivity patterns are not fully defined at design time. Instead, a generative description is provided which specifies how the architecture could be generated "on-the-fly". A generative architecture specification is similar to the generate statement used in VHDL: it is essentially a program that, when executed, generates an architecture by instantiating components and connecting them together.

The generative description is especially powerful when it is combined with architectural parameters and hierarchical decomposition. In a component one can generatively represent an architecture, and the generation "algorithm" can receive architectural parameters from the current or higher levels of the hierarchy. These parameters influence the architectural choices made (e.g. how many components to use, how they are connected, etc.), but they might also be propagated downward in the hierarchy to components at lower levels. There the process is repeated: architectural choices are made, components are instantiated and connected, and possibly newly calculated parameters are passed down further. Thus, with very few generative constructs one can represent a wide variety of architectures that would be very hard, if not impossible, to pre-enumerate.

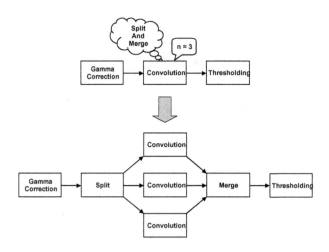

Fig. 3. Generative Modeling

As a simple example for generative modeling, consider a data parallel algorithm, where the data set needs to be split N ways and the results need to be merged. If N can change during runtime, instead of modeling the structure for every possible instance of N, we can explicitly model the parameter N and create a generator that does the split and merge operations (Fig. 3). Even if models do not change at runtime, but they do change frequently at design time, this generative technique provides a convenient approach to modeling.

Naturally, not every architectural alternative is viable in all circumstances. The infrastructure allows for representing architectural descriptions that constrain the selection process, thus limiting the search needed while forcing the process to obey other requirements.

Generative modeling naturally allows for system modifications along dimensions fixed at design time. While this is sufficient for most applications, the EMI can be configured to allow even more liberty in modifying running models. In this mode, an external agent is allowed the same power to specify models as is possible during the boot phase.

To be able to make arbitrary modifications, however, requires extensive kernel support to safely deal with the transient effects and ensure integrity of scheduling communications during system changes. This support is usually not universal, and it is the responsibility of the external agent not to go beyond the abilities of the kernel.

6   Self-Adaptive EMI Configurations

One of the design goals of the embedded modeling infrastructure is to provide convenient support for self-adaptive computing. We define self-adaptive computing architecture as one that is able to measure and detect changes in its own performance and respond to these changes by performing structural changes on its configuration. According to this definition, an adaptive system must contain *monitoring, decision making,* and *configuration modification* functionality. The EMI system provides capabilities for each of these three tasks.

To facilitate the implementation of monitoring algorithms, convenient access to operational parameters is required. Operational parameters in embedded systems belong to one of two distinct categories:

- The momentary status of the embedded operating system itself: resource utilization, timing relations, availability of peripherals and remote nodes in a distributed system, etc.
- The parameters representing the performance of the application algorithms, such as the control error rates of a control system, the amount of missed/ discarded packets of a communication system, cost functions, etc. A common feature of these parameters is that they are application-specific, and their values are usually highly dependent on the environment of the embedded system.

Our decision was to use the embedded models as a place for uniform representation of these parameters. Objects in the model may have designated attributes (monitor attributes) set by the underlying modules: either by the embedded kernel (in case of most operation system parameters), or by any of the application specific task modules that have information on the operation of the algorithm.

The third component, configuration modification, is supplied by generative models and generators described in the previous chapter. This allows, the model designer to efficiently control the degrees of freedom in the model by providing generators where adaptive modifications in the model are foreseen. This decision also reflects the fact that self-adaptive modifications are usually similar or identical to alterations executed by an external management system (or a human operator) on a non-self-adaptive system. Model changes made by the generators are translated towards the kernel by the embedded interpreter.

The most critical component of self-adaptive applications is the one making reconfiguration decisions. In our embedded infrastructure, this is the evaluator, a kernel process itself, which is responsible for interpreting the monitor parameters and for setting architectural parameters for the generators. It is obvious that, depending on the complexity of the application domain and level of adaptivity implemented, the knowledge of such an evaluator may range from some simple mapping operations to real intelligence comparable to that of a human expert. This also means that the programming model may be chosen from a wide range of alternatives: data tables, procedural code, data-flow network, or some more esoteric techniques, such as genetic algorithms or neural nets.

These considerations led us to leave the selection of the evaluator to the application designer: from the EMI system's point of view, the evaluator is a native module accessing the model through the standard EMI API. It is expected to take input primarily from the monitor parameters in the model, and produce its outputs by setting the values of the generator parameters.

The evaluator is a full-fledged task of the kernel, thus nothing inhibits it from interacting with the kernel and with other modules. While this form of direct access may not be an elegant programming practice, we believe that it is helpful if special interactions are required that cannot be efficiently implemented through the monitor variables (e.g. large amount of data, I/O access etc.). Another use of direct communication is the case where the evaluator itself is not monolithic, but rather consists of several tasks communicating with one another.

While we find native application-dependent evaluators necessary and efficient, certain tasks may be implemented by standard modules where no native application-specific programming is needed. Upon initial investigation, adaptive responses to events in the operating system itself (node down, timing specifications not met, etc.) seem to be an area where a parameterized, but otherwise application independent solution may be feasible. We are currently seeking a technique to model evaluator functionality for these problems.

7   Operation of the EMI

Figure 4 presents a detailed view of the embedded model-integrated architecture extended with constructs supporting self-adaptivity. The Embedded Modeling

Infrastructure (EMI), which is the focus of our research, has the following functions:

- Loading the initial version of the model from an external source (typically a modeling/management computer) or from some internal storage facility,
- Booting the embedded system based on the model loaded. This includes executing the built-in generators, which, in-turn, create the dynamic parts of the model through the embedded interpreter,
- Checking model constraints and implementing emergency measures in case of failures,
- In the case of self-adaptive systems, evaluating the operation of the embedded programming modules and setting generative parameters accordingly. Again, the model generators are tasked to implement these changes on the model itself,
- Receiving and executing model updates from external sources, and
- Communicating status information to external management agents.

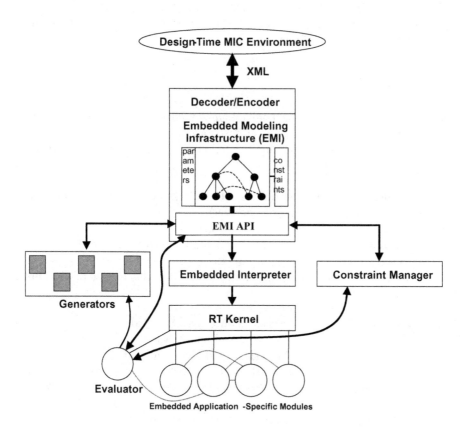

Fig. 4. Self-Adaptive Embedded System

During the load/boot phase the EMI builds the data structures of the initial model and, based on this information, instructs the kernel to instantiate the computing objects accordingly. Generators execute and generate the structure that corresponds to the initial status of the generative parameter objects. Generators are hybrid objects. While they are part of the embedded model, the compiled object code of the generator scripts cannot be represented as paradigm independent modeling objects in the EMI. These scripts, therefore, are located outside of the EMI. Note that they use the same EMI API as, for example, the embedded interpreter. From a programmers point of view, generative modeling and interpreter implementation are similar activities.

The Constraint Manager is a module responsible for ensuring that modeling constraints are met. There are two principal questions about constraints: when to check them, and what to do when (resulting from modifications by the self-adaptive control loop or from external modification commands) they are violated. The answer to these questions is highly application dependent, therefore, the Constraint Manager is designed to be a flexible component with its own API. The evaluator, for example, can request constraint checking for any subset of constraints and/or models at any time.

Network model loading functionality and other forms of external communications are detailed in the following section.

8   Communications

Since the proportion of network-enabled embedded systems is constantly on the rise, we find it essential for the model-based architecture to fit into a networked environment. Our goal is to provide the following functions over the network:

- Model download,
- Model queries, including attributes subject to modification by the embedded system (status/operational information),
- Initiating run-time model modifications,
- Sending notification or alarm messages from the embedded system,
- User-interface-like input/output communication, and
- Interprocess communication and remote function calls in case of distributed embedded systems.

In addition to the above, we envision the future addition of features that support the distributed operation of model-based systems.

Our most important goal in designing the communication interface was to find technologies that can cover most of the above tasks, thus making the implementation of communications *relatively simple* and *lightweight* (especially from the resource utilization point of view on the embedded system's side).

Standard compliance was another goal with the promise of easy communication to other open-protocol systems (web-browsers, management stations) and the ability to reuse publicly available solutions to implement them.

When designing networked applications, there is a pretty obvious but somewhat drifting division line in the hierarchical layers of the OSI reference model: lower levels usually belong to the 'infrastructure', while higher levels are typically handled by the application [10]. While the EMI system is an infrastructure in itself, from the networking point of view it is positioned as an application of the underlying operating system. This means that for the lower levels we rely on operating system support, or support by an external communication library. Since for most practical cases (serial line, TCP/IP) good packages are available, this saves a lot of work, and enables us to focus on the higher level interfaces (presentation layer or above).

For the transfer syntax of the presentation layer protocol, the Extensible Markup Language (XML [3]) was selected. This young, but already widely adopted and continually developed presentation technology is a good fit to our needs. XML provides a presentation layer, but the structure of the information carried also needs to be further defined. This process usually involves the definition of a schema (DTD) above XML. Since there is currently no standard data format for our specific application domain (models of information systems and especially embedded software models), we defined a schema based on our experience and specific needs. In case a standard schema emerges, we expect it fairly straightforward to convert our system to support it. Even in this case, there will likely be specific issues to be addressed as extensions of the standard schema.

Given XML as the selected presentation transfer syntax, we tried to simplify the implementation of the networking functions by creating a uniform, application-level protocol above it as well. This protocol is based on communicating sections of the model tree. To enable subsequent modifications, the XML schema is extended so that objects can not only be added, but other editing operations (e.g. update, delete, move) also become available. Management is also provided by means of the model representation, where the management agent is able to query any desired section of the actual model tree. The same technology can also be applied for building user interfaces where a part of the model tree is sent to/from the user agent that provides a schema interpreter for appropriate visualization.

While we found the strict adherence to an appropriate presentation technology crucial, relying on external networking services at the lower levels makes us independent of the type of networking used, which practically means, that the infrastructure is able to communicate both over a simple serial line and a complete TCP/IP or OSI protocol stack [10].

When using TCP/IP, we still had to make some decisions about the transfer protocol used. HTTP has been selected (with the embedded system playing role of an HTTP server), partly because of its popularity (a simple browser can connect to the modeling system) and also because of the availability of practically transparent secure communication (SSL/TLS). These advantages made other researchers create similar solutions.

With our stated goal of manageability, existing *management protocols* must not be completely neglected. Unfortunately the ruling management protocol (SNMP) is not XML-based, but uses another presentation technology (ASN1/BER) instead. Nonetheless, we are committed to provide SNMP compliance in the future, either by the embedded model infrastructure itself, or by providing a proxy to translate between SNMP and our XML-based communication system.

Of course the initial version of the embedded modeling infrastructure we are currently working on will not support all these functions at the same time. However, we intend to build the backbone of the networking architecture: the services to parse and generate XML data, and the underlying HTTP support, which in turn relies on the TCP/IP networking support available in our current development platform. These will be sufficient to provide the most important networking functions: the downloading of models and reconfiguration commands to the embedded system, and providing access to the system status for XML capable browser clients. We are also confident, that the architecture makes it fairly straightforward to extend the capabilities for other protocols, in case there is low-level support available in the kernel or an external library.

9   Application Example

The model-based approach is a suitable for implementing most embedded systems, since it provides a well-identified object of focus both for designing the architecture and for analyzing the status of a running application. These features are getting even more important, if run-time configurability and adaptablity are part of the requirements. Among the many possible applications are the different kinds of multi-channel multi-function data analysis systems, an example of which is outlined below.

The example system is used for screening radio signals, i.e. detect and analyze signals from unknown sources (Fig. 5). It is a distributed architecture containing groups of aerial dishes. Each aerial is connected to a *wideband data-filtering unit*. Wideband units have a fixed architecture that enables them to detect frequencies that exceed a given threshold of intensity, cut out selected signals and forward them, with significantly reduced bandwidth, on high-speed network channels. These signals are processed by low-bandwidth signal-processing units (*analysis units*), that identify the encoding type (AM/FM/PCM), decode the data, and depending on its type (voice, music, data or unknown/encrypted data) perform further analysis, and/or store them on a recording device.

On a separate input, the system continually receives a list of frequencies currently used by known/friendly communication that are not to be analyzed. For the unknown ones however, it may be necessary to combine several signals (e.g. signals from different aerials) before analysis. The number of signals under simultaneous analysis tends to be vary, and so do the types and resource requirements of the operations used to analyze them. The system is definitely unable to handle all data under all circumstances.

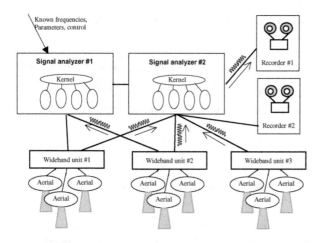

Fig. 5. Radio signal analysis architecture

The number of all components (aerials, wideband units, analysis units) varies depending on the deployment configuration. In addition, any of the components, as well as communication lines between the components are prone to failure, leaving the system mangled or separated.

As mentioned above, there is a significant difference in intelligence between the wideband and the analysis units. The former are fixed architecture, externally managed devices that operate on external commands to select the frequencies to be separated. The signal analysis units on the other hand are versatile, embedded computers operating on a real-time, multiprocess kernel [9]. So, it is the task of the signal-processing units to decide which signals are to be analyzed, and also to configure wideband units, distribute analysis tasks among each other, and to start up the necessary analysis algorithms. Although the network topology makes several units able to receive data from each of the wideband units, network bandwidth is also a resource to economize on.

Although the environment described above is not an existing system, we believe that it realistically contains most features expected from an up-to-date signal-processing infrastructure.

The proposed model-based approach calls for modeling the system from several aspects. First, the *static architecture* of the hardware components are modeled:

- Aerials: location, direction, type, availability
- Wideband units: model description (channel number, sensitivity), aerials connected (represented by connections in the model), network identifier
- Signal processing units: model description (number of processors, memory, network interfaces), network identifier

- Recording devices: channel number, network identifier, data speed
- Network links: bandwidth, connected units

Another aspect of the system is the run-time status of its components:

- their availability status,
- for the wideband units the active threshold, the selected frequencies, and the associated network channels
- the enabled channels on the recording device
- the utilization factors of the network links

This kind of data is stored as dynamic attributes added to the architectural model.

The status of the signal processing units is a more complex collection of information, thus it is stored in a separate modeling category, and linked to the architectural model by references only. This category includes:

- the currently selected frequencies, with timing, priorities, signal description data, and reference to the processes/recorders associated. This also contains frequencies for which analysis has been skipped due to unavailable resources.
- The list of friendly frequencies whose analysis is to be suppressed.
- the status of processes in each unit, along with their timing characteristics, resource allocations and reference to the frequency (frequencies) being analyzed.
- Other operational characteristics that describe the overall status of the system: the load system factor and the availability of resources.

As expected, the models describe the startup and the operation of the architecture. The static architecture data forms the 'skeleton' of the modeling information. This is to be assembled by a human expert (using related tools described in [2]), to reflect deployment configuration of the system.

The dynamic attributes of the model are initialized to reasonable defaults. The startup model also contains information on those processes that are expected to be running in the initial state of the system. When the model is read during startup (from internal storage or via a network session), the corresponding processes are automatically started with the supplied operational parameters.

The embedded model remains a central component of control reconfiguration during the further operation of the system as well. A process that is responsible for evaluating new frequencies will insert a new modeling object (atom) for each new frequency found. At the same time, this object is also assigned estimated attribute values for priority and resource usage (discussed below in detail).

The appearance of a new object triggers a generator to create a new analysis process object in the model, eventually creating a new process in the real-time kernel. This will start the analysis the data, and while doing that, it will set attributes in the model to represent the type of data found and the success rate of the analysis. If the contents of the data indicates that it is worth recording, another modeling object is generated that will result in a recorder channel being opened. In case there are several analysis units available, the system assigns the analysis task to the one which has sufficient resources available and which has a connection of sufficient bandwidth towards the data emitter wideband unit.

Different types of encoded information are to be processed by different algorithms. So if the evaluator component in the model finds that the data type detected needs a special analyzer (e.g. fax data decoder), it will insert a new object into the model to startup a new process.

If an analysis task is not discarded earlier, when signal strength decays below a given level, the process initiates termination by removing/inactivating objects in the model. This will result in switching off the corresponding frequency or frequencies in the wideband unit and removing the process used for analysis.

Assigning analysis tasks get more challenging when the evaluator runs into resource limitations, e.g. all nodes run out of process tables, free memory, or their load factor indicates, that they cannot accept further tasks. The evaluator calculates a so-called gain value for each of the frequencies analyzed. A simple formula for gain value G_i of the frequency i is

$$G_i = P_i / \max(\frac{T_i}{T_{\text{all}}}, \frac{M_i}{M_{\text{max}}}, \frac{B_i}{B_{\text{dir}}})$$

where P_i is the priority of the frequency, T_i is the is the processing time (or estimated processing time) used for the frequency i, T_{all} is the total processing time, M_i is the approximate memory allocation, M_{max} is the memory available for the most powerful node in the system, and B_i is the bandwidth utilization, which is compared to the total bandwidth B_{dir} available in that direction. The gain function is purposely simple, since the calculation and (in case of not-yet analyzed frequencies) the estimation of the input values for the equation are rather inaccurate anyway.

The utility function enables the evaluation to select the most important analysis tasks, and drop the rest. Since the function incorporates the bandwidth availability between the data source and the processing nodes, it is calculated for the best node initially, yielding the possibly highest gain value. It is automatically recalculated if the processing is about to be assigned to another node.

Before a frequency is analyzed, the gain value is based on estimation. For running processes however, gain value is calculated for actual (measured) resource usage. This can lead to the election of frequencies that are later discarded based on high resource usage, which practically results in the waste of resources. This side-effect may be reduced by including an additional 'entry cost' for new frequencies (or by simply providing somewhat pessimistic estimates), but it is obvious that a more thorough pre-analysis step might be necessary to provide more realistic gain value estimates.

The mechanisms outlined above suggest, that even if the system is distributed (in terms of containing several analysis nodes), the high-level model-based control operates in a centralized manner. This is true, since the cooperation of the nodes is based on an elected master policy: while each analysis unit has the capabilities to do the modeling decisions by itself, a single node from among them will always have the authority to coordinate the operation of the whole system.

All units, however, contain a replica model of the static modeling information, which is set up during startup and evolves through later operations initiated by external sources (most notably, the static architectural model, and the list of friendly frequencies). This information is used in case of system breakdowns: if a group of processing nodes determine that they have lost contact to the modeling master, they elect a new master (this process is simply based on preset priorities). This new master first determines the available architecture: availability of wideband, analysis, and recording units, along with the usable network links, and then restarts the assignment of frequencies among the remaining nodes. This scheme works both for broken analysis units and for separated network topologies.

The presented scheme for distributed operation may be considered somewhat rudimentary in the sense, that the change of the elected master node practically causes a complete restart in the analysis process. Another possible alternative would be to decentralize the modeling operations, thus making smooth transitions feasible. The primary reason for not going this way is that the processing overhead of a distributed model is significantly higher even for a single node, not to mention a group of nodes all repeating identical operations. The other reason is that we consider component breakdowns highly exceptional events: the fact that the system automatically resumes operation seems to be sufficient for all practical cases.

10   Conclusion

Migrating model-integrated computing from design-time towards run-time helps in the design and implementation of dynamic embedded systems. The presented Embedded Modeling Infrastructure is a paradigm-independent, general framework that is highly applicable to reconfigurable architectures. This configurability is a necessary precondition for self-adaptivity, and we demonstrated a way to incorporate adaptive behavior.

Self-adaptivity can have different manifestations, ranging from systems that are able to put themselves into either of two "modes of operation", to ones that generate a significant portion of their code "on the fly" and operating in ways never planned by their designers. Although the latter approach seems to be intellectually more challenging, we find that application areas where embedded systems are used (telecommunications, vehicles, high-risk environments) are unlikely to become customers for such unpredictable (and practically not testable) behaviors in the foreseeable future. That is why both the proposed system architecture and the demonstrated example application exhibit just a limited, designer-controlled form of self-adaptability.

Finally it is important to point out, that self-adaptivity is not the only gain in following the proposed model-based approach. Architectures based and operated on models also offer significantly improved manageability, serviceability and configurability, features welcome in practically all possible application areas of embedded and self-adaptive systems.

References

1. Sztipanovits J., Karsai G.: Model-Integrated Computing. IEEE Computer, April, 1997
2. Nordstrom G., Sztipanovits J., Karsai G., Ledeczi, A.: Metamodeling - Rapid Design and Evolution of Domain-Specific Modeling Environments. Proceedings of the IEEE Conference and Workshop on Engineering of Computer Based Systems, April, 1999
3. Bradly, N.: The XML Companion. Addison-Wesley, 1998
4. Ledeczi, A., Karsai, G., Bapty, T.: Synthesis of Self-Adaptive Software. Proceedings of the IEEE Aerospace Conference, March, 2000 (to appear)
5. Bapty T., Sztipanovits J.: Model-Based Engineering of Large-Scale Real-Time Systems. Proceedings of the Engineering of Computer Based Systems (ECBS) Conference, Monterey, CA, March, 1997
6. Oreizy, P. et al.: An Architecture-Based Approach to Self-Adaptive Systems. IEEE Intelligent Systems and their Applications Journal, May/June 1999
7. Karsai, G., Sztipanovits J.: Model-Integrated Approach to Self-Adaptive Software. IEEE Intelligent Systems and their Applications Journal, May/June 1999
8. Tornado/VxWorks operating system by the WindRiver System. http://www.windriver.com/products/html/vxwks54.html
9. The ChorusOs Operating System. http://www.sun.com/chorusos
10. Larmouth, J.: Understanding OSI. International Thomson Computer Press, 1996, ISBN 1-85032-176-0
11. Davis, J., Scott, J., Sztipanovits, J., Karsai, G., Martinez, M.: Integrated Analysis Environment for High Impact Systems. Proceedings of the Engineering of Computer Based Systems, Jerusalem, Israel, April, 1998

Coordination of View Maintenance Policy Adaptation Decisions: A Negotiation-Based Reasoning Approach

Prasanta Bose[1] and Mark G. Matthews[2]

[1] Information and Software Engineering Department, George Mason University,
Fairfax, VA 22030
bose@isse.gmu.edu
[2] The MITRE Corporation, 1820 Dolley Madison Blvd.,
McLean, VA 22012
mmatthew@mitre.org

Abstract. In mission critical applications of distributed information systems, autonomous information resources are coordinated to meet the information demands of client specific decision-support views. A major challenge is handling dynamic changes in QoS constraints of the clients and/or changes in QoS properties of the resources. This paper presents a negotiation-based adaptive view coordination approach to address such run-time changes. The three key ideas are as follows. a) A negotiation-based reasoning model for adapting view maintenance policies to meet changes in QoS needs and context constraints. b) A dynamic software architecture of the collaborating information resources supporting the client task of maintaining a specific view. c) Coordination mechanisms in the architecture that realize negotiated changes in the policies for view maintenance. The paper describes an initial prototype of the support system for the supply-chain task domain.

1 Introduction

In mission critical applications of distributed information systems, autonomous information resources are coordinated to meet the information demands of client specific decision-support views. . A major challenge is handling dynamic changes in quality of service (QoS) properties and constraints of the clients, information resources, and shared infrastructure resources. Current view coordination approaches are static in nature and cannot be dynamically changed to meet changing demands. Consider the following scenario from the supply-chain domain.

A decision-support view for inventory management is maintained from multiple autonomous information resources within the supply-chain. Customer order information from customer sites, product assembly information from manufacturer sites, and parts inventories from parts supplier sites are configured to support an "Order-Fulfillment" view used by inven tory managers of the suppliers and consumers. As orders, product assembly requirements, and parts inventories constantly change, changes in the view must be coordinated to achieve consistency and to support management decisions.

P. Robertson, H. Shrobe, and R. Laddaga (Eds.): IWSAS 2000, LNCS 1936, pp. 116–133, 2000.
© Springer-Verlag Berlin Heidelberg 2000

There are multiple view change coordination policies available to support the above inventory management task. When selecting a policy to implement, one must consider tradeoffs between consistency, communications costs, and processing costs. Currently, the view coordination policy is set at design-time and is static. Suppose a high-cost complete consistency view maintenance policy was selected for implementation at design-time. Further suppose that several inventory managers are simultaneously executing intensive on-line analytical processing queries against the `Order-Fulfillment` view. The queries are competing with the view coordination policy for system resources. Under these conditions, both the queries and the view maintenance task are likely to suffer from poor performance. Short of shutting down, reconfiguring, and restarting the system, current view coordination approaches have no way of prioritizing preferences and dynamically responding to changing preferences and constraints.

1.1 Self-Adaptive Software: Requirements and NAVCo Approach

Self-adaptive software systems that can dynamically adapt internal mechanisms and components in response to changing needs and context are required for addressing the above problems. There are four major requirements that a self-adaptive software system must meet. i) *Detecting a change* in context or a change in needs. It should be able to monitor its behavior and detect deviations from commitments or the presence of new opportunities. It should be able to accept new needs from external sources and evaluate for deviations with respect to current commitments. ii) *Knowing the space of adaptations*. It must have knowledge of the space of self-changes it can choose from to reduce deviations. iii) *Reasoning for adaptation decision*. It should be able to reason and make commitments on the self-changes and commitments on revised goals. iv) *Integrating the change*. It should be able to package the change if required and do assembly/configuration coordination to insert the change into the existing system with minimal disruption to existing behaviors.

The NAVCo approach described in this paper considers a family of adaptive systems that involve information view management and makes specific design choices to meet the requirements. In particular, the approach considers the following. a) Changes in committed preferences and context assumptions to trigger the adaptation process. b) An adaptation space defined by a set of view coordination policy objects. c) Reasoning for change as a negotiation-based process involving client and information resource agents. d) Use of assembly plans for change integration. Our current change integration approach relies on forcing the active view coordination objects to a quiescent state and then, based on the results of the negotiation-based reasoning, dynamically switching to an alternate set of objects within the space of adaptation.

The following sections of the paper focus primarily on the negotiation-based coordination to decide on the adaptation. Section 2 presents background information. Section 3 presents the NAVCo approach and architecture. An initial prototype of the support system for the supply-chain task domain is described in Section 4. Related work is discussed in Section 5. A summary is presented and future work discussed in Section 6.

2   Multi-Resource View Coordination Architecture

Multi-resource view maintenance falls within the domain of distributed decision-support database systems. A simplified model of this domain is illustrated in Figure 1. As illustrated in Figure 1, a view (V) is maintained from a set of autonomous data sources $(S_1, S_2,\ldots ,S_n)$. The view is a join of relations $(r_1, r_2,\ldots ,r_n)$ within the data sources. The update/query processor and view coordination object execute a distributed algorithm for incrementally maintaining the view. As data within a source changes, the associated update/query processor sends notification of the update to the view coordination object in Figure 1 which in turn queries the other sources to compute the incremental effect of the source update. After the incremental effect of the update has been computed, it is propagated to the client view. Client applications, such as on-line analytical processing and data mining applications, execute queries against the view. The data sources also support transactional environments, which result in updates to source relations that participate in the view.

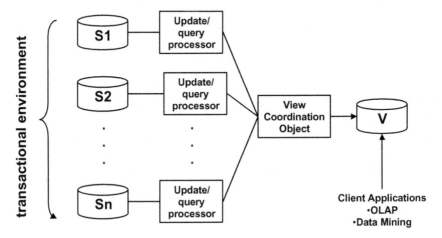

Fig. 1. Distributed Decision-Support Database System Domain

2.1   View Coordination Objects: Background

View coordination object (VCOs) are algorithmic objects that correspond to different policies for view maintenance. These view maintenance algorithms focus on maintaining a materialized view at the client in the presence of concurrent updates to the data resources. Four VCOs are briefly discussed and compared in this section. A complete description of these algorithms can be found in [1, 27] and is beyond the scope of this paper.

View coordination objects can be differentiated based on the level of consistency provided. Four levels of consistency (convergence, weak, strong, and complete) have been defined [1]. Here we consider VCOs that provide either a strong or a complete level of consistency. Strong consistency requires the order of the view states to match the order of source updates. Strong consistency allows global states to be skipped (i.e., every source update need not result in a distinct view update). Complete consistency is more restrictive requiring every source state to be reflected as a distinct view state. With complete consistency there is a complete order-preserving mapping between view states and source states.

The Strobe algorithm is an incremental algorithm that achieves strong consistency. The Strobe algorithm processes updates as they arrive, sending queries to the sources when necessary. However, the updates are not performed immediately on the materialized view; instead, a list of actions to be performed on the view is generated. The materialized view is updated only when it is certain that applying all of the actions in the action list as a single transaction at the client will bring the view to a consistent state. This occurs when there are no outstanding queries and all received updates have been processed.

The Complete-Strobe (C-Strobe) algorithm achieves complete consistency by updating the materialized view after each source update. The C-Strobe algorithm issues compensating queries for each update that arrives at the VCO between the time that a query is sent from the VCO and its corresponding answer is received from a source. The number of compensating queries can be quite large if there are continuous source updates.

The SWEEP algorithm achieves complete consistency of the view by ordering updates as they arrive at the VCO and ensuring that the state of the view at the client preserves the delivery of updates. The key concept behind SWEEP is on-line error correction in which compensation for concurrent updates is performed locally by using the information that is already available at the VCO. The SWEEP algorithm contains two loops that perform an iterative computation (or sweep) of the change in the view due to an update.

The Nested SWEEP algorithm is an extension of the SWEEP algorithm that allows the view maintenance for multiple updates to be carried out in a cumulative fashion. Nested SWEEP achieves strong consistency by recursively incorporating all concurrent updates encountered during the evaluation of an update. In this fashion, a composite view change is computed for multiple updates that occur concurrently.

The performance of VCOs can be compared based on the communications and processing costs required to maintain a given level of consistency. Communications costs can be measured with respect to the number and size of messages required per update. Processing costs must be measured with respect to the processing burden that the algorithm places on both the client and the data sources.

Table 1 compares the communications and query processing cost of the four view maintenance algorithms discussed above. The cost of the algorithms is dependent on the number of data sources, n. The costs of the C-Strobe and Nested SWEEP algorithms are highly dependent on a workload characterization factor, a where $0 \leq a \leq 1$, which reflects the rate of updates received. If updates arrive infrequently $a=0$ and if updates arrive continuously $a=1$. The client processing cost of a delete update in the Strobe and C-Strobe algorithms is highly dependent on the number of pending updates, p. The costs in Table 1 depict the case in which the VCO is co-located with the client.

Table 1. View Coordination Object Comparison

Algorithm	Consistency Level	Update Type	Comm Cost	Client Cost	Server Cost
Strobe	Strong	delete	1	1+p	0
		insert	2n-1	(n-1)+1	1
C-Strobe	Complete	delete	1	1+p	0
		insert	2(n-1)+ 2a(n-1)!+1	(n-1)+ a(n-1)!+1	1+a(n-2)!
SWEEP	Complete	delete/insert	2n-1	(n-1)+1	1
Nested SWEEP	Strong	delete/insert	2(1-a)(n-1)+1	(1-a)(n-1)+1	(1-a)

2.2 Order-Fulfillment Scenario Revisited

To better understand the costs and demands of the algorithms we consider a supply-chain view coordination scenario with databases at client, manufacturer, and parts supplier locations.

A customer orders database is maintained at client locations for orders that get handled by an automobile manufacturer. Each time an order is placed for an automobile, a tuple is inserted into the Orders relation. When an order is filled, it is deleted from the Orders relation and an appropriate tuple is inserted into a FilledOrders relation. There is only one end-item (automobile) allowed per order. If a customer wishes to order two automobiles, then two separate orders are generated. The database schema for the Orders relation is as follows:

```
Orders(OrderID(PK),CustomerID,ModelNumber)
```

A product assembly database is maintained at manufacturer locations. This database maintains a ProductAssembly relation that captures the dependency of each assembled product on supplier parts. Each end item (automobile) that is ordered must be assembled from a set of sub-items. Each time the manufacturer offers a new automobile model, new tuples are inserted into the ProductAssembly relation. When a manufacturer discontinues a model, the tuples associated with the automobile model are deleted from the ProductAssembly relation. The database schema for the ProductAssembly relation is as follows:

```
ProductAssembly(ModelNumber(PK),PartNumber(PK),
QuantityRequired(PK))
```

A parts inventory database is maintained at parts supplier locations. This database maintains an inventory of the number of automobile parts (sub-items) that are in stock in the warehouse. As the quantity of parts at the warehouse changes, the corresponding tuples are updated in the PartsInventory relation. Tuples are inserted into the PartsInventory relation as the warehouse begins storing new parts and tuples are deleted as the warehouse discontinues the storage of particular parts. The database schema for the PartsInventory relation is as follows:

```
PartsInventory(PartNumber(PK),QuantityAvailable)
```

A decision-support database is maintained at management locations to support inventory management decisions. This database maintains a materialized view (MV) of the inventory of parts available to fill automobile orders. The database schema for the materialized view is as follows:

```
MV=Orders|x|ProductAssembly|x|PartsInventory
=(OrderID, CustomerID, ModelNumber, PartNumber,
QuantityRequired, QuantityAvailable)
```

The materialized view is maintained as orders are placed and filled, manufacturer models and model-part dependencies change, and as supplier inventories change. Supplier and consumer inventory managers utilize this view to perform on-line analytical processing tasks in support of their inventory management decisions.

2.3 Run-time Policy Switching: Cost-Benefit Analysis

As illustrated in Table 1, VCO cost is highly sensitive to the workload characterization (i.e., the volume and types of updates received). To illustrate the effect of workload on VCO cost, consider the order fulfillment scenario discussed earlier. Assume that there are four data resources and one client view. Further assume that over a period of time the system experiences the following workload.

? Period 1 -high vol., high insert, 100 inserts and 0 deletes over X seconds
? Period 2 - low vol., balanced, 50 inserts and 50 deletes over 3X seconds
? Period 3 - medium vol., high delete, 0 inserts and 100 deletes over 2X seconds

The cost of each algorithm over these periods can be calculated using the formulas in Table 1. The value of the parameter p is assumed to be 0 for low traffic, 10 for medium traffic, and 100 for high traffic. The value of the parameter a is assumed to be 0 for low traffic, 1/3 for medium traffic, and 1 for high traffic. The cost of the four algorithms over Periods 1-3 is illustrated in Table 2:

Table 2. View Coordination Costs in the Supply-Chain Example

Algorithm	Consistency Level	Comm Cost	Client Cost	Server Cost
Strobe	Strong	1200	1750	150
C-Strobe	Complete	2400	2350	350
SWEEP	Complete	2100	1200	300
Nested SWEEP	Strong	1250	775	158

With current technology a single algorithm is implemented during system configuration and can not be changed without shutting down and reconfiguring the system. The selection of an algorithm can have a profound effect on the processing and communications requirements to support the view. Tradeoffs must be made at design-time with respect to consistency versus client, server, and communications costs. If, however, the algorithm can be dynamically changed at run-time, these tradeoffs can be made continuously as preferences and constraints change. As illustrated in Table 3, the ability to dynamically switch algorithms can result in significant cost savings and improved performance in a constrained environment.

The first row in Table 3 shows that communications cost can be minimized by initially implementing the Nested SWEEP algorithm and then dynamically switching to the Strobe algorithm between periods 1 and 2. This results in a reduction of 450 messages over a static implementation of the Strobe algorithm.

The second row in Table 2 shows that client processing cost can be minimized by implementing the Nested SWEEP algorithm during periods 1 and 3, and the Strobe algorithm during period 2. This results in a reduction of over 1000 queries over a static implementation of the Strobe algorithm. This would free up valuable resources for the processing-intensive analysis users and result in a significant performance improvement for those users.

Table 3. Results of Dynamic Switching of View Coordination Algorithms in the Example

Preferences/ Constraints	Comm Cost	Client Cost	Server Cost	Period 1	Period 2	Period 3
Minimize comm cost	750	1525	75	Nested Sweep	Strobe	Strobe
Minimize client cost	950	625	108	Nested Sweep	Strobe	Nested Sweep
Minimize server cost	750	1525	75	Nested Sweep	Strobe	Strobe
Minimize comm cost and complete consistency	1200	1750	150	Sweep	C-Strobe	C-Strobe
Minimize client cost and complete consistency	1350	825	175	Sweep	C-Strobe	Sweep
Minimize server cost and complete consistency	1200	1750	150	Sweep	C-Strobe	C-Strobe

3   The NAVCo Approach

The NAVCo approach to adapting view coordination policies in response to changes in needs of the clients or change in constraints imposed by the resources is based on negotiation reasoning between the client and resource objects. The approach introduces negotiation reasoning models and adaptive policy reconfiguration mechanisms to the existing view coordination application architecture. The architecture, shown in Figure 2 as a UML class diagram, introduces a negotiation layer to perform dynamic negotiation-based selection of coordination policies. Additional software mechanisms are introduced to bring about the dynamic switching of the coordination objects.

The key elements of the architecture are: a) Models and reasoning support for model-based coordination negotiation via Role Negotiation Agents (RNAs) and a Negotiation Facilitator Agent (NFA) that communicate via the shared coordination negotiation data space (CNspace). b) Models and support for switching based on negotiated switching decisions. The change reasoning and change coordination views are integrated via a shared data space whereby the negotiation facilitation agent communicates with team level coordination agents via the CNspace [6]. The Change Coordination Agent (CCA) aids in coordinating the switching.

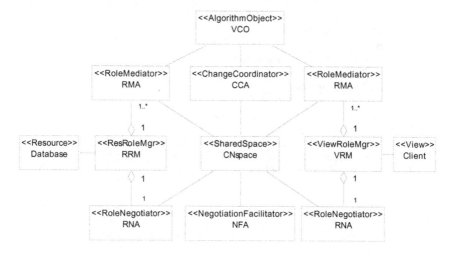

Fig. 2. Architecture To Support Adaptive View Coordination

3.1 Negotiation Reasoning

The model for negotiation reasoning used in our approach is based on the WinWin [2, 3] model used in requirements negotiation. In such a model, the participating agents collaboratively and asynchronously explore the WinWin decision space that is represented by four main conceptual artifacts. i) *WinCondition* - capturing the preferences and constraints of a participant. ii) *Issue* - capturing a conflict between WinConditions or their associated risks and uncertainties. iii) *Option* - capturing a decision choice for resolving an issue. iv) *Agreement* - capturing the agreed upon set of conditions which satisfy stakeholder WinConditions and/or capturing the agreed options for resolving issues. The object model for the WinCondition object developed for negotiating VCOs is shown in Figure 3. The object explicates attributes relevant to expressing preferences and constraints for the view coordination problem.

NAVCo incorporates three types of negotiation reasoning schemes that extend the WinWin model to consider a reactive model of negotiation. The first scheme, illustrated in Table 4, is used during the initial establishment of the task and subsequent negotiation of the initial policy. This scheme is triggered when a new WinCondition of a client is submitted. The WinCondition contains the task parameters and any client preferences and constraints. The negotiation facilitator agent then generates issues and the associated options and then sends the options to the client and resources role negotiation agents for evaluation. An agreement is reached and propagated to the change coordinator agent for implementation if all the role negotiation agents accept the option. Otherwise the client or resources can trigger further negotiation through the submission of revised WinConditions.

Win Condition
WinConditionID : String
ComponentID : String
Role : one of {Provides, Requires}
View : QueryObject
InsertVolume : Integer
DeleteVolume : Integer
UpdateMode : one of {Incremental, Batch}
BatchPeriod : Integer
ConsistencyLevel : one of {Convergence,Weak,Strong,Complete}
ComponentCostTolerance : one of {Low,Medium,High}
LatencyTolerance : one of {Low,Medium,High}

Fig. 3. The WinCondition Object Model

Table 4. Task Driven Negotiation Protocol

1. Client RNA submits a WinCondition to NFA. The WinCondition identifies the task preferences and constraints of the Client
2. The NFA analyzes the posted WinCondition and identifies Issue(s)
3. The NFA generates potential Options that Resolve the Issue(s)
4. The Resource and Client RNAs evaluate the Option(s)
5. If an option is accepted by all RNAs
Then {Agreement = Accepted Option
Agreement propagated to CCA for implementation}
Else {Client and/or Resource RNAs post revised WinConditions
Go To Step 2 }
End If
6. If timeout_event received
Then initiate priority driven protocol
End If

The second scheme (illustrated in Table 5) is conflict-driven and is used for run-time dynamic renegotiation of policies. This scheme can be triggered by any client or resource through the submission of a revised WinCondition representing changing component preferences and/or constraints. The negotiation facilitator agent then analyzes the revised WinCondition against the current set of WinConditions and the current agreement to identify issues and associated options. If this results in an option other than the current agreement, a negotiation among the components ensues.

The third scheme is priority-driven and is triggered by the occurrence of a timeout_event during the execution of either the task-driven or conflict-driven protocols. NAVCo supports two priority-driven schemes, competitive and cooperative. In both schemes, a list of possible preferences is identified (e.g., x_1 = complete consistency, x_2 = low communications, etc.). Each component maintains a weighted list of the local preferences (e.g., $a_{i,j}$ is the weight assigned by component i to preference j). Each component is also assigned a global weight (e.g., w_1 = 1.0, w_2 = 0.95, etc.). Table 6 details the steps in the competitive scheme and Table 7 details the steps in the cooperative scheme.

Table 5. Conflict Driven Negotiation Protocol

1. Resource or Client RNA submits a revised WinCondition to the NFA. The revised WinCondition reflects a local change in preferences and/or constraints
2. The NFA analyzes the revised WinCondition against the set of current WinConditions to generate Issue(s) resulting from (pairwise) conflicting interaction
3. The NFA generates potential Options that resolve the Issue(s)
4. If there is no change in Option (i.e., Option = current Agreement)
Then {NFA marks the Issue as resolved}
Else {Resource and Client RNAs evaluate the Option(s)
If an Option is accepted by all RNAs
Then {Agreement = Accepted Option
Agreement propagated to CCA for implementation}
Else {Client and/or Resource RNAs post revised WinConditions
Go To Step 2 }
End If
End If
5. If timeout_event received
Then initiate priority driven protocol
End If

Table 6. Competitive Priority Driven Negotiation Protocol

1. Each RNA generates a weighted list of local preferences
(e.g., $a_{1,1}x_1$, $a_{1,2}x_2$... a_jx_j for component number 1)
2. As part of WinCondition, each RNA submits top weighted preference to the NFA (e.g., $a_{1,1}x_1$, may be submitted by component 1)
3. NFA applies global component weighting factors to submitted preferences
(e.g., $w_1a_{1,1}x_1$ would be the weighting for component 1's preference)
4. The NFA selects the component preference with the highest overall weighting
(i.e., the preference associated with $\max(w_ia_{i,j})$ is selected)
5. The NFA identifies the policy that most satisfies the selected preference
6. The selected policy is propagated to CCA for implementation

Given the above reasoning methods three major questions arise. 1) How do *issues* get generated? 2) How do *options* get generated? 3) How do *options* get evaluated?

The NAVCo approach exploits the context and the view coordination problem domain to address the questions as follows. a) Given one or more WinConditions, *issue generation* involves formulating a query to identify VCO specification objects that satisfy the WinConditions. Here the issue is formalized as a query object. b) Given the formulation of the issue, *option generation* involves evaluation of the query to retrieve plausible VCO specification objects and their refinements. c) Given the options, *option evaluation* involves checking for consistency of an option against a database of committed WinConditions.

Table 7. Cooperative Priority Driven Negotiation Protocol

1. Each RNA generates a weighted list of local preferences   (e.g., $a_{1,1}x_1, a_{1,2}x_2\ldots a_jx_j$ for component number 1)   2. As part of WinCondition, each RNA submits entire list of weighted preferences to the NFA   3. NFA applies global component weighting factors to submitted preferences   4. The NFA sums the weights associated with each preference   (e.g., $(w_1a_{1,1} + w_2a_{2,1}+\ldots + w_na_{n,1})x1$ would be the cooperative sum for preference 1)   5. The NFA selects the preference with the highest overall cooperative sum   5. The NFA identifies the policy that most satisfies the selected preference   6. The selected policy is propagated to CCA for implementation

3.2 Models to Support Negotiated Selection of VCO

In order to support the reasoning approach outlined above, NAVCo requires the following. a) Declarative models of preferences and constraints at the clients and resources as a database of facts. b) Rules for issue generation, option generation, and option evaluation. We briefly describe below the data models and some examples of the rules that have been formulated and prototyped in our initial experiments.

The class diagram shown in Figure 4 captures the data model underlying the information maintained by the role negotiation agents of the clients and resources. The model in essence articulates the WinCondition as consisting of two parts. a) The *task part* is of type "provides" for a resource or of type "requires" for a client. The task part explicates the role to be played, prioritization of tasks, task preferences, and update volume and distribution submitted in support of the task. b) The *QoS constraint part* articulates the constraints imposed on the task. The QoS schema specifies the component workload to support the task and the component QoS constraints based on the status of component resources captured as QoS metrics. The data model also specifies global integrity constraints.

The data model specifying the content of the information in the negotiation facilitation agent is given in Figure 5. The data model captures VCO specifications and associated costs. The data model also contains models of the WinConditions, Issues, and Options that get posted or generated by the NFA. Some of the important data elements are a) identification, characteristics, and costs of available coordination policies, b) task-specific meta-data, and c) overall team-level workload characterization, preferences, and constraints.

The rules for issue and option generation and option evaluation are modeled as database trigger rules that analyze WinCondition updates to identify issues and options and to trigger option evaluations. The trigger rule in Table 8 creates an Issue, whose semantics is that of a query assertion to select a VCO policy, in the Issues table when there is an update to the WinCondition table. The rule accesses relevant constraints imposed by a task specific WinCondition that must be met by a VCO. A trigger rule for option generation, as shown in Table 9, adds entries to the Options table and is triggered by issue entries in the Issues table.

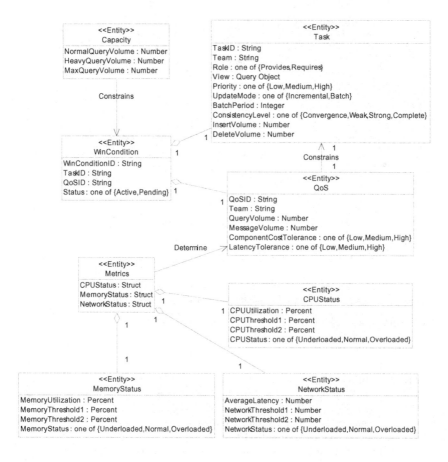

Fig. 4. RNA Data Model of Preferences and Constraints

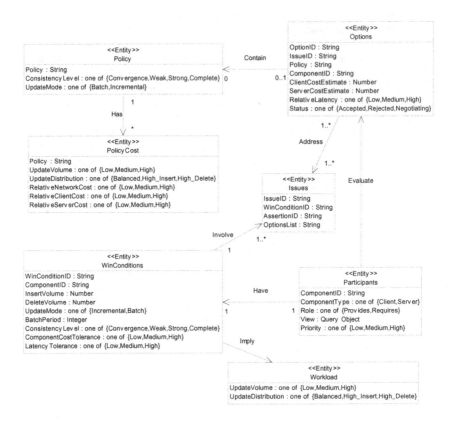

Fig. 5. NFA Data Model of Preferences and Constraints

Table 8. An Example of an Issue Generation Rule modeled as a Trigger Rule

```
TRIGGER <Issue generation> on INSERT into WinConditions
(INSERT into Issues (…  )
   WHERE Issue.Assertion =
   (SELECT Policy
    FROM PolicyCost |x| Policy
WHERE UpdateVolume = WinCondition.UpdateVolume
AND UpdateDistribution =WinCondition.UpdateDistribution
AND ConsistencyLevel = WinCondition.ConsistencyLevel
AND UpdateMode=WinCondition.UpdateMode
AND RelativeClientCost < =WinCondition.ComponentCostTolerance))
```

Table 9. An Example of an Option Generation Rule modeled as a Trigger Rule

```
TRIGGER <VCO-Option-with-Evaluation>
on INSERT into Issues
(INSERT into Options (... )
WHERE Policy=Evaluate(Issues)
AND ClientCostEstimate=
[estimated client update volume based on policy and workload]
AND ServerCostEstimate=
[estimated server query volume based on policy and workload]
AND RelativeLatency=
(SELECT RelativeNetworkCost
FROM PolicyCost WHERE Policy=Issues.Option))
```

3.3 Mechanisms for Dynamic Switching of VCO

Figure 6 depicts an object collaboration diagram for the dynamic switching of view coordination objects. The event sequence is further elaborated below.

1. Once an option has been successfully negotiated the NFA writes a dynamic switching plan (DSP) into the CNspace. The DSP identifies the VCO that has been negotiated and includes a plan for dynamically switching between VCOs.
2. The CNspace sends a notification event to the CCA upon receipt of the DSP from the NFA.
3. The CNspace sends notification events to each RMA upon receipt of the DSP from the NFA.
4. Upon receipt of the notification event, the CCA reads the DSP from the CNspace and begins executing the plan.
5. Upon receipt of the notification event, each RMA reads the DSP from the CNspace and begins executing the plan. RMAs associated with resources begin queuing updates at this point.
6. The CCA sends a message to the current VCO to destroy itself. The VCO will continue to execute its algorithm until its queue of unprocessed queries is empty. At this point the VCO will send a return variable to the CCA indicating that it is about to destroy itself.
7. After the VCO is destroyed, the CCA using meta-data contained in its knowledge base will create a new VCO of the type indicated in the DSP. The meta-data contains task specific information to include the identity and location of team participants.
8. Upon instantiation, the VCO will bind itself to the RMI Registry.
9. The CCA writes a status event to the CNspace. The status event contains the name of the instantiated VCO.
10. The CNspace sends notification events to each RMA.
11. Upon receipt of the notification event, each RMA reads the status event from the CNspace.
12. Each RMA establishes a dynamic binding to the VCO through the use of the RMI Registry. Resource RMAs begin sending updates to the VCO.

4 Prototype

The adaptive view coordination architecture has been modeled using Rationale Rose 98 Enterprise Edition. Use cases, class diagrams, object collaboration diagrams, and sequence diagrams have been developed. Initial prototypes have been developed for both the negotiation and application views (layers). Prototypes for role mediator, role negotiation, change coordinator, and negotiation facilitator agents have been developed. Each prototype agent consists of a Java application and a Microsoft Access database.

All agent-to-agent coordination is accomplished through the use of the CNspace, which is implemented using JavaSpaces technology. WinConditions, options, dynamic switching plans and other objects are written as entries into the CNspace. The CNspace notify and read methods are utilized to route the entries to the appropriate agents. The prototype agents currently utilize input and output text files to simulate interactions with clients and resources. Initial results show that the NAVCo reactive reasoning methods can exploit the JavaSpaces based design environment to make negotiated decisions on the policy objects.

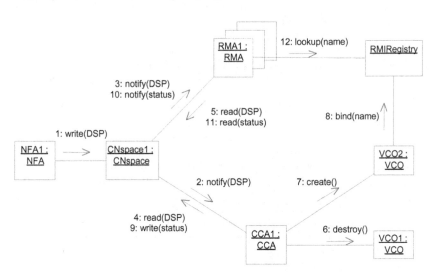

Fig. 6. Object Collaboration Diagram for Dynamic VCO Switching

5 Related Work

There has been a significant amount of work conducted in the area of view maintenance resulting in a spectrum of solutions ranging from a fully virtual approach where no data is materialized at one extreme to a fully replicated approach where full base relations are copied at the other extreme. These two extreme solutions are inefficient in terms of communications cost at one extreme and storage cost at the other extreme. Incremental view maintenance policies, such as ECA [26], Strobe [27], and SWEEP [1], are a hybrid of these two extremes. Incremental view maintenance policies maintain a materialized client view consisting of the relevant subset of data from the base relations at the data sources. Client decision-support applications, such as on-line analytical processing and data mining, then directly access the data contained within the materialized view at the client. The ECA family of algorithms is designed for a centralized database system, while the Strobe and SWEEP families are designed for distributed systems. Our research focuses on developing a self-adaptive architecture for distributed decision-support database systems. The NAVCo architecture described in this paper supports run-time policy changes between the Strobe and C-Strobe algorithms. The architecture is robust enough and can be scaled to support additional algorithms, such as SWEEP and Nested SWEEP.

The NAVCo work builds on the negotiation research performed by the community in requirements negotiation as well as automated negotiation. Negotiation is a complex and difficult area of active research pursued by researchers in different fields of study. Research progress has been made in different approaches to negotiation: a) Human factors approach where the major focus is understanding methods and techniques employed by humans to negotiate so as to manage the human factors of pride, ego, and culture [7, 19, 20]. The work on understanding people factors in requirements negotiation falls in this category. b) Economics, Game Theory and bargaining approach where research progress has been made on theoretical models of process driven negotiation [18], outcome driven negotiation, and self-stabilizing agreements to achieve some equilibrium [14]. Research on negotiation focuses on the group decision context where the power to decide is distributed across more than one stakeholder/agent as opposed to group decision making where a single decision maker relies on a set of analysts [15]. Two key aspects of the negotiated decision studied in most of the research are conflict and interdependence of decisions. Conflict has been used constructively in cooperative domains to explore negotiation options [3]. c) Artificial agents approach where the focus has been on developing computational agents that negotiate to resolve conflict [5], to distribute tasks [22, 24], to share resources [28], and to change goals so as to optimize multi-attribute utility functions [23]. In general, the models for agent cooperation and negotiation consider negotiation between multiple agents driven by global utility functions or independent local utility functions. The WinWin [2, 3] model used in NAVCo consider both types of drivers typical of negotiating teams having local preferences as well as global constraints.

The NAVCo approach is similar in spirit to the work on architecture-based run-time evolution [16]. Our approach and reasoning tools differ from [16] in terms of the nature of automation. The work in [16] focuses on providing a support environment where the necessary analysis for dynamic change and consequent operationalization can be performed. Automated switching based on automated negotiation reasoning motivates the NAVCo approach and prototype discussed in the paper.

The requirements for self-adaptive software included in Section 1.1 are derived from the DARPA "Broad Agency Announcement on Self-Adaptive Software" (BAA-98-12, December 1997). Due in part to the DARPA BAA the area of self-adaptive software has been an active area of research over the last several years [9, 10, 11, 13, 17, 21]. Most of the current research relies on the use of control theory to some extent [11]. A reflective agent architecture has been developed to support the run-time change of filters for the aerial surveillance domain [21]. The approach taken in [21] utilizes both reflection and control system theory. The use of control theory as a feedback loop for change reasoning was proposed in [10]. The control theory approach taken by others appears to be most applicable for embedded systems and domains with hard real time requirements. Since our domain of distributed decision-support database systems does not display these characteristics, we have taken a different approach based on negotiation reasoning followed by change coordination.

6   Summary and Future Work

This paper develops a Negotiation-based Adaptive View Coordination (NAVCo) approach for a class of distributed information management systems. The NAVCo approach allows view coordination to be dynamically adapted at run-time to meet changes in QoS preferences and constraints. The paper presents the key ideas and models developed and prototyped in our initial experiments with the approach. The key ideas of the NAVCo approach are as follows. a) A negotiation-based reasoning method for adapting view maintenance policies to meet dynamic changes in context (e.g., constraints). b) A dynamic software architecture of the collaborating information resources supporting the client task of maintaining a specific view. c) Coordination mechanisms in the architecture that realize negotiated changes in the policies for view maintenance.

This paper focuses primary on the negotiation-based reasoning models used in NAVCO and only briefly describes the NAVCo change coordination mechanisms. The change coordination mechanisms described in Section 3.3 rely on forcing the view coordination objects to a quiescent state prior to the dynamic switching. Our current work is focused on developing more sophisticated change coordination mechanisms that can gracefully transition on-going workload between view coordination objects without forcing the objects to a quiescent state. The main challenge is to ensure that the transitions support certain safety and correctness properties during and after the dynamic switching.

References

1. D. Agrawal, A. El Abbadi, A Singh, and T. Yurek, "Efficient View Maintenance at Data Warehouses," In Proceedings of the ACM SIGMOD 97, pp. 417 -427, 1997.
2. B. Boehm, P. Bose, E Horowitz and M. J. Lee, 'Software Requirements Negotiation and Renegotiation Aids: A Theory-W Based Spiral Approach," In IEEE Proceedings of the 17th ICSE Conference, 1995.
3. P. Bose and Z. Xiaoqing, "WinWin Decision Model Based Coordination," Internat ional Joint Conference on Work Activities Coordination and Collaboration," 1999.
4. W. R. Collins et. al., "How Good is Good Enough?" Communications of the ACM, pp. 81-91, January 1994.

5. E. H. Durfee, V. R. Lesser, and D. D. Corkill, "Cooperation Through Communication in a Distributed Problem Solving Network," In M. N. Huhns ed., Distributed Artificial Intelligence, Chapter 2, 29-58.
6. J. Farley, "Java Distributed Computing," O' Reilly Press, 1998.
7. R. Fisher and W. Ury, "Getting to Yes," Houghton-Mifflin, 1981. Also Penguin Books, 1983.
8. R. Hull and G. Zhou, A Framework for Supporting Data Integration Using the Materialized and Virtual Approaches. In Proceedings of the ACM SIGMOD International Conference on Management of Data, pp. 481-492, June 1996.
9. G. Karsai and J. Sztipanovits, "A Model-Based Approach to Self-Adaptive Software," IEEE Intelligent Systems, volume 14, number 3, May/June 1999.
10. M. Kokar, K. Baclawski, and Y. Eracar, "Control Theory-Based Foundations of Self-Controlling Software," IEEE Intelligent Systems, volume 14, number 3, May/June 1999.
11. R. Laddaga, "Creating Robust Software Through Self-Adaption," IEEE Intelligent Systems, volume 14, number 3, May/June 1999.
12. T. W. Malone and K. Crowston, "The Interdisciplinary Study of Coordination," ACM Computing Surveys, Vol. 26, No. 1, pp. 87-119, Mar. 1994.
13. D. J. Musliner, R. P. Goldman, M. J. Pelican, and K. D. Krebsbach, "Self-Adaptive Software for Hard Real-Time Environments," IEEE Intelligent Systems, volume 14, number 4, July/August 1999.
14. J. F. Nash, "The Bargaining Problem," Econometrica 28, pp. 155-162, 1950.
15. J. F. Nunamaker, A. R. Dennis, J. S. Valacich and D. R. Vogel, "Information Technology for Negotiating Groups: Generating Options for Mutual Gain," Management Science, October 1991.
16. P. Oreizy, N. Medvidovic, and R. N. Taylor, "Architecture-based Runtime Evolution," In Proceedings of ICSE 1998.
17. P. Oreizy et. al., "An Architecture Based Approach to Self-Adaptive Software," IEEE Intelligent Systems, volume 14, number 3, May/June 1999.
18. M. J. Osborne and A. Rubinstein, "A Course in Game Theory," MIT Press, MA, 1994.
19. M. Porter, "Competitive Strategy: Techniques for Analyzing Industries and Competitors," Free Press, NY, 1980.
20. H. Raiffa, "The Art and Science of Negotiation,, Harvard University Press, Cambridge, MA, 1982
21. P. Robertson and J. M. Brady, "Adaptive Image Analysis for Aerial Surveillance," IEEE Intelligent Systems, volume 14, number 3, May/June 1999.
22. R. G. Smith, "The Contract Net Protocol: High-level Communication and Control in a Distributed Problem Solver," IEEE Transactions on Computers, 29, pp. 1104-1113, 1980.
23. K. P. Sycara, "Resolving Goal Conflicts Via Negotiation," In Proceedings of AAAI, pp. 245-250, 1988.
24. M. P. Wellman, "A General Equilibrium Approach to Distributed Transportation Planning," In Proceedings of AAAI-92, San Jose, CA 1992.
25. T. Winograd, "Bringing Design to Software," Addison Wesley Publishers, 1996.
26. Y. Zhuge, H. Garcia-Molina, J. Hammer, and J. Widom. View Maintenance in a Warehouse Environment. In Proceedings of the ACM SIGMOD International Conference on Management of Data, pp. 316-327, May 1995.
27. Y. Zhuge, H. Garcia-Molina, and J. Wiener, "The Strobe Algorithms for Multi-Source Warehouse Consistency," In Proceedings of the International Conference on Parallel and Distributed Information Systems, December 1996.
28. G. Zlotkin, and J. S. Rosenschein, "Mechanism Design for Automated Negotiation and Its Application to Task Oriented Domains," Artificial Intelligence, Vol. 86, pp. 195-244, 1996.

Dynamic Self Adaptation in Distributed Systems

Israel Ben-Shaul, Hovav Gazit, Ophir Holder, and Boris Lavva

Technion, Israel Institute of Technology, Haifa 32000, ISRAEL,
issy@ee.technion.ac.il,
WWW home page: http://www.dsg.technion.ac.il

Abstract. The emergence of global network connectivity has motivated the investigation of models and techniques for dynamic self adaptive distributed software for two reasons: to enable adjustment of deployed components to previously unknown and possibly dynamically changing hosting environments, and to adapt the inter-component distributed architecture in order to improve application scalability, performance and availability. Several issues impact the quality of self-adaptation, including the degree of adaptation, programming transparency, performance, and monitoring facilities. We discuss these issues and describe two approaches to self adaptation, one focusing on intra-component adaptation and the other on inter-component adaptation. Both approaches were fully implemented in the Hadas and FaRGo projects, respectively.
Keywords: Dynamic adaptability; Self adaptive components; Engineering Distributed Systems; Java; Reflection; Mobile Objects;

1   Introduction and Motivation

The emergence of global network connectivity has motivated the investigation of models and techniques for designing distributed systems in which components can be dynamically deployed. In this context, dynamic self adaptive software is instrumental in two aspects. First, adaptability of structure and behavior at the *individual software component* level is highly desirable, so as to adjust a deployed component to a previously unknown and possibly dynamically changing hosting environment, without having to reengineer it. The autonomous nature of the hosting environment implies that deployed components cannot anticipate in advance all possible changes, hence the need for adaptation. The autonomous nature of the deployed components, on the other hand, implies that such adaptation should be performed with minimum dependence on the the environment, hence self-adapt.

Second, there is a need to support dynamic self adaptation at the *inter-component distributed application level*, i.e., at the architectural level, so as to adjust the location and relationships between components to changes in the distributed environment. Since the deployment space might be arbitrarily large and heterogeneous, the designer is unlikely to know at design time how to structure the application in a way that best leverages the available sites. Moreover, characteristics such as bandwidth, site and resource availability, and processor load

P. Robertson, H. Shrobe, and R. Laddaga (Eds.): IWSAS 2000, LNCS 1936, pp. 134–142, 2000.

might change dynamically among Internet-connected sites, further demanding dynamic reconfiguration capabilities.

Thus, a generic framework for self dynamic adaptation is highly desirable, but it raises many issues that need to be properly addressed before such a framework can prevail. In the rest of this paper we present these issues, and describe two approaches for addressing some of them, which were embodied in two frameworks, Hadas and FARGO. Although both frameworks provided self-adaptation, the different goals and orientation led to different design and focus. Hadas focused on intra-component self adaptability, whereas FARGO focused on inter-component self adaptability. We compare these approaches and explain the rationale behind the decisions made in each system.

2   Issues in Dynamic Self Adaptation

Before discussing issues in dynamic self adaptive software, one has to define the term, both for individual components and for a multi-component distributed systems, and distinguish it from non-adaptive software. In particular, it might be argued that if the software has the logic to "adapt" itself and all the code ultimately pre-exists in the component (we do not consider here automatic generation of new code, as in genetic programming [1]), then this is not really (self) adaptation but merely flexibility.

The main distinction is that in self-adaptive software the behavior of a given operation can be dynamically modified by changing the code of the operation, as opposed to pre-embedding the different behaviors inside an operation. In object-based terminology, this means that the implementation of a given interface can be replaced at runtime. Furthermore, advanced self-adaptive software may even permit the interface to be mutable, allowing addition and removal of operations and state.

The change in behavior (and possibly in structure that is manipulated by the behavior) is often triggered by changes in the environment, and is controlled by a dedicated monitoring (meta) component that is used solely for the internal management of the component. Such an "evaluator", in DARPA's terminology [2], may either contain the alternative functionality within its scope, or import it from external sources.

Finally, we extend the notion of self-adaptation to distributed systems as an evolution of the location and relationships between components.

Self adaptive software, as defined above, raises the following important issues.

- *Programming transparency* — A critical aspect in designing a framework for programming self-adaptive software is the programming (and object) model used to encode the application. Clearly, it is desirable to keep the model as close as possible to the conventional object-based programming model, to avoid drastic changes in the syntax, tools and methods used to design and implement applications. However, it is also clear that support for dynamic adaptation necessarily implies some deviation from any non adaptive model, both in the programming model and in the runtime support for adaptation. In particular, it requires an *introspection* facility that enables it to examine an interface and select the proper method (as in Java), and it is highly desirable to provide mutability of data structures and methods, which is not common in strongly typed languages. This implies the need to use reflection [3].

- *Performance overhead* — Adaptability can impact performance in two major ways. First, monitoring support requires some level of interception and thus indirection, which incurs a performance penalty. Second, if the interface is mutable, then there must be a lookup mechanism for locating a data member (or method) before accessing (invoking) it, whereas in static non-mutable models the location is determined at compile time as a fixed offset.

- *Granularity of mutable objects* — This is related to both the programming model and to performance. In the context of the programming model, it is important to identify the smallest unit of mutability on which the modified object is applied. In the extreme case, every programming-language object can be mutable, which implies a whole new programming language, such as Self [4] or Cecil [5]. A preferred approach is to adopt a component-based approach. A component may be loosely defined as a collection of encapsulated objects that perform a certain task, and is accesssible through well-defined interface objects. An example compoent is a CORBA [6] object, which is distinct from the programming language objects that are used to implement it. By restricting self adaptation to the component level, the programming model needs to be altered only at the component level, thus preserving conventional language and object models to implement objects.

- *Object vs. class adaptation* — self-adaptability implies dynamic evolution of runtime objects, which conflicts with classes as static, compile time entities. At the same time, classless models have their own limitations. In particular, since a component's structure can divert from its original class definition, type-safety is considerably weakened and might lead to runtime mismatches between the caller's formal expectation of the component's structure and the component's actual structure. Furthermore, unrestricted adaptability provides no guarantees as to what functionality or structure a certain component will have at a given time, thereby reducing its usability significantly.

- *Degree of "selfness"* — Another aspect of self-adaptability is who conducts the adaptation (as opposed to who initiates the change). This can be done internally, using mutability functionality that is part of the component, or externally by another component.

- *Monitoring facilities* — An important element in a self-adaptive framework is its support for "sensing" both the environment and the specific performance of the components, and the interface it provides for applications to gain access to the monitored information as a basis for making judicious adaptability decisions.

- *Secure Adaptability* — Finally, adaptability clearly raises serious security concerns, particularly when the adapted components interact with components that are owned by a different authority. This issue, however, is beyond the scope of this paper.

3   Intra-component Adaptation in Hadas

The Hadas framework [7,8,9] was designed for assembling (widely) distributed applications from (possibly existing) components, addressing site autonomy and supporting dynamic deployment. Self adaptation is a major element of the system. In particular, every user-defined Hadas component is mutable, and the system supports a special class of highly adaptive Hadas objects termed Ambassadors, which are dynamically deployed to remote sites and serve as representatives of their counterpart "base" components.

Hadas components are relatively coarse-grained. Each component has an interface consisting of (Hadas) methods and (Hadas) data members, each of which can be evolved at runtime, but implementation of particular Hadas methods and data members are done with regular (Java) objects and classes.

In order to enable object-based adaptation without sacrificing completely type safety, Hadas employs the following hybrid approach that balances the *object vs. instance* conflicting demands. Each component is split into two sections, Fixed and Extensible. Data items and methods defined in the Fixed section of the component are treated as conventional class-based items that may not be changed during the component's lifetime. This portion of the component can be used to store its fundamental state and behavior. In contrast, the Extensible section comprises the mutable portion of the component through which component's structure and behavior can be changed, and in which new items (data, objects or methods) can be added, removed or changed on-the-fly. For example, a plausible methodology is to use Fixed elements for interface-related functionality, in order to ensure proper interaction with other components, and to use Extensible elements for implementation-level functionality, which can be adjusted dynamically. The distinction between Fixed and Extensible sections of a component impacts also specialization (or inheritance): the Fixed section can be reused by other components, whereas the Extensible section cannot.

Hadas provides a high *degree of "selfness"* in its adaptation mechanism. Each component performs the requested changes on itself through built-in meta methods that are responsible for structural and behavioral changes. Although external mutability may be simpler to implement, the main advantage of self-mutability is that it minimizes the reliance on the external environment which might be owned by other authorities, hence promoting autonomy. A related question is *where* to store component behavior, both regular and meta (i.e., component manipulation) methods. Conventional class-based languages maintain state in instances and the behavior resides separately in classes. The main advantage of this instance-class separation is in maintaining the common knowledge in a single shared structure. However, having committed to dynamic adaptability, this approach is not applicable. In addition, any centralized repository of behavior is problematic. If an instance has been deployed to a remote site, we would like to ensure that its *operational context is nearby*. Thus, Hadas adopts a self-containment approach, whereby components store state, behavior, and meta-behavior inside themselves. In order to preserve built-in semantics for meta-methods, they are always stored in the immutable Fixed section of components, and the programmer decides where to store other methods and data items.

Technically, Hadas implements mutability by representing each method and each data item as singleton object of a corresponding method and data member classes, respectively. Using Java's dynamic class loading capabilities, these methods and data items can be modified. In addition, every Hadas component inherits from the built-in Component class, which contains the built-in meta-methods and containers for Fixed and Extensible (Hadas) items.

Figure 1 shows sample code that changes the behavior of a component when the load on its site increases beyond a certain threshold. The component is locked (setting a mutex to prevent concurrent access to the component while it is being modified); then the (built-in) method removeMethod removes the application's buy method (line 3); this is followed by addition of a new initialized message data-item (line 4) and an addition of a new buy method that takes the message as a parameter (lines 6); completed by an unlock operation.

```
      . . .
(1) if (systemLoad() > threshold) {
(2)     selfObject.lock();
(3)     selfObject.invoke("removeMethod", p("buy"));
(4)     selfObject.invoke("addDataItem",  p("message",
(5)                 "Our shop is temporarily closed"));
(6)     selfObject.invoke("addMethod", p("buy", "message"))
(7)     selfObject.unlock();
(8) }
      . . .
```

Fig. 1. Dynamic Adaptability in Hadas

As can be seen, the adaptive component model requires a special invocation mechanism (in fact, Hadas' invocation mechanism is itself reflective, similar to [3], enabling to adapt even the invocation "method", but this is beyond the scope of this paper; see [9]). This is similar to the invocation mechanism used in the (read-only) Java Reflection API.

The changes to the invocation mechanism have implications on both performance and on programming transparency. In terms of performance, although the invocation time is shorter than Java 1.1 reflection [10], it is still an order of magnitude slower than regular Java invocation. This means that indeed, the Hadas object model is not a substitute for regular programming-language objects and should be restricted to the implementation of components.

In terms of programming transparency, Hadas clearly requires a new programming model for components, including new invocation, parameter passing, and visibility modifiers.

In order to ease the programming task, Hadas provides a component builder tool that assists component developers to encode Hadas components by generating automatically part of the code. Still, the significant deviation from conventional programming model, even if restricted to programming coarse-grained components, may be viewed as the main shortcoming of the otherwise powerful framework. Thus, one of the design goals in FARGO, the successor to Hadas, was to preserve the syntactic transparency of Java as much as possible.

Hadas was fully implemented and is available for download. For more information see http://www.dsg.technion.ac.il/hadas.

4   Inter-component Adaptation in FarGo

The FARGO system [11,12], which has been under development since 1997, also targets Internet-based applications, but with focus on dynamic inter-component structure. The scale and variability of global environment, which is characterized by constant changes in network bandwidth, machine loads, and availability, implies that assumptions that are made early at *design time* are unlikely to hold during deployment time, let alone throughout the application's lifetime. Thus, the conventional static determination of the local-remote partitioning of components and the general mapping of the distributed application (logic) onto a set of (physical) processes/hosts, which we generically term the *layout of the application*, is undesirable and likely to impact its scalability.

FARGO addresses these issues by a comprehensive programming model and corresponding runtime support for dynamic relocation of components. At the basic system level FARGO provides component mobility, attachment of remote components into the same address space, and detachment of co-located components into different address spaces. During these activities, all references between components remain valid using a tracking mechanism that is embedded in the (compiler-generated) reference between components.

On top of the basic relocation support, FARGO provides the unique capability to specify various co-location constraints on components by placing semantics on the reference between components. For example, a `pull` reference from component α to β implies that both components must always be co-located. Furthermore, when component movement occurs, FARGO automatically relocates related components in order to comply with the new configuration. Thus, a movement of α implies a movement of β (and all components `pulled` from β, recursively) to α's new location. Another type of FARGO reference is `dup`, which means that a copy of the target component follows the source component to its new destination.

Self adaptation is provided in FARGO at two levels. First, the dynamic relocation itself may be viewed as an adaptation of the architecture. Second, FARGO enables dynamically evolution of the semantics of inter-component reference. A technical challenge was to support dynamic evolution without changing the invocation syntax or the object model in general, unlike Hadas. The general idea was to reflect upon the reference, instead of the object. Specifically, each reference has a meta reference object that reifies its semantics and allows it to change it. As shown in Figure 2, this object is contained by the stub (which is

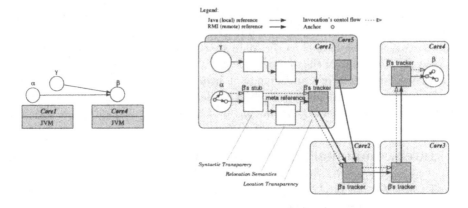

Fig. 2. The Structure of a FARGOReference

auto-generated by the FARGO compiler) and is accessible using a system method. (The other parts of the reference structure shown in the Figure support
relocation and syntactic transparency and are beyond the scope of this paper).

For example, Figure 3 shows a code fragment that retrieves the meta reference
of the msg reference, and then checks whether the type of that reference is link
(the default FARGO reference), in which case it changes the type to pull. The
meta reference's methods getRelocator (setRelocator) get (set) an object
that reifies the reference relocation type.

```
(1) MetaRef metaRef = Core.getMetaRef(msg);
(2) if (metaRef.getRelocator() instanceof Link)
(3)    metaRef.setRelocator(new Pull());
```

Fig. 3. Dynamic Reference Adaptability in FARGO

The key point is that the rest of the program preserves the component reference's transparency, and no changes are needed to the invocation mechanism,
i.e., the standard Java "." is used to invoke methods along FARGO references.
This reflects one of FARGO's major design goal, to retain as much as possible the
local Java programming model for encoding the logic of the application. Thus,
components are constructed and referenced using normal construction and invocation, respectively, and co-location constraints are encoded separately with
minimal interference with the encoding of the application logic.

Another emphasis in the FARGO project that was not part of the Hadas
project is the *monitor*, which enables application to make relocation decisions
based on sensing the environment. The FARGO monitor consists of three layers.
The bottom layer provides "environment sensors" such as detectors of network

delay and host load, and instant events such as planned shutdown or an arrival of new components to a given site. The sensing layer can be accessed directly by an application, or indirectly using the intermediate event layer. This layer allows applications to register interest in certain events, get notified asynchronously when these events occur, and react with possible self-relocation operations. Finally, the top layer provides high-level access to the event and sensing layers in three ways: through an API, through a graphical monitor view which enables manual relocation, or through a scripting language that enables encoding of relocation policies, possibly after the deployment of the application. For example, Figure 4 shows a script that recalculates the best location of an Engine component upon movement of related components, and relocates it if necessary.

```
Script EngineScript {
  on completDeparture(complet, target) do {
    engine = thisComplet();
    userInterfaces += complet;
    best = Locator.findBest(userInterfaces);
    move(engine, best);
  }
}
```

Fig. 4. FARGO Script

Performance-wise, FARGO does not suffer from the overhead of Hadas. The only overhead is in the extra invocations that are made inside a FARGO reference. Notice that when two components happen to be co-located, the references between them are all local and do not require a traversal of the TCP stack, as with sockets.

Finally, FARGO also adopts a coarse-grained component model, which defines the smallest granularity of relocation. Thus, programmers can distinguish between intra-component references, which are guaranteed to always be local, and inter-component references, which may be at times local and at times remote (hence the parameter passing semantics is uniformly remote). This distinction eases the programming task considerably. For more information on FARGO and to download the current version see http://www.dsg.technion.ac.il/fargo.

5   Conclusions

The explosive growth in networked mobile devices promises increased interest in models and techniques for designing software that can adapt itself to the environment in which it (currently) operates. However, for such technology to prevail, several important constraints and requirements on adaptability need to be properly addressed. In this paper we have listed some of these requirements and showed how they were addressed in two systems, Hadas and FARGO. From the adaptability perspective, the major distinction between the two approaches was the focus on the FARGO reference as the subject of adaptability, as opposed to the Hadas component. Although adaptability in FARGO is more limited, it is by far more convenient programming-wise (due to the syntactic transparency) and more efficient (using few extra standard invocations, as opposed to costly reflective invocations). The monitoring capability has further made FARGO more usable. A major objective is then to apply these lessons to improve component self adaptability.

References

1. W. Langdon, *Genetic Programming And Data Structures*. Boston, Massachusetts: Kluwer Academic Publishers, 1998.
2. "Self adaptive software," 1998. DARPA, BAA 98-12, Proposer Information Pamphlet.
3. P. Maes, "Concepts and experiments in computational reflection," *OOPSLA '87 Conference Proceedings, SIGPLAN Notices*, vol. 22, pp. 147–155, December 1987.
4. D. Ungar and R. B. Smith, "Self: The power of simplicity," *OOPSLA '87 Conference Proceedings, SIGPLAN Notices*, vol. 22, pp. 227–242, December 1987.
5. C. Chambers, "Object-oriented multi-methods in Cecil," in *ECOOP '92 Conference Proceedings*, pp. 33–56, 1992.
6. Object Management Group, *The Common Object Request Broker: Architecture and Specification. Revision 2.2*, February 1998. Available at: http://www.omg.org/corba/corbaiiop.html.
7. I. Ben-Shaul, A. Cohen, O. Holder, and B. Lavva, "HADAS: A network-centric system for interoperability programming," *International Journal of Cooperative Information Systems (IJCIS)*, vol. 6, no. 3&4, pp. 293–314, 1997.
8. O. Holder and I. Ben-Shaul, "A reflective model for mobile software objects," in *Proceedings of the 17th International Conference on Distributed Computing Systems (ICDCS'97)*, (Baltimore, Maryland), pp. 339–346, IEEE Computer Society Press, May 1997.
9. I. Ben-Shaul, O. Holder, and B. Lavva, "Dynamic adaptation and deployment of distributed components in hadas," tech. rep., technion:dsg, 2000. Submitted for Publication.
10. Sun Microsystems Inc., *Java Core Reflection: API and Specification*. Available at: http://java.sun.com/products/jdk/1.2/docs/guide/reflection/spec/java-reflectionTOC.doc.html.
11. O. Holder, I. Ben-Shaul, and H. Gazit, "System support for dynamic layout of distributed applications," in *Proceedings of the 19th International Conference on Distributed Computing Systems (ICDCS'99)*, (Austin, TX), pp. 403–411, May 1999.
12. O. Holder, I. Ben-Shaul, and H. Gazit, "Dynamic layout of distributed applications in FarGo," in *Proceedings of the 21st International Conference on Software Engineering (ICSE'99)*, (Los Angeles, CA), pp. 163–173, May 1999.

Imposing Real-Time Constraints on Self-Adaptive Controller Synthesis

David J. Musliner

Automated Reasoning Group
Honeywell Technology Center
3660 Technology Drive, Minneapolis, MN 55418*
david.musliner@honeywell.com

Abstract. Self-adaptive systems must reconfigure themselves, at runtime, to compensate for changing environments, objectives, and system capabilities. This paper discusses how the SA-CIRCA architecture for intelligent autonomous systems can automatically synthesize customized control software on the fly, and how that synthesis process itself can be managed to conform to real-time deadlines that may constrain the time available for reconfiguration. By restricting the scope of the problems it is trying to solve, by using incremental improvement algorithms, and by trading off solution quality against computation time, SA-CIRCA operates as a self-aware, self-adaptive system responding in real-time to perceived changes.

1 Introduction

Self-adaptive systems must reconfigure themselves, at runtime, to compensate for changing environments, objectives, and system capabilities. At first glance, this concept poses the major problem that the self-adaptive system must be able to understand its own objectives, capabilities, and environment in order to both detect changes and reconfigure itself. Upon further consideration, it becomes clear that this raw self-adaptation ability alone is not enough: the self-adaptive system must actually perform its self-adaptation online, as the deployed system is operating. Hence the real-time demands of the world are also applicable to the reconfiguration process itself! Clearly, it will be extremely challenging to deploy self-adaptive software into mission-critical applications, where any violation of real-time deadlines can have catastrophic consequences.

The Self-Adaptive Cooperative Intelligent Real-time Control Architecture (SA-CIRCA) can automatically synthesize customized controllers for autonomous systems, on the fly. This paper discusses how that synthesis process itself can be brought under soft real-time control, so that the synthesis of new controllers is accomplished within real-time deadlines (i.e., the time available for reconfiguration). The key to this control of deliberation is SA-CIRCA's ability to reason

* This work was supported by the Defense Advanced Research Projects Agency under contracts F30602-98-C-0212 and F30602-00-C-0017, and by a National Science Foundation Graduate Fellowship.

P. Robertson, H. Shrobe, and R. Laddaga (Eds.): IWSAS 2000, LNCS 1936, pp. 143–160, 2000.

about resource restrictions and modify the control problems for which it synthesizes controllers. Because SA-CIRCA is able to explicitly and accurately reason about its own predictable performance, it can not only recognize overconstraining domains, it can also analyze the potential effects of various changes to its goals or plans. By restricting the scope of the problems it is trying to solve, by using incremental improvement algorithms, and by trading off solution quality against computation time, SA-CIRCA is designed to operate as a self-aware, self-adaptive system responding in real-time to perceived changes.

In the next section, we present a brief overview of the SA-CIRCA architecture and outline how its controller-synthesis algorithms work. We then discuss the various means available to control the complexity and resource usage of the controller synthesis algorithms, describing the performance tradeoffs that result. To demonstrate these effects, we present several implemented examples showing the tradeoffs that can be made to meet real-time restrictions.

2   Self-Adaptation via Automatic Synthesis of Controllers

Building on the proven CIRCA architecture for intelligent real-time systems [12, 13], SA-CIRCA is an architecture for intelligent self-adaptive systems that must meet real-time deadlines [14]. Many intelligent agent architectures (e.g., RAPs [4], PRS [7], 3T [3]) essentially provide customized programming environments that make it easier for humans to write complex programs that behave appropriately. In contrast, SA-CIRCA *automatically synthesizes* its control programs (or plans) from primitive descriptions of the system it is controlling, the system objectives, and the environment in which the system operates.

2.1   The Example Domain

To help the reader understand this distinction clearly, and to set the stage for later examples, consider the domain illustrated in Fig. 1. The Puma robot arm is assigned the task of packing parts arriving on the conveyor belt into the nearby box. The conveyor moves at a fixed rate and the parts are spaced apart on the belt so that they arrive with some maximum frequency. Once at the end of the belt, each part remains motionless until the next part arrives, at which time it will be pushed off the end of the belt (unless the robot picks it up first). If a part falls off the belt because the robot does not pick it up in time, the system is considered to have failed. Thus, the arriving parts impose hard deadlines on the robot's responses; it must always pick up parts before they fall off the conveyor.

The parts can have several shapes (e.g., square, rectangle, triangle), each of which requires a different packing strategy. The control system may not know a priori how to pack all of the possible types of parts. If parts of a new shape arrive, the system can stack those parts on the nearby table until it has derived an appropriate box-packing strategy. The derivation of the packing method may involve search algorithms with potentially unbounded complexity. This aspect of

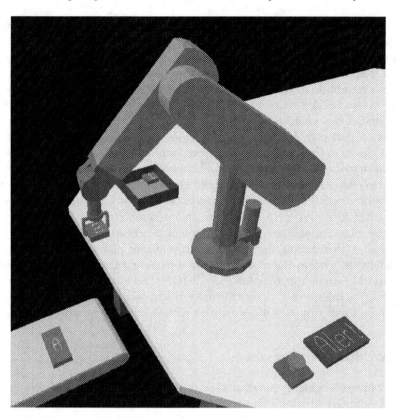

Fig. 1. The example Puma domain, in which the robot packs objects from the conveyor into the box.

the domain is used to exercise CIRCA's ability to combine arbitrary AI methods with real-time response guarantees.

The robot arm is also responsible for reacting to an emergency alert light. If the light goes on, the system has only a limited time to push the button next to the light, or it fails. This portion of the domain represents a completely asynchronous interrupt with a hard deadline on its service time.

To cope with this domain properly, the robot control system must be able to provide real-time responses to unsynchronized domain events (part arrivals and emergency alerts) while also performing complex search algorithms (deriving packing methods and reaction plans in general). To complicate matters further, the speed of the Puma robot and the domain sensors are limited. Variations of the domain can be set up with different part arrival rates, emergency alert rates, robot speeds, etc. To be truly intelligent and real-time in this domain, the control system will need to be able to evaluate its capabilities, its goals, and the domain behavior restrictions. With that information, an intelligent system should provide some measure of useful performance, possibly involving tradeoffs that sacrifice aspects of the system behavior as necessitated by resource restrictions.

Applying a reactive control architecture such as PRS, RAPs, or 3T to this domain would require a human to write complex control rules specifying what the Puma should do in the many different situations that may arise. The human would have to build a control program (or plan, or set of concurrent behaviors) that manages the asynchrony of the environment. Even if the control program was written perfectly, however, none of these systems could provide guarantees that all the domain's real-time deadlines would be met. While PRS and the Rex/Gapps system [15, 8] can provide bounded response times on reactive execution, they have no way to reason about the timing characteristics of a domain to understand whether that bounded response time will be *fast enough*.

In contrast, applying SA-CIRCA to this domain requires the human to describe the robot capabilities, the environment processes, and the overall system goals. Rather than telling the system *when it should* pick up a part, the human simply tells the system that it *can* pick up a part, and that if it does not pick up a part quickly enough, it may fail. SA-CIRCA then automatically synthesizes a set of reactive rules and performs formal verification processes to guarantee that the domain's real-time deadlines are all satisfied by the new reactive controller.

2.2   Architecture Overview

Figure 2 presents a highly abstract view of the SA-CIRCA architecture, showing how the Adaptive Mission Planner (AMP), Controller Synthesis Module (CSM), and Real-Time Subsystem (RTS) interact to provide intelligent, adaptive, real-time control. All of the SA-CIRCA subsystems operate in parallel. At the top, the AMP reasons about long-term goals, problem structures, and approaching deadlines to decide what the near-term goals should be, and what problems the near-term reasoning should be focused on. For example, in the Puma domain the AMP is responsible for reasoning about what part-packing algorithms should be developed for different part types, and what new robot control plans are necessary to implement those part-packing algorithms.

The AMP sends subgoals and problem configurations to the CSM, which develops real-time controllers to accomplish near-term goals. The controllers are in the form of a set of reactive rules that specify what actions the system should take in all of the possible different world situations. Each reaction that is critical to avoiding a potential failure includes a timing constraint. For example, in the Puma domain, the control plan might say what to do if the emergency alert light goes on and the robot is not holding a block (*push the button!*), and how quickly that action must be taken (*before the emergency results in failure!*).

The CSM sends these control plans to the RTS, which reactively executes the automatically-generated plans and enforces guaranteed response times. Meanwhile, the AMP and CSM continue to reason ahead about future contingencies and phases of the problem. In the Puma domain, the AMP might try to predict what new types of parts will arrive, and generate suitable control plans in

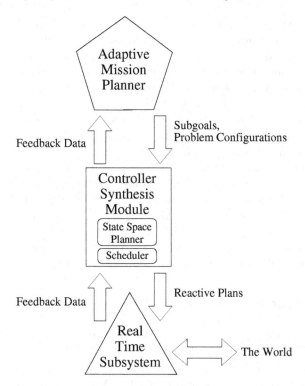

Fig. 2. The SA-CIRCA architecture includes three major components operating at different levels of abstraction and responsiveness.

advance. The RTS contains a plan cache mechanism that allows it to store additional reactive plans that are not currently executing, and switch to executing one of those plans with a (very fast) constant time operation.

Thus SA-CIRCA is designed to adapt its runtime behavior through both on-line, runtime planning and runtime selection of pre-built plans. In essence, if the AMP and CSM can build a plan ahead of time to handle a particular contingency, they will cache it in the RTS. If a contingency occurs for which no cached plan exists, the system will invoke its best available plan and the AMP will direct the CSM to synthesize a new, customized plan as quickly as possible. To the degree that a domain is accurately modeled and can be successfully controlled by the available execution resources, SA-CIRCA will provide safety guarantees and high-quality performance. When the real world diverges from the domain model, or the execution resources prove insufficient to control the domain, SA-CIRCA is designed to monitor its own performance, detect these problems, and gracefully degrade its plans to adapt.

The controller synthesis algorithms are extremely complex and potentially undecidable. Thus one of the keys to making CIRCA's safety guarantees is that each controller executed on the RTS must keep the system safe while waiting for the CSM to generate the next controller. Some nicely-structured domains make it possible to build reactive controllers that preserve safety indefinitely while waiting for the CSM. For example, in some formulations of the Puma domain, the robot can respond to all types of arriving parts (by simply putting them down on the table) and all emergency alerts for an essentially unlimited amount of time. The only practical limitation is the number of parts the table can hold, and if this is made infinite, the domain allows perfect "holding patterns." Of course, real worlds do not offer infinite tables (or infinite amounts of fuel for aircraft to circle in holding patterns).

Practical applications of the SA-CIRCA architecture will require the CSM to provide some level of predictable response, so that the RTS only needs to remain safe and stable for a limited time horizon. In this paper, our focus is on bringing the controller-synthesis activities of the CSM under this type of soft real-time control. When faced with limited time to reconfigure the RTS with a new reactive control plan, how can SA-CIRCA control its deliberation processes and ensure that it will synthesize a new controller in time?

3   Controlling the Synthesis Process

As illustrated in Fig. 2, the CSM includes a State Space Planner (SSP) and a Scheduler component. The SSP builds control plans based on a world model and a set of formally-defined safety conditions that must be satisfied by feasible plans [13, 6]. To describe a domain to SA-CIRCA, the user inputs a set of transition descriptions that implicitly define the set of reachable states. For example, Fig. 3 illustrates several transitions used in the Puma domain.

```
EVENT emergency-alert                    ; ; Emergency light goes on.
      PRECONDS: ((emergency F))
      POSTCONDS: ((emergency T))

TEMPORAL emergency-failure               ; ; Fail if don't attend to
      PRECONDS: ((emergency T))          ; ; light by deadline.
      POSTCONDS: ((failure T))
      MIN-DELAY: 30 [seconds]

ACTION push-emergency-button             ; ; Pushing button cancels emerg.
      PRECONDS: ((part-in-gripper F))    ; ; Requires empty gripper.
      POSTCONDS: ((emergency F))
      WORST-CASE-EXEC-TIME: 2.0 [seconds]
```

Fig. 3. Example transition descriptions given to SA-CIRCA.

The SSP builds plans by generating a nondeterministic finite automaton (NFA) from these transition descriptions. The SSP assigns an action to each reachable state. These actions are selected to drive the system towards states that satisfy as many goal propositions as possible and to *preempt* transitions that lead to failure. For example, Fig. 4 shows graphically how a planned action can preempt a temporal transition to failure, if the action is constrained to *definitely occur* before the temporal transition *could possibly occur*. System safety is guaranteed by planning action transitions that preempt *all* transitions to failure [13]. Action assignments determine the topology of the NFA (and so the set of reachable states): preemption of temporal transitions removes edges, and assignment of actions adds them.

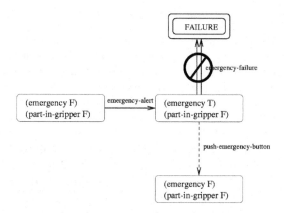

Fig. 4. Preemptive actions are planned to keep the system safe.

The control plan for the RTS is extracted from the set of planned actions in the NFA and cast in the form of Test Action Pairs (TAPs). Each TAP has a test expression that recognizes a subset of the NFA (world) states, and a single action that has been planned for those states. TAPs that preempt failures have timing constraints, and the Scheduler builds them into a fixed, looping schedule to be executed by the RTS. TAPs that do not preempt failures, but are planned only to achieve other non-safety-critical goals, are executed in a best-effort, "if-time" fashion.

3.1   Control Inputs

There are currently two different versions of the SA-CIRCA SSP: the evolved original SSP that reasons about nondeterministic worlds without explicitly representing quantitative uncertainty, and the Probabilistic State Space Planner (PSSP) from CIRCA-II [1, 2], that reasons explicitly about the probabilities of different transitions and states [10]. In both cases, the controller synthesis activity can be controlled by adjusting aspects of the SSP inputs: the problem configuration it is required to solve, and the parameters that describe precisely the nature of an acceptable solution.

For the non-probabilistic SSP, the problem configuration consists of :

Action Transitions — representing potential actions that the SSP can plan to invoke, with guaranteed results after some maximum amount of time.

Event Transitions — representing uncontrollable, instantaneous events.

Temporal Transitions — representing uncontrollable environmental processes that take at least some minimum amount of time.

Reliable Temporal Transitions — representing processes that are guaranteed to occur, given a certain amount of time.

Start States — describing possible states in which the system may start, or "wake up."

Goals — describing desirable state features.

The Probabilistic State Space Planner (PSSP) uses additional input information, including probability rate functions associated with each transition, and a single probability threshold parameter that controls how conservative the PSSP should be in worrying about low-probability states.

3.2   Triggering Tradeoffs

SA-CIRCA has several ways of recognizing that the domain is overconstrained, and that the system cannot build a plan that accomplishes all of its goals and guarantees system safety. During the controller-synthesis process, the SSP may finish a complete search of the space of possible reaction plans and find that there are no suitable plans that can prevent failure. Or, if the SSP spends too much time trying to build a controller, it may time-out and be alerted by a timer interrupt. Finally, the SSP may come up with a set of desired reactions which are then rejected as unschedulable by the Scheduler. This is the most common way of recognizing an overconstrained domain: a suitable reaction plan exists, but its execution cannot be guaranteed with the limited resources of the RTS. At this point, the SSP would backtrack by default to make a different choice and produce a modified reaction plan. Alternatively, the AMP might decide to make a tradeoff instead, simplifying some aspects of the control problem so that the CSM can generate a feasible controller.

We have designed several experiments to illustrate and evaluate this tradeoff capability. Note that these tradeoff methods are not heuristics themselves; they can be implemented by simple procedures making bounded changes to the SA-CIRCA data structures describing the world model, the current control plan, etc. Furthermore, the effects of those changes are well-understood; SA-CIRCA can explicitly reason about the impact of applying its various tradeoff methods on the system's performance. However, choosing *which* tradeoff method to apply in a particular situation remains a heuristic decision we have not yet addressed.

3.3   Ignoring a Temporal Transition to Failure

One of the most obvious and powerful tradeoffs is to simply delete or ignore one or more temporal transitions that lead to failure in the world model. This corresponds to the SSP not even considering that some ongoing process will ever lead to failure. As a result, the TAP that was planned to preempt that temporal transition to failure (TTF) may be affected in several ways. In the following material, we will examine in detail one example of the types of performance tradeoffs that result from simply ignoring a TTF. We then outline several other possible outcomes, but do not investigate them in depth because they represent minor variations.

One Result of Ignoring a TTF If the SSP is not told about a TTF from a particular state, it is possible that the SSP will still choose the same action for that state, but that the action will no longer be preventing a failure. Because the action is not preempting a TTF, it will be implemented by an if-time TAP (see Sect. 3) that does not need to be scheduled, so the scheduling problem will be easier. However, performance will suffer because the system no longer guarantees to execute the affected TAP and prevent one particular type of failure.

In the Puma domain, for example, the AMP might decide to ignore the possibility of a part falling off the conveyor, perhaps because it is highly unlikely that the part will really fall. As a result, when examining a state in which a part is waiting on the conveyor, the SSP will no longer be required to plan a **pickup-part-from-conveyor** action to avoid failure. However, the action will still be planned because it is useful in achieving the system's goals: the robot must pick up the part in order to pack it in the box, which satisfies the goal **(part-in-box T)**. Note that the system can still make guarantees about other types of failures. For example, it can guarantee that it will avoid failures resulting from the emergency alert, because the actions preempting the **emergency-failure** TTF are still guaranteed.

Schedulability Effects of Ignoring a TTF To quantify the effects of this type of tradeoff method, we make the CSM try to build controllers for parametric variations of the Puma domain. Figure 5 shows the effect on schedulability over a range of arrival rates for emergency alerts and parts. If the arrival rates match a point below the lower, "normal plan" curve, then the system can build a schedule that will guarantee to both avoid emergency failures and prevent parts from falling off the conveyor. The form of this curve illustrates the tradeoff that the scheduling mechanism can make between tasks; when the emergency rate is relatively high, the system will still build a schedule, as long as the part arrival rate is sufficiently low that the Scheduler can allocate more resources to the tasks that respond to the alert. Conversely, when the emergency rate is lower, the system can deal with a faster rate of arriving parts. If the arrival rates match a point above the lower curve, then the system cannot build a schedule that will guarantee to avoid both emergency failures and dropping parts. However, if the system ignores the **part-falls-off-conveyor** TTF, then it can build guaranteed schedules for all of the instances below the upper line, the maximum rate of emergency alert arrivals that can be handled with the given primitives. The part arrival rate is no longer critical to the scheduling problem, because the **pickup-part-from-conveyor** TAP, with a period determined by the **part-falls-off-conveyor** TTF, is no longer being scheduled and guaranteed.

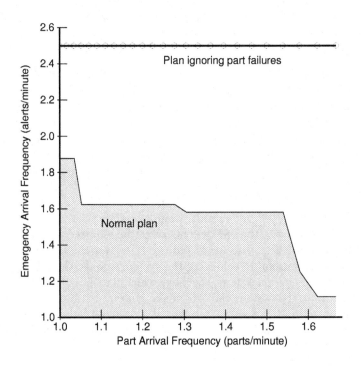

Fig. 5. The improved schedulability achieved by ignoring a TTF.

Performance Effects of Ignoring a TTF To illustrate the non-guaranteed nature of the resulting behavior, we implemented this tradeoff method in the Puma domain, increasing the rate of emergency alerts and part arrivals so that the original plan of actions is not schedulable. The SSP was told that the worst-case rate was 2.4 alerts/minute, well above the limit of schedulability for the entire problem, as shown in Fig. 5. The AMP then removes the **part-falls-off-conveyor** TTF from the SSP's world model, re-plans, and builds a new TAP plan in which the **pickup-part-from-conveyor** action is implemented by an if-time TAP rather than a guaranteed TAP. Figure 6 illustrates the results from several hundred trials on the Puma simulator, with emergency alerts arriving with random delays uniformly distributed in the range of 25 to 30 seconds (2 to 2.4 alerts/minute). As we expected, when parts arrived more frequently, the number of parts falling off the conveyor would increase, as the system had less and less free time to apply to if-time behaviors.

Interestingly, the if-time TAP that implemented the **pickup-part-from-conveyor** action was always executed frequently enough to prevent failures when the parts arrived no more frequently than two parts/minute. Referring back to Fig. 5, we can see that the actual simulated execution was more robust than the Scheduler predicted; the "normal plan" plot in the graph indicates that even with the **pickup-part-from-conveyor** TAP in the schedule, the system could not be guaranteed to handle part arrivals faster than about 1.65 parts/minute. This result may indicate that the worst-case situations the SSP considered never occurred in the tests, or that the Scheduling or SSP algorithms were overly conservative. We plan to investigate further.

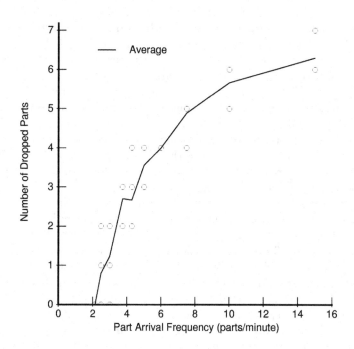

Fig. 6. The system behavior after ignoring the **part-falls-off-conveyor** TTF, with the emergency light frequency between 2 and 2.4 alerts/minute.

Alternative Results of Ignoring a TTF Several other outcomes are possible when the AMP chooses to ignore a TTF. For example, it is possible that, by ignoring one TTF from a state, a different temporal transition becomes dominant and still causes the planned action for that state to meet a deadline. In general this will mean that the deadline for the planned reaction will be longer, but the

TAP will still need to be scheduled. The resulting tradeoffs are similar to those above, in that the system can no longer guarantee to avoid all types of failures. In this case, however, no TAPs are moved out of the guaranteed list: instead, the reaction deadline of one of the TAPs will be increased, thus decreasing the desired utilization, and making the scheduling problem easier.

In the extreme case, ignoring a TTF may cause the planner to completely eliminate one or more planned actions, thus removing TAPs from the list to be scheduled. If an action was only planned originally to preempt failure (or as a "precursor" to that preemption), and was not instrumental in achieving any other system goals, then the action may be removed entirely. For example, if SA-CIRCA ignores the **emergency-failure** transition in the Puma domain, it will completely alter the world model and avoid planning the **push-emergency-button** action. Depending on the frequency of part arrivals, it may also eliminate the need to put parts on the table temporarily, and thus ignoring this one TTF could also remove the **stop-moving** and **place-part-on-table** actions from the plan. These latter actions are precursors that were included in the plan to establish the preconditions of the action that was planned to preempt the **emergency-failure** TTF, and thus they are also unnecessary.

While moving a TAP to the if-time list means that, in non-worst-case situations it may be still executed quickly enough, deleting a TAP altogether provides no such potential. Since if-time TAPs do not use any resources when the RTS is pressed for time, avoiding building if-time TAPs does not save any significant RTS execution-time resources. However, this tradeoff can significantly reduce the complexity of the controller synthesis problem, and thus it provides a powerful method for managing the CSM's responsiveness.

An important feature of this tradeoff method, and of the SA-CIRCA approach in general, is that the system can introspectively examine the predicted effects of a particular tradeoff. In other words, SA-CIRCA might evaluate the worth of various tradeoff methods by examining the expected results in the world model. If the AMP considers ignoring a TTF, it can immediately recognize that the failure resulting from that TTF will be possible with the modified TAP plan. In addition, the AMP can examine the new world model and TAP plan to recognize more detailed aspects of the tradeoff. For example, if the new plan still includes all the same guaranteed TAPs as the original plan, then the AMP can conclude that the reaction previously planned to preempt the TTF is still being enforced, but at a lower rate. If the AMP knows that the worst-case rate of the ignored TTF is rarely achieved, this tradeoff option may be very attractive, because it has exchanged a decrease in one TAP's response rate for the ability to schedule and guarantee the entire reactive plan.

3.4   Ignoring an Event Transition

Just as the AMP may decide to alter its treatment of temporal transitions, it may also choose to change how it considers event transitions. Ignoring an event transition may have many of the effects described above for temporal transitions: it may cut off parts of the world model state space, possibly making some goals unreachable. Ignoring an event transition can thus reduce the planning time and decrease the number of TAPs planned, allowing the system to make guarantees for some subset of desired behaviors which were not previously schedulable.

For example, in the Puma domain, ignoring the **emergency-alert** event transition provides a large reduction in the planning time, because many states are eliminated from the model— in fact, the state space for our running example is reduced from 330 enumerated states and 158 reachable states to 106 enumerated and a mere 58 reachable states. Furthermore, a large number of contingency reactions are eliminated from the plan, and thus the complexity of the TAPs is reduced, and the scheduling problem is eased. Because the emergency alert is no longer of concern, the system is able to react to parts on the conveyor belt even more quickly than if the predicted alert rate is very slow (as in the extreme right edge of Fig. 5). While the example of Fig. 5 could handle parts arriving at most every 36 seconds, the plan built by ignoring the **emergency-alert** transition can handle parts arriving every 27 seconds, a significant improvement in capacity. Of course, the tradeoff is that the system is no longer monitoring the emergency light, and it will not react to an alert. If the AMP thinks that an alert is unlikely, or finds that the cost of failing to respond to an alert is sufficiently low, it may judge that the reduced planning time and improved part-packing reaction time are worth the risk involved in ignoring alerts.

More generally, we can see that ignoring an event transition can have the desirable effects of reducing the SSP's planning time and simplifying the scheduling problem. The disadvantage, of course, is that this tradeoff method removes planned contingency actions entirely, as opposed to just moving the relevant TAPs to the if-time list (as ignoring a TTF can do). Because event transitions represent instantaneous events in the world, as opposed to the ongoing processes represented by temporal transitions, it seems plausible that the AMP could have knowledge of event probabilities that would be helpful in guiding the use of this tradeoff method. Ignoring highly improbable event transitions would obviously be a good approach, in order to ensure that the system is least likely to encounter world situations for which it is not prepared. The PSSP takes this idea one step further, using probabilistic information to provide uniform, unified pruning of the SSP model when necessary.

3.5   The Probabilistic State Space Planner

At the University of Michigan, colleagues have been working on a new version of the SSP that uses probabilistic information to guide the system in considering the most-probable states first [10]. The Probabilistic State Space Planner (PSSP) builds partial plans that are only probabilistically safe, because they only consider those states whose likelihood is above a given threshold. By explicitly pruning least-probable areas of the state space, the PSSP approach allows SA-CIRCA to optimize its allocation of controller-synthesis effort and runtime reactive resources against the most-probable types of failure. The AMP can adjust the probability threshold to alter the complexity of the controller synthesis problem. Moreover, if additional planning-time resources are available and the

RTS capabilities are actually the limiting factor, the system can build contingency plans to handle pruned areas of the state space and swap those plans in when the pruned, less-likely situations arise.

The PSSP techniques resemble work on developing policies for Markov Decision Processes, with the added complexity of a non-Markovian temporal model and the resulting looping automata. This problem formulation leads to more compact world models, but complex reasoning.

The probabilistic approach is less coarse and "heavy-handed" than simply ignoring an entire TTF. For example, the PSSP may realize that in one world state a TTF is highly unlikely (and thus can be ignored), but that same TTF is more likely in a different state (and should be handled). Furthermore, this approach retains the advantages of the general CIRCA approach, in that the system can introspectively examine the predicted effects of a particular tradeoff. We have not yet implemented any experiments in the Puma domain to demonstrate and evaluate this approach. However, tests in related domains (e.g., controlling simplified autonomous aircraft) show promise for this approach.

3.6   Modifying Action Transitions (Method Selection)

The AMP can also make changes to the action transitions that are available to the CSM for use in synthesizing controllers. The AMP may have several different methods for performing an action (or a test), and it can choose amongst them according to the resources available. For example, suppose that the Puma control system provides the RTS with two different implementations of the **place-part-in-box** operator: a slow, high-accuracy, "fine-motion" version; and a faster, lower-accuracy, "coarse-motion" version. Using the fine-motion operator allows the system to place the parts very close together, thus yielding densely-packed boxes. But the fine-motion operator needs four seconds to finish the placement operation. Using the coarse-motion operator requires the system to leave more space between the parts, since the placement is less-certain. As a result, the system will produce less-densely packed boxes, but it can produce them more quickly, because the coarse-motion operator only needs 2.5 seconds. Thus, in this example, selecting different operators will allow the system to trade off the quality of its results (the packing density) for the timeliness of its long-term and short-term behaviors (the speed of packing whole boxes and individual parts). This tradeoff method is equivalent in many ways to the "configuration selection" [9], "version selection" [11], and "design-to-time" [5] approaches. Given the faster coarse-motion operator, the system may be able to guarantee to respond in time to a higher frequency of emergency alerts than with the slower operator.

Experimental Results of Method Selection To provide a more quantitative demonstration of this tradeoff, we ran experiments using the coarse/fine operators described above. The fine-motion operator was defined to require no space at all surrounding parts being placed in the box: essentially, it could achieve 100% packing density with a fortuitous series of part arrivals. The coarse-motion operator, on the other hand, required one inch of clearance on all sides of the parts in order to place them in the box. Naturally, the achievable packing density is lower with this operator, since parts necessarily occupy spaces larger than their actual size.

Figure 7 shows the improvement in response-time achieved by using the coarse-motion operator, displayed here by the increased rate of emergency alerts and part arrivals that can be handled. The lower curve shows the performance for the fine-motion operator used in the earlier examples (and previously graphed in Fig. 5). The upper curve shows the larger range of domains that can be handled using the faster, coarse-motion packing operator. The coarse-motion operator reduces the time allocated to the **place-part-in-box** TAP, and therefore the system can respond in time to more frequent part arrivals, emergency alerts, or both.

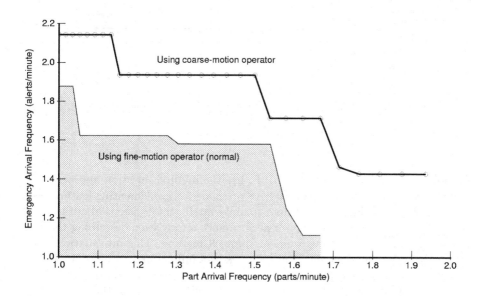

Fig. 7. Schedulability variations using different TAP implementations.

However, Fig. 8 shows the corresponding decrease in performance quality that resulted from the coarse-motion operator, when applied to 100 trials using randomly ordered arrivals of four different part shapes. On average, the density of the packed box was reduced from 70% using the fine-motion operator to 59% with the coarse-motion operator. In these experiments, simulations of the box-packing algorithm were continued until the first arrival of a part that did not fit in the box. The fine-motion version was able to pack an average of 45 parts in the box, while the coarse-motion version packed an average of only 26 parts.

Thus we can see that the improved schedulability and response time illustrated in Fig. 7 are only achieved at the cost of stiff performance degradation.

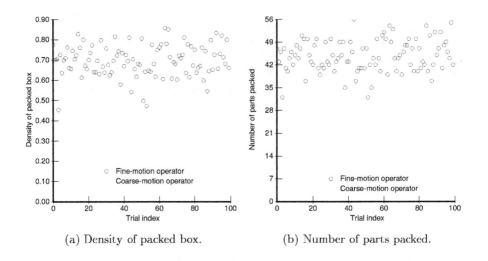

(a) Density of packed box.   (b) Number of parts packed.

Fig. 8. Performance variations using different TAP implementations.

Generalizing Method Selection To use the method selection approach, the system obviously must have alternative methods for implementing feature tests and actions on the RTS. In addition, to make intelligent decisions about method selection, the system would require performance information describing the output quality and resource requirements of each method. This information could be relatively simple, or could be as complex as a full performance profile. In any case, because method selection retains the consideration of all world model states and does not remove any TAPs from the schedule, it is one of the more subtle tradeoff techniques, capable of altering the resource needs of the system without drastic effects on its performance guarantees. Depending on the assortment of different methods available, the method-selection approach can alter almost any quality measure of the reactive system's performance, including precision, accuracy, etc.

4   Summary and Future Directions

The ability to make performance tradeoffs in the face of resource limitations is a fundamental requirement for intelligent real-time systems, since the very nature of real-time domains includes resource constraints. We have presented a variety of ways in which SA-CIRCA can make such performance tradeoffs, actively managing its allocation of deliberation and reaction resources. Our experiments in the Puma domain have demonstrated several different strategic tradeoff methods that the AMP can use to modify the problems it poses to the SSP, adjusting the difficulty of the controller synthesis problem, and thus the performance of the SSP itself.

In the probabilistic version of the SSP, the fundamental technique for controlling the search process is adjusting the threshold of state probabilities below which the SSP ignores states. An alternative or supplemental approach, which has not yet been implemented, is to impose a time horizon limit on the SSP's projective search as well. An explicit time horizon would tell the SSP that it only needs to build a reactive controller that can keep the system safe for a limited amount of future time, and this could be used to truncate the SSP search forward through the space of possible future worlds. In fact, if the AMP could tell for sure what would be an appropriate and feasible time horizon for a particular SSP problem configuration, these horizon limits would be a feasible simplification, not reducing the completeness or performance guarantees of an SSP's plan. As such, time horizon control could be even preferable to probability threshold adjustments for domains in which the expected progress through a mission plan can be sufficiently predicted.

References

[1] E. Atkins, R. H. Miller, T. Van Pelt, K. D. Shaw, W. B. Ribbens, P. D. Washabaugh, and D. S. Bernstein, "Solus: An Autonomous Aircraft for Flight Control and Trajectory Planning Research," in *Proc. American Control Conference*, volume 2, pp. 689–693, June 1998.

[2] E. M. Atkins, *Plan Generation and Hard Real-Time Execution with Application to Safe, Autonomous Flight*, PhD thesis, University of Michigan, 1999.

[3] R. P. Bonasso, D. Kortenkamp, D. Miller, and M. Slack, "Experiences with an Architecture for Intelligent, Reactive Agents," in *Journal of Experimental and Theoretical AI*, 1996.

[4] R. J. Firby, "An Investigation into Reactive Planning in Complex Domains," in *Proc. National Conf. on Artificial Intelligence*, pp. 202–206, 1987.

[5] A. Garvey and V. Lesser, "Design-to-time Real-Time Scheduling," *IEEE Trans. Systems, Man, and Cybernetics*, vol. 23, no. 6, , 1993.

[6] R. P. Goldman, D. J. Musliner, K. D. Krebsbach, and M. S. Boddy, "Dynamic Abstraction Planning," in *Proc. National Conf. on Artificial Intelligence*, pp. 680–686, 1997.

[7] F. F. Ingrand, M. P. Georgeff, and A. S. Rao, "An Architecture for Real-Time Reasoning and System Control," *IEEE Expert*, pp. 34–44, December 1992.

[8] L. P. Kaelbling and S. J. Rosenschein, "Action and Planning in Embedded Agents," in *Robotics and Autonomous Systems 6*, pp. 35–48, 1990.

[9] T.-W. Kuo and A. K. Mok, "Load Adjustment in Adaptive Real-Time Systems," in *Proc. Real-Time Systems Symposium*, pp. 160–170, December 1991.

[10] H. Li, E. Atkins, E. Durfee, and K. Shin, "Resource Allocation for a Limited Real-Time Agent Using a Temporal Probabilistic World Model," in *Working Notes of the 2000 AAAI Spring Symposium on Real-Time Autonomous Systems*, 2000.

[11] N. Malcolm and W. Zhao, "Version Selection Schemes for Hard Real-Time Communications," in *Proc. Real-Time Systems Symposium*, pp. 12–21, December 1991.

[12] D. J. Musliner, E. H. Durfee, and K. G. Shin, "CIRCA: A Cooperative Intelligent Real-Time Control Architecture," *IEEE Trans. Systems, Man, and Cybernetics*, vol. 23, no. 6, pp. 1561–1574, 1993.

[13] D. J. Musliner, E. H. Durfee, and K. G. Shin, "World Modeling for the Dynamic Construction of Real-Time Control Plans," *Artificial Intelligence*, vol. 74, no. 1, pp. 83–127, March 1995.

[14] D. J. Musliner, R. P. Goldman, M. J. Pelican, and K. D. Krebsbach, "Self-Adaptive Software for Hard Real-Time Environments," *IEEE Intelligent Systems*, vol. 14, no. 4, pp. 23–29, July/August 1999.

[15] S. J. Rosenschein and L. P. Kaelbling, "The Synthesis of Digital Machines with Provable Epistemic Properties," in *Proc. Conf. Theoretical Aspects of Reasoning About Knowledge*, pp. 83–98, 1986.

Software Mode Changes for Continuous Motion Tracking*

Deepak Karuppiah[1], Patrick Deegan[2], Elizeth Araujo[2],
Yunlei Yang[2], Gary Holness[2], Zhigang Zhu[1],
Barbara Lerner[3], Roderic Grupen[2], and Edward Riseman[1]

[1] Dept. of Computer Science, Computer Vision Research Laboratory,
University of Massachusetts, Amherst, MA 01003 USA
{zhu, riseman}@cs.umass.edu
http://vis-www.cs.umass.edu/projects/safer
[2] Dept. of Computer Science, Laboratory for Perceptual Robotics,
University of Massachusetts, Amherst, MA 01003 USA
grupen@cs.umass.edu
http://www-robotics.cs.umass.edu/rob_safer
[3] Dept. of Computer Science, Lab. for Advanced Software Eng. Research,
University of Massachusetts, Amherst, MA 01003 USA
lerner@cs.umass.edu
http://laser.cs.umass.edu/SAFER.htm

Abstract. Robot control in nonlinear and nonstationary run-time environments presents challenges to traditional software methodologies. In particular, robot systems in "open" domains can only be modeled probabilistically and must rely on run-time feedback to detect whether hardware/software configurations are adequate. Modifications must be effected while guaranteeing critical performance properties. Moreover, in multi-robot systems, there are typically many ways in which to compensate for inadequate performance. The computational complexity of high dimensional sensorimotor systems prohibits the use of many traditional centralized methodologies. We present an application in which a redundant sensor array, distributed spatially over an office-like environment can be used to track and localize a human being while reacting at run-time to various kinds of faults, including: hardware failure, inadequate sensor geometries, occlusion, and bandwidth limitations. Responding at run-time requires a combination of knowledge regarding the physical sensorimotor device, its use in coordinated sensing operations, and high-level process descriptions. We present a distributed control architecture in which run-time behavior is both preanalyzed and recovered empirically to inform local scheduling agents that commit resources autonomously subject to process control specifications. Preliminary examples of system performance are presented from the UMass Self-Adaptive Software (SAS) platform.

* This work was supported by AFRL/IFTD under F30602-97-2-0032 (SAFER), DARPA/ITO DABT63-99-1-0022 (SDR Multi-Robot), and NSF CDA-9703217 (Infrastructure).

P. Robertson, H. Shrobe, and R. Laddaga (Eds.): IWSAS 2000, LNCS 1936, pp. 161–180, 2000.

1   Introduction

Much of current software development is based on the notion that one can correctly specify a system a priori. Such a specification must include all input data sets which is impossible, in general, for embedded sensorimotor applications. Self-adaptive software, however, modifies its behavior based on observed progress toward goals as the system state evolves at run-time [10]. Achieving self-adaptation requires knowledge of software structure as well as a means of measuring progress toward the goal. Current research in self-adaptive software draws from two traditions, namely control theoretic and planning.

The control theoretic approach to self-adaptive software treats software as a plant with associated controllability and observability issues[9]. Time-critical applications require the ability to act quickly without spending large amounts of time on deliberation. Such reflexive behavior is the domain of the control theoretic tradition. Control output decisions are based on observations of the plant's state. A goal is reached when the controller drives error between an input reference state (software specification) and the current system state to zero. Traditionally, control theoretic approaches to physical plants ignore issues of resource allocation and scheduling - robust control seeks to guarantee bounded performance degradation in the face of bounded parameter variation and adaptive control seeks to estimate the parameters of the controller and/or the plant in order to optimize closed-loop behavior.

Traditions in planning are also meaningful to self-adaptive software. Planning enumerates process state, possible actions, and desired goals in an effort to find a sequence of actions which advance it toward the goal. As actions are carried out, various artifacts can be predicted and resources can be scheduled to optimize performance. In the planning approach to self-adaptive software, software components are treated as resources [13]. A particular schedule may not be reasonable because it violates resource limits or causes the system to diverge from its goal. In this situation, a planning system may find a sequence of actions which advances (partially) toward a goal specification. The ability to make tradeoffs and perform such higher level reasoning is the domain of the planning tradition. Planning for large complex systems is both time and compute intensive.

How can a system react to time critical events while at the same time, make tradeoffs and perform high level reasoning? This is known as the planning versus reaction dilemma. In the UMass Self-Adaptive Software (SAS) research project, we take an approach which combines the control theoretic and planning traditions where appropriate to manage complex self-adaptive software systems.

High-level deliberation and low-level reactivity are valuable in the control of autonomous and self-adaptive systems. A successful implementation of such a hybrid architecture would permit the system to make use of prior knowledge when appropriate and to respond quickly to run-time data. The central open question appears to be deciding how reacting and deliberating should interact in a constructive fashion. We have adopted a perspective in which the control hierarchy is adaptive at every level. Low-level control processes parameterized by resources interact with the domain continuously and recover run-time context observable by the working set of control. This kind of context feedback permits a high-level process planner to re-deploy resources. Over time, robust plans for interacting with specific problem domains are compiled into comprehensive reactive policies. State descriptions evolve to express likely run-time context at the highest levels and reactive policies adapt to handle run-time contingencies at the lowest levels [14].

We are concentrating on how resources, distributed in a non-uniform manner over multiple robot platforms can be coordinated to achieve mission objectives. Our approach relies on technologies that produce flexibility, resourcefulness, high performance, and fault tolerance. Specifically, we are interested in (1) how cross-modal sensory front-ends can be designed to provide mission-specific percepts, (2) how perceptual behavior can incorporate sensory information derived from two or more robotic platforms carrying different sensors and feature extraction algorithms, and (3) how team resources can be organized effectively to achieve multiple simultaneous objectives.

A family of resource scheduling policies, called Behavior Programs (B-Pgms), is downloaded into members of a working group of robots as part of the configuration process. Each B-Pgm contains a set of (previously evaluated) contingency plans with which to respond to a variety of likely run-time contexts and is responsible for orchestrating the run-time behavior of the system in response to percepts gathered on-line. If required, run-time contexts may be handled by making use of contingency plans in the B-Pgm, or by re-deploying resources at the process planning level.

The UMass hybrid SAS architecture is based on a set of primitive, closed-loop control processes. This framework allows hierarchical composition of the controllers into behavior programs (B-Pgms) for tracking, recognition, motion control, and for a more complex human tracking scenario. The multi-robot platform is designed to respond to multiple, simultaneous objectives and reasons about resources using a high-level process description and control procedure using the little-JIL process description language. Our goal is an ambitious, vertically integrated software environment in which run-time data sets drive the organization of behavior and contribute to the management of large and comprehensive software systems. This document describes the very first experiments employing this paradigm.

2   Sensory Primitives for Motion Tracking

A multi-objective system requires that the sensory algorithms are flexible to support adaptation and reconfigurable on-line to facilitate fault-tolerance. Our approach is designed to provide a set of sensor processing techniques that can fulfill both low-level and high-level objectives in an open environment. Cooperative interaction among members of the robot team requires the mission planner to be effective in utilizing system resources across team members, including robot platforms, sensors, computation, and communication. In particular, we are constructing robot behaviors across multiple coordinated platforms and sensors.

To achieve the desired robustness, the platform is configured with a variety of sensors and algorithms. Vision is the primary sensing modality, but it is complemented by inexpensive pyroelectric sensors, sonar, infrared proximity sensors, and (in the future) acoustic sensors. Multiple types of sensors are considered to be distributed across several robot platforms to allow flexibility in mission planning and resource scheduling in response to hardware and algorithm failures.

2.1   Panoramic Imaging

Effective combinations of transduction and image processing is essential for operating in an unpredictable environment and to rapidly focus attention on important activities in the environment. A limited field-of-view (as with standard optics) often causes the camera resource to be blocked when multiple targets are not close together and panning the camera to multiple targets takes time. We employ a camera with a panoramic lens[1] to simultaneously detect and track multiple moving objects in a full 360-degree view [3,12,16].

Figures 1 and 2 depict the processing steps involved in detecting and tracking multiple moving humans. Figure 1 shows a panoramic image from a stationary sensor. Four moving objects (people) were detected in real-time while moving in the scene in an unconstrained manner. A background image is generated automatically by tracking dynamic objects through multiple frames [5]. The number of frames needed to completely build the background model depends on the number of moving objects in the scene and their motion. The four moving objects are shown as an un-warped cylindrical image of Figure 2, which is a more natural panoramic representation for user interpretation. Each of the four people were extracted from the complex cluttered background and annotated with a bounding rectangle, a direction, and an estimated distance based on scale from the sensor. The system tracks each object through the image sequence as shown in Figure 2, even in the presence of overlap and occlusion between two people. The dynamic track is represented as an elliptical head and body for the last 30 frames of each object. The final position on the image plane is also illustrated in Figure 2. The human subjects reversed directions and occluded one another during this sequence. The vision algorithms can detect change in the environment, illumination, and sensor failure, while refreshing the background accordingly. The detection rate of the current implementation for tracking two objects is about 5Hz. The motion detection algorithm relies heavily on the accuracy of the background model at any given time in order to detect moving objects. Types of changes in the background can be broadly grouped into two categories: changes due to the illumination affecting pixel intensities at a fine scale; and changes of surfaces in the environment such as the movement of objects.

It is quite difficult to take care of both cases simultaneously because the first type requires a constant update while the second type requires a context-dependent update. The low-level background estimation procedure is quite simple. The constant update is done on those regions of the image that are not

---

[1] PAL-3802 system, manufactured by Optechnology Co.

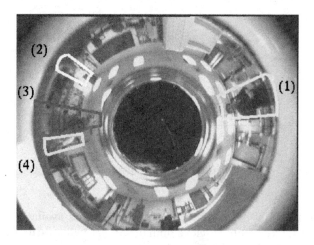

Fig. 1. Original panoramic image (768 x 576)

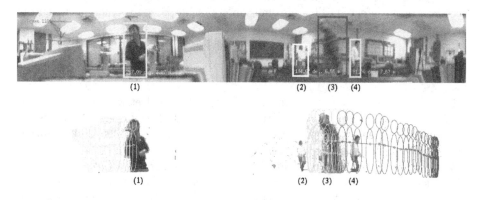

Fig. 2. Un-warped image, four moving people detected - top image; and track through image sequence for the last 32 frames - bottom image.

classified as a moving object by the motion detection algorithm. We track each region and keep a history of velocity for each as well. When the velocity falls below a threshold and remains so for a period of time, it becomes a suitable candidate for part of the background. The assumption is made that humans will be not be still for a long period of time. Therefore, they do not become part of the background. Similarly, only when the velocity of an object exceeds a threshold, is it classified as a possible human subject. This helps to avoid detecting some objects that should remain part of background but are not completely stationary, like the motion of tree branches, or the flicker of a computer monitor.

The adaptive background update improved the performance of the panoramic sensors considerably. The above adaptation only provides a low-level mechanism to handle the problem of maintaining an accurate background model. A more elegant way would be to use the context as inferred by the reasoning at higher

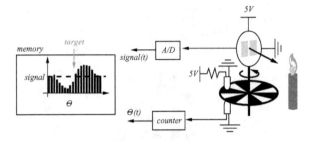

Fig. 3. Pyroelectric sensor.

levels of knowledge-based planning where all resources available might be employed. For example, an unconscious human subject will be still, so the low level will include them in the background. However, using the pyroelectric sensor, we might guess where the human is, particularly if the previous motion of the subject had been detected. This information could be passed to the vision sensors to update the background accordingly.

2.2   Pyroelectric Sensor

The pyroelectric sensor[2] is a Lithium Tantalate pyroelectric parallel opposed dual element high gain detector with complete integral analog signal processing. The detector is tuned to thermal radiation in the range that is normally emitted by humans. Since the pyroelectric detector itself only responds to changes in heat, the detector must be scanned. As shown in Figure 3, a thermal target is identified as a zero crossing in the sensor's data stream. We have implemented such a sensor on a scanning servo motor with two control modes; the sensor may saccade to a region of space designated by another sensor or pair of sensors, and it can track the thermal signature (even when the subject is still) by oscillating around the target heading. The result is a sensor that responds quite precisely to human body temperature but with a rather poor lateral bandwidth. This is due primarily to the scanning required to measure a zero crossing. To use this sensor appropriately, it must be applied only when the predicted lateral bandwidth of the subject is relatively small.

2.3   Stereo Head System

The stereo head platform[3] is a high-performance binocular camera platform with two independent vergence axes. As shown in Figure 10, it has four mechanical degrees of freedom and each lens has three optical degrees of freedom.

---

[2] Model 442-3 IR-EYE Integrated Sensor, manufactured by Eltec Instruments, Daytona Beach, FL

[3] BiSight System, manufactured by HelpMate Robotics, Inc., Danbury, CT

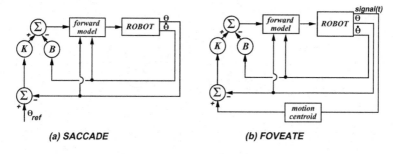

Fig. 4. Closed-Loop Primitives for Controlling Attention.

There are several state-of-the-art tracking algorithms in the literature [1,11, 2]. Our tracking algorithm uses one of the cameras as an active eye and the other as an passive eye. The active eye detects subsampled pixels of greatest change in intensity between two consecutive frames. The passive eye correlates multi-resolution fovea with the frame from the active eye. The stereo head is then servoed to bring the pixel of greatest change into the fovea of the active eye. Subsequently, the passive eye is verged to point its fovea to the same world feature as the fovea of the active eye, extracting the spatial location of the object.

The accuracy of the spatial location of the object is dependent on its distance from the stereo head system. This algorithm can only track single moving objects.

2.4 SACCADE-FOVEATE B-Pgm for Recovering Heading

The most primitive software process in this approach is an asymptotically stable closed-loop *controller* [4,7]. Controllers suppress local perturbations by virtue of their closed-loop structure. Some variations in the context of a control task are simply suppressed by the action of the controller. Controllers also provide a basis for abstraction. Instead of dealing with a continuous state space, a behavioral scheme need only worry about control activation and convergence events. When a control objective is met, a predicate is asserted in an abstract model of the system behavior. The pattern of boolean predicates over a working set of controllers constitutes a functional state description in which policies can be constructed. The "state" of the system is a vector of such functional predicates, each element of which asserts convergence for some control law and resource combination. The state vector also, therefore, represents the set of discrete subgoals available to a robot given these native control laws and resources.

Two closed-loop primitives are employed for motion tracking (see Figure 4). The first, *saccade*, accepts a reference heading in space and directs the sensor's field-of-view to that heading. The second, *foveate*, is similar except that it accepts heading references determined by a sensor signal. For example, the pyroelectric sensor scans a small region centered on the current gaze and identifies the *zero crossing* in the sensor output. The heading to the zero crossing is used as the

168   D. Karuppiah et al.

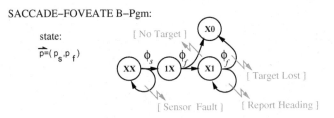

Fig. 5. Behavior Program for Detecting and Measuring the Heading to a Motion Cue.

reference heading to control the sensor's gaze. Within bandwidth limitations, the result is that the pyroelectric sensor tracks the thermal source.

Localizing and tracking the motion of objects in the world is an important, reusable behavior that can be realized in a number of different ways using a variety of different sensors. Each sensor in a stereo pair recovers the heading to a feature in the environment. When the imaging geometry of the pair is suitable, the sensors can, in principle, be used to triangulate the spatial location of the feature. Moreover, the control process for each sensor can be completely independent of the other sensor processes. We have hand-crafted a B-Pgm for accomplishing this task that is parametric in sensory resources. This B-Pgm is illustrated in Figure 5 - it represents a family of run-time hardware configurations for estimating the location of moving objects in space.

The state in the nodes of Figure 5 is the convergence status of the saccade controller, ϕ_s, and the foveate controller, ϕ_f. That is, if ϕ_s is converged and ϕ_f is not, then the state of the saccade-foveate process is 10. An X in the state representation represents a "don't care" or "don't know" condition.

Given R, the set of sensor resources, the saccade-foveate B-Pgm (or template) begins by directing a sensor $r_1 \in R$ to saccade to an interesting region of space. If this process fails for some reason, it is presumably an error in the motor component for the sensor and it reports a fault. If no hardware fault is detected and the sensor achieves state $1X$, then an independent, periodic, closed-loop process ϕ_f is engaged whose goal it is to bring the centroid of the local motion cue to the center of sensor r_1's field of view. If no motion cue is detected, then a report of *"no target"* is generated. If a target motion cue is detected and foveated, then the sensor achieves state $X1$ where the target is actively tracked. Consequently, sensor r_1 is likely no longer at the position specified by the original saccade. As long as subsequent foveation cycles preserve this state, a heading to the motion cue is reported. If, however, the sensor state becomes $X0$, then the target may be moving too quickly and a *"target lost"* report is generated. When two sensors are simultaneously in state $X1$, then the pair of active B-Pgms are reporting sufficient information for estimating the spatial location of this motion cue by triangulation. Each unique resource allocation $r_1, r_2 \in R$ produces a hypothesis of varying quality depending on the context of the localization query.

This policy does not rely on the physical quantity that is transduced; optical flow, thermal radiation, acoustic, etc. It assumes, however, that the two participating observers are foveated on the same entity in the world. While incorrect correspondence can lead to anomalous results, cross-modality can be used to advantage. For example, if the location is computed from consistent visual motion and pyroelectric information, then we may detect *"warm-moving"* bodies. Such a strategy may be attractive when detecting and localizing human beings as opposed to other types of moving objects.

2.5   "Virtual" Stereo Pairs

Any fixed-baseline stereo vision system has limited depth resolution due to the imaging geometry, whereas a system that combines multiple views from many stationary or movable platforms allows a policy to take advantage of the current context and goals in selecting viewpoints. A *"virtual stereo"* policy is a policy that engages different sensor pairs as the target moves through ill-conditioned sensor geometries. Although this policy is more flexible than a fixed pair, this approach requires dynamic sensor (re)calibration and accuracy in the depth of a target is limited by the quality of calibration. The virtual stereo strategy may be particularly effective with a pair of mobile panoramic sensors because they have the potential of always seeing each other and estimating calibration parameters[16]. Once calibrated, they can view the environment to estimate the 3D information of moving targets by triangulation, and maintain their calibration during movement by tracking each other. Suppose we have two panoramic cameras with the same parameters. Both of them are subject to planar motion on the floor and are of same heights from the floor. If they can see each other and at the same time see a target T, then we can compute the bearing and distance of the target after a dynamic calibration of the two cameras. Suppose that O_1 and O_2 are the viewpoints of the two cameras and they can be viewed by each other (as $M_2 1$ and $M_1 2$). B is the baseline (i.e. distance $O_1 O_2$) between them. The projection of a point T is presented by T_1 and T_2 in the two cameras. Then a triangulation $O_1 O_2 T$ can be formed (Fig. 7) so that the distances from the two cameras to the target can be calculated as

$$D_1 = B\frac{\sin \phi_2}{\sin \phi_0} = B\frac{\sin \phi_2}{\sin(\phi_1 + \phi_2)} \quad , \quad D_2 = B\frac{\sin \phi_1}{\sin \phi_0} = B\frac{\sin \phi_1}{\sin(\phi_1 + \phi_2)} \quad (1)$$

By defining an arbitrary starting orientation for each cylindrical image, angles ϕ_1, ϕ_2 (and ϕ_0) can be calculated from the following four bearing angles: θ_1 and θ_2, the bearings of the target in image 1 and image 2 respectively, β_{12} and β_{21}, the bearing angles of camera 1 in image 2 , and camera 2 in image 1 respectively. In order to estimate the distance of a target, we need first to estimate the baseline and the orientation angles of the two panoramic cameras by a dynamic calibration procedure. Several practical approaches have been proposed for this purpose [14]. The basic idea is to make the detection and calculation robust and simple. One of the approaches is to design the body of each robot as a cylinder with some vivid colors that can be easily seen and extracted in the image of the other robot's camera. The estimated triangulation error can be computed

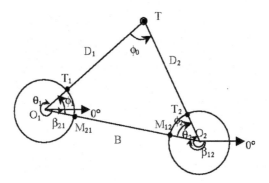

Fig. 6. Panoramic stereo geometry

by partial differentials of 1 as

$$\partial D_1 = \frac{D_1}{B}\partial B + D_1\left|\cot(\phi_1 + \phi_2)\right|\partial\phi_1 + \frac{D_2}{\sin(\phi_1 + \phi_2)}\partial\phi_2 \qquad (2)$$

where ∂B is the error in computing the baseline B, and $\partial\phi_1$ and $\partial\phi_2$ are the errors in estimating the angles ϕ_1 and ϕ_2 from the two panoramic images. Basically, the distance error is determined by both the error of the baseline and the errors of the angles in the triangulation approach. Given the dynamic calibration method, we can use Equation 2 to find the error bound of the distance estimation in any triangulation configuration, and further to find an optimal configuration of the virtual stereo with minimum estimating error.

We have developed the algorithms for mutual calibration and 3D localization of motions using a pair of panoramic vision systems each running the saccade-foveate B-Pgm. The first implementation has been carried out by cooperation between two stationary cameras. Figure 7 shows a stereo image pair from two panoramic sensors.

2.6   Peripheral and Foveal Vision Integration

The human eye has a wide-angle, low resolution field in its peripheral view, and a high resolution narrow field in its foveal view, a combination that works cooperatively in a highly robust manner. We can find a moving object within the peripheral view and then start a tracking behavior by peripheral-foveal cooperation. The key point here is the natural cooperation of peripheral and foveal vision as a real-time behavior operating within a common coordinate system.

As we consider a computer implementation of this behavior, we note differences with human capability. Humans must rotate the head so that the peripheral system covers the moving object in its field of view. Furthermore, multiple objects in very different directions cannot be tracked simultaneously. The panoramic-panoramic sensor pair (or any other pair applicable under the runtime context) can provide the spatial reference for a saccade-foveate B-Pgm on a

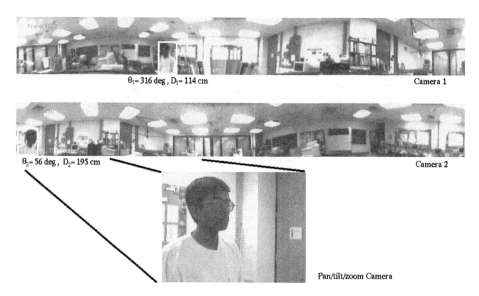

$\theta_1 = 316$ deg, $D_1 = 114$ cm   Camera 1

$\theta_2 = 56$ deg, $D_2 = 195$ cm   Camera 2

Pan/tilt/zoom Camera

Fig. 7. 3D localization by the panoramic stereo system - top two images; and a closeup image of the Human Subject (the first author) localized - bottom image.

standard zoom camera mounted on a small pan/tilt platform. The pan/tilt/zoom imaging system may then undergo a saccade to the interesting motion cue. From here it can foveate on the cue and zoom if necessary for detailed processing.

High resolution color images obtained from the pan/tilt/zoom camera can be used to determine the identity of the object of interest. In particular, a challenging problem is to separate and track individuals in a group (or even a crowd). Using contour extraction algorithms based on motion cues, the pixels that correspond to the object can be extracted from the background.

We have successfully set up a peripheral and fovea vision system, and implemented a cooperative algorithm for processing moving objects. The system detects any moving object in the view of the panoramic camera, and tracks and identifies it through the zoom camera. Figure 7 illustrates the image resulting from such a process where the spatial reference to a motion cue is provided by the panoramic-panoramic image pair. The suspicious character in this panoramic image pair has been scrutinized successfully using the pan/tilt/zoom camera.

3   The Containment Unit

B-Pgms can be used to coordinate the behavior of a fixed set of resources. In [6], we show how to build B-Pgms automatically using reinforcement learning that approach optimal policies for a fixed resource allocation. The hierarchical generalization of a B-Pgm is the Containment Unit (CU). The CU is an active entity designed to represent a family of optimal contingency plans (B-Pgms)

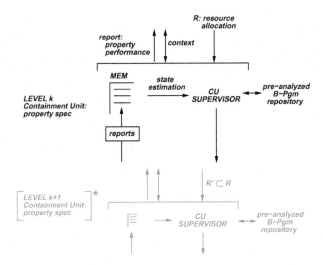

Fig. 8. The Structure of a Containment Unit.

parameterized by resource commitments. Its objective is to "contain" faults. A fault is generally construed to be any functional violation of the behavior associated with the CU: real-time constraints, liveness of constituent hardware, or performance constraints. If a sensor fails, it is the role of the CU to select an alternative B-Pgm to provide the same *type* of information and to inform the process that activated the CU of the impact on the expected performance.

The structure of a CU is presented schematically in Figure 8. It accepts reports from subordinate CUs and estimates the state necessary to make local resource allocation decisions. Multiple instances of a CU may be active concurrently, each with a resource specification that determines the range of variation permitted locally in the strategy for executing the CU directive. Global resource constraints are achieved by limiting the range of autonomy each CU enjoys through careful specification of its proprietary resources. In general, specific B-Pgms may be applicable only in prescribed contexts. For example, adequate illumination may be necessary to employ B-Pgms that use vision sensors, or limited target velocity may be required in order to track with a scanning pyroelectric sensor. These "contexts" can be loaded when a CU is activated and then verified at run-time, or they may be recovered by monitoring the active B-Pgm's performance. The CU determines how to reconfigure lower-level CUs and/or whether to report recovered context to high-levels.

3.1   CU Supervisor: Domain-Independent Behavioral Expertise

Some aspects of a particular B-Pgm's performance *in situ* are determined entirely by attributes of the participating resources. The most obvious example of critical local state is the *liveness* of the participating hardware. Other locally determined attributes can also be important with respect to overall performance.

Consider a pair of vision sensors performing as a virtual stereo pair to localize a moving target. Localization will be poor if the uncertainty in the position of the participating sensors is large or the saccade-foveate B-Pgm may behave poorly if the target approaches a collinear spatial relationship with the sensor pair. These conditions are entirely determined by examining attributes of the sensors (their relative spatial arrangement) and the result of the B-Pgm coordinating them (the target position). Circumstances such as these are completely determined in the local state of the CU supervisor without higher-level deliberation. We will develop an example of the CU supervisor in Section 5.

The memory structure illustrated in Figure 8 records the reported results of all subordinate CUs, estimates state information required to make local resource allocation decisions, and supports the interpretation and reporting of context from the CU. Task specific information such as target location and current fault conditions are stored. The structure is maintained by a communication protocol over Internet sockets between the active B-Pgms and the CU. If resources reside on disparate architectures and operating systems, the memory structure will also provide the CU with a common communication interface to all subsystems and forms the basis for the High Level Interface.

3.2 Context: Domain-Dependent Behavioral Models

Open environments present data sets to sensorimotor processes that cannot be predicted at process configuration time in general and must be observed at run-time. When peculiar or unexpected environments cause the behavior of the system to deviate from expectations, a higher-level reconfiguration must modify system performance while remaining within specifications. If a specific B-Pgm proves to be inadequate in a particular run-time context, the context is passed upward in the control hierarchy to a process manager which may choose to reallocate resources. Over time, some of these reconfiguration decisions that depend strongly on controllable system components might be compiled into appropriate CU supervisors. However, other contexts will be determined by the run-time environment, and the deliberative process planner must model these dependencies at a higher level. We are studying mechanisms where the process description can incrementally model these environmentally determined contexts and manage resources so as to recover critical run-time, environmentally determined contexts in the course of the mission.

4 The Little-JIL Agent Coordination Language

Little-JIL provides rich and rigorous semantics for the precise specification of processes that coordinate multiple agents [15,8]. In the context of our SAS platform, the agents consist of individual sensors, individual robots, or combinations thereof. Little-JIL provides constructs for proactive and reactive control, exception handling, and resource management.

A Little-JIL process defines a high-level plan to coordinate agents to act as a team. A process is constructed of steps that are hierarchically decomposed into finer-grained substeps. The steps and substeps are connected with dataflow and control flow edges. Each step has a declaration identifying resources needed to carry out that step and allows reasoning over interactions between resource specifications including the sensors, computational platforms, and communication hardware that constitute a team of robots.

A process description typically specifies parts of the coordination policy precisely while deferring some choices until run-time. In this way, a step may be implemented in several ways using different resources. Which choice is most appropriate depends on resource availability, timeliness and performance constraints, and run-time context. These high-level decisions require reasoning across the collection of robots as the task unfolds. This approach is particularly useful for exception handling - a certain amount of reaction can be handled within the CUs by dynamically selecting the appropriate B-Pgms. Some situations, however, require higher level support. For example, consider a process intended to track multiple people. Such a process might designate one sensor to watching for new motion cues entering at a door and allocate the balance of the resources to track targets already in the room. If a new motion cue occurs, the process reacts by reassigning resources. The actual selection of resources and CUs and thus the actual instantiation of the system is made by the integrated capability of robot planning and scheduling technologies whose description is outside the scope of this paper.

The Little-JIL process control language as discussed above, provides a powerful means of exploiting knowledge to structure planning and learning by focusing policy formation on a small set of legal programs. Moreover, at lower levels, new and enhanced processes are constructed. The objective is to constantly optimize and generalize the active B-Pgm during training tasks, and to return it at the end of the task better than we found it. These B-Pgms actually consist of many coordinated primitive controllers but are thought of as discrete abstract actions. Subsequent plans and learning processes can exploit this abstraction.

Figure 9 shows a sample Little-JIL process that uses sensors to track multiple humans. We assume that this process specification is in the context of a partial model of the run-time environment. The root step of the process is Track Humans. This step is decomposed into two steps that run concurrently (denoted by the parallel lines). One step is to track a human while the other step is to watch the door. The Watch Door step requires use of the panoramic camera.

Track Human is a choice step. Dynamically, the system will decide which of the three substeps to use. This decision is based on the resources available, what time constraints there are on the tracking, and contextual issues, such as whether there is good lighting or whether the target is moving quickly. One might easily imagine many more than three choices here. Each choice requires one or more resources and has some expected performance. The scheduler and runtime system use knowledge about the context to assist in making the decision.

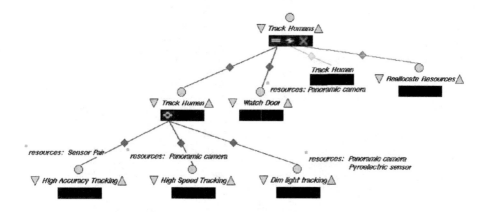

Fig. 9. Sample Little-JIL Process Description for Tracking a Human Subject.

If another human enters the room, this results in an event that is handled by a second Track Human step. This is simply a reference to the original track human step and will result in a new instance of Track Human starting with a new set of resources. This results in an exception, causing some replanning and reallocation of resources to occur. Other exceptions can be used to adapt locally (within the CU) during execution. For example, if there had been normal lighting and the lights were turned off, we would expect an exception within the currently active containment units that employ vision sensors.

5   Self-Adaptive Software (SAS) Experimental Platform

In our experimental platform, we have implemented three types of motion detectors that are deployed at fixed and known positions in an indoor office-like environment. The platform consists of an articulated stereo vision system, and scanning pyroelectric sensor, and two panoramic vision sensors, as shown in Figure 10. In each instance of the saccade-foveate B-Pgm observations are collected from sensor pairs that are sufficient to determine a spatial location of the moving feature in the field of view. This family of functionally equivalent programs produces a spatial estimate of a motion cue with varying quality that could serve as a spatial position reference to a subsequent sensory or motor control task. Indeed, combinations of these strategies are themselves B-Pgms with reserved resources for corroboration or for fault tolerance. Which of these to use in a particular context is dependent on the task, the resources available, and the expected performance based on accumulated experience.

5.1   Designing the CU Supervisor for Tracking Human Subjects

The CU Supervisor determines which B-Pgm (sensor pair) is recommended for triangulation and tracking given the current state of the process. In our demon-

Motion Tracking Sensors:
- 1 Pyroelectric Sensor;
- 1 Stereo Head Sensor;
- 2 Panoramic Vision Sensors.

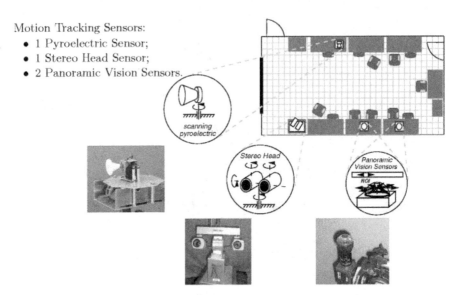

Fig. 10. The "Smart Room" - Motion Tracking Platform.

stration, there are six unique pairs of sensors available. A boolean state predicate describes the "liveness" of each pair. For a given pair, if both sensors are functioning and they are not in a collinear configuration with the target subject, the corresponding predicate is set to 1, otherwise it is set to 0. This is the role of the state estimation component of Figure 8. Given a pattern in the "liveness" state vector, the CU supervisor always chooses the pair of sensors with the highest value with respect to the process' objective function.

We have hand-crafted a Human Tracking CU supervisor for engaging sensor pairs that deploys resources in the following priority-based hierarchy:

- Panoramic - stereo head (camera 1);
- Panoramic - stereo head (camera 2);
- Stereo-head (camera 1 and 2);
- Panoramic - pyroelectric;
- Stereo-head (camera 1) - pyroelectric;
- Stereo-head (camera 2) - pyroelectric.

Each resource allocation in this hierarchy, in turn, instantiates two concurrent containment units for tracking motion with a single sensor. These subordinate CUs execute the saccade-foveate B-Pgm described earlier and report to the track human CU. Each CU in this hierarchical control process has the authority to manage the resources reserved for them.

5.2   Experimental Results

The Human Tracking CU supervisor has been implemented to control the various sensors in order to track a single moving person seamlessly through failure modes captured in the liveness assertion. Some preliminary results are presented below.

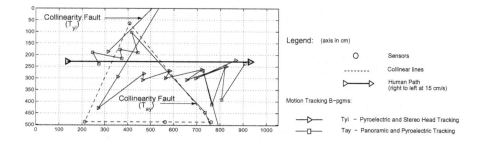

Fig. 11. Motion Tracking for the Pyroelectric-Stereo head and Pyroelectric-Panoramic sensor pairs.

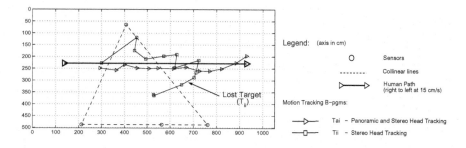

Fig. 12. Motion Tracking for the Panoramic-Stereo head and Stereo Head sensor pairs.

Accuracy and Repeatability Experiments. To design any CU supervisor that depends on the coordinated activity of multiple sensors, it is necessary to model the performance of the individual sensors. We conducted a series of experiments to determine the accuracy and repeatability of the sensors. At known spatial locations, a motion cue was generated and observed from the different sensors.

It was observed that the panoramic sensors were both accurate and repeatable, the stereo head is accurate but not repeatable, and the pyroelectric sensor was repeatable but not accurate. The data was also used to examine the quality of triangulation on the motion cue by different sensor pairs. As expected the quality degraded as the motion cue approached the line joining a sensor pair or a collinear configuration. Because such a configuration is not desirable we call this a collinearity fault.

Tracking a Human Subject. The next set of experiments evaluated the task of tracking a single moving person using combinations of the four sensors. The results are shown in Figures 11, 12, 14 and 13. Figure 11 shows the tracks of the Panoramic-Pyroelectric pair (T_{ay}) and the Pyroelectric-Stereo head pair (T_{yi}). As the motion track crosses collinear sensor geometries, the performance degrades as expected.

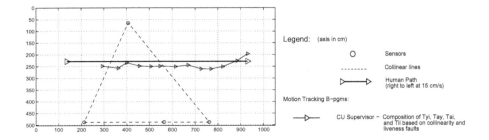

Fig. 13. Motion Tracking Performance during Mode Changes in the Motion Tracking CU supervisor.

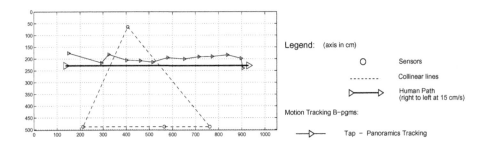

Fig. 14. Motion Tracking for the Panoramic-Panoramic sensor pair.

Figure 12 shows the tracks of Panoramic-Stereo head pair (T_{ai}) and Stereo head alone (T_{ii}). Target tracking using stereo head alone can be quite bad due to its small stereo baseline and mechanical properties [2].

Our next demonstration shows the performance of the CU supervisor. The CU supervisor is designed to address run-time contexts (e.g. tracking precision, sensor liveness faults, and collinearity faults) by effecting software mode changes in response to feedback from the sensors. Figure 13 shows that the Track Human CU supervisor was effective in handling these run-time contexts.

Figure 14 shows preliminary localization results using the Panoramic virtual stereo pair (T_{ap}). This sensor pair is highly reliable and is capable of accurate, high velocity tracking for large regions of the room because of its tracking precision and the complete field of view they provide. Our current CU supervisor does not include the Panoramic virtual stereo pair (T_{ap}). However, as shown in Figures 13 and 14, T_{ap} performs as well as the current multi-sensor CU under the conditions tested and so it will introduce a great deal of robustness when T_{ap} is integrated into the Track Human CU - since other sensors can fill in regions where T_{ap} performs badly or when other forms of sensor faults occur. In future we plan to include our Panoramic virtual stereo pair into the SAS platform. This addition will allow for multiple Human tracking at higher velocities.

These results indicate the potential of our hierarchical self adaptive software architecture in handling faults at both lower level (i.e. sensors) and higher level (i.e. context of the motion cue).

6   Summary, Conclusions, and Future Experimental Work

Multi-robot scenarios present significant technical challenges regarding sensing, planning, computing, and software methods and must support both reactivity and predictability. Ultimately, one of the most desirable characteristics of a multi-robot system is its ability to adapt to changes in the environment and to internal faults - in hardware components and in end-to-end performance specifications. Thus, reconfigurability is critical.

Our current work presents preliminary results towards the responsiveness to novel data sets and robustness that are critical to a multi-robot application. The CU supervisor for tracking a human subject was able to handle individual sensor faults gracefully as well as faults due to run-time context. Future experimental work is underway currently to demonstrate the ideas presented in this paper more thoroughly. Some of the dimensions along which we will enhance the experimental effort are described in the following sections.

Multiple Target Corroboration. When a single subject is tracked, excess resources can be allocated to enhance robustness. However, when multiple subjects are tracked, decisions must be made in order to allocate the right sets of resources to the right targets. For example, if a subject stops moving, we may be able to assign a single observer to it to verify that it remains stationary. When movement is detected, it can trigger another re-distribution of resources. We are developing process descriptions and resource scheduling algorithms that will reallocate resources in a manner that depends on target type.

Inter-Process Communication. In related work, we are developing an inter-process communication mechanism that guarantees that data will be shared between distributed processes within a specified time bound. In this application, it is less critical that communication events occur at precise times and more important that reports from multiple sensors happened at roughly the same time. Many techniques for relative process synchronization are being examined.

Hierarchical Process/Device Models. We already motivated a collinearity fault for pairs of sensors. We also intend to build models of each individual sensor's lateral bandwidth since it is this information that speaks directly to whether and how well a particular sensor can track a moving target. If context (e.g., $[\dot{x} \ \dot{y}]$) recommends against using a slow sensor, it can unilaterally "take itself out of the game." On the other hand, if a rapidly moving subject changes to a slower or stationary target, relatively high-performance and expensive resources may be released and used more effectively elsewhere. We feel that models will naturally reside at many levels of abstraction and we intend to both build this information into the CU supervisors and acquire it empirically over time.

Self Calibration. Eventually, some of our sensors will be mobile and will take action prophylactically to avoid predictable faults. In order to do this, there must be sufficient resources to identify the new and changing sensor geometries. Resources previously used to track human subjects must be orchestrated to track spatially reconfigurable sensors.

References

1. D. Coombs and C. Brown. Real-time binocular smooth pursuit. *Int. J. of Computer Vision*, 11(2):147–164, 1993.
2. K. Daniilidis, C. Krauss, M. Hansen, and G. Sommer. Real time tracking of moving objects with an active camera. *J. of Real-time Imaging*, 4(1):3–20, Feb. 1998.
3. P. Greguss. *Panoramic Imaging Block for 3D space*, Jan. 1986. U.S. Pat. 4566763.
4. R. A. Grupen, M. Huber, J. A. Coelho Jr., and K. Souccar. A basis for distributed control of manipulation tasks. *IEEE Expert*, 10(2):9–14, Apr. 1995.
5. I. Haritaoglu, D. Harwood, and L. S. Davis. W4s: A real-time system for detection and tracking people in 2.5d. In *Proc. of the 5th European Conf. on Computer Vision*, Freiburg, Germany, Jun. 1998.
6. M. Huber and R. A. Grupen. A feedback control structure for on-line learning tasks. *Robotics and Autonomous Systems*, 22(3-4):303–315, Dec. 1997.
7. M. Huber, W. S. MacDonald, and R. A. Grupen. A control basis for multilegged walking. In *Proc. of the Int. Conf. on Robotics and Automation*, volume 4, pages 2988–2993, Minneapolis, MN, Apr. 1996.
8. D. Jensen, Y. Dong, B. S. Lerner, E. K. McCall, L. J. Osterweil, S. M. Sutton Jr., and A. Wise. Coordinating agent activities in knowledge discovery processes. In *Proc. of the Int. Joint Conf. on Work Activities Coordination and Collaboration*, pages 137–146, San Francisco, CA, Feb. 1999.
9. M. M. Kokar, K. Baclawski, and Y. A. Eracar. Control theory based foundations of self controlling software. *IEEE Intelligent Systems*, 14(3):37–45, May 1999.
10. R. Laddaga. Creating robust software through self-adaptation. *IEEE Intelligent Systems*, 14(3):26–29, May 1999.
11. A. Maki, T. Uhlin, and J. Eklundh. Phase-based disparity estimation in binocular tracking. In K. Heia, K. A. Høogdra, and B. Braathen, editors, *Proc. of the 8th Scandinavian Conf. on Image Analysis*, pages 1145–1152, Tromsøo, Norway, May 1993. Norwegian Society for Image Processing and Pattern Recognition.
12. S. K. Nayar and S. Baker. Catadioptric image formation. In *Proc. of DARPA Image Understanding Workshop*, pages 1431–1437, May 1997.
13. P. Oreizy, M. M. Gorlick, R. N. Taylor, D. Heimbigner, G. Johnson, N. Medvidovic, A. Quilici, D. S. Rosenblum, and A. L. Wolf. An architecture-based approach to self-adaptive software. *IEEE Intelligent Systems*, 14(3):54–62, May 1999.
14. J. Sztipanovits, G. Karsai, and T. Bapty. Self-adaptive software for signal processing: evolving systems in changing environments without growing pains. *Communications of the ACM*, 41(5):66–73, May 1998.
15. A. Wise, B. S. Lerner, E. K. McCall, L. J. Osterweil, and S. M. Sutton Jr. Specifying coordination in processes using little-JIL. Tech. Report TR 99-71, Univ. of Massachusetts, Amherst, Dept. of Comp. Sci., 1999.
16. Z. Zhu, E. M. Riseman, and A. R. Hanson. Geometrical modeling and real-time vision applications of panoramic annular lens (pal) camera systems. Tech. Report TR 99-11, Univ. of Massachusetts, Amherst, Dept. of Comp. Sci., Feb. 1999.

Port-Based Adaptable Agent Architecture

Kevin R. Dixon, Theodore Q. Pham, and Pradeep K. Khosla

Department of Electrical and Computer Engineering and
Institute for Complex Engineered Systems
Carnegie Mellon University
Pittsburgh, PA 15213

Abstract. To facilitate the design of large-scale, self-adaptive systems, we have developed the Port-Based Adaptable Agent Architecture. This distributed, multi-agent architecture allows systems to be created with the flexibility and modularity required for the rapid construction of software systems that analyze and dynamically modify themselves to improve performance. This architecture provides user-level access to the three forms of software adaptability: parametric fine tuning, algorithmic change, and code mobility. In this paper, we present the architecture, describe port-based agents, and outline several applications where this flexible architecture has proven useful.

1 Introduction

In the monolithic programming model, increasingly capable systems require increasingly complex software. Multi-agent systems achieve sophisticated capability through complex interactions, not complex software. As such, modularity, reconfigurability, and extensibility are more achievable, and components can largely be tested in isolation. However, most implementations of multi-agent systems do not take advantage of this modularity and reconfigurability because they depend too heavily on the foresight of the author at design time. Reconfiguration is typically a time-consuming manual process that often involves changes to the components themselves. Use of multiple processing nodes further complicates design and reconfiguration. The creation of a general multi-agent software architecture that can learn from its own interactions with the world, evaluate its performance, and adapt itself to achieve its goals better, would find natural use in the distributed system, real-time control, and proxy computing arenas. We propose a distributed system supporting port-based agents as such an architecture.

Analysis of the last five years in computing leads to two key insights. First, the phenomenal growth of computing power, the advancement of miniaturization technologies, and the advent of commodity computers guarantee that computers will permeate every facet of life. Second, the growth of the Internet, fueled by this commodity computing, has redefined what a computer is and how computers are used.

Computers started as large, cumbersome machines which were little more than ballistics calculators. As technology progressed, the mainframe computer was born, which was a calculator that multiple people could use simultaneously via time sharing or batch processing. However, the coupling of networking with the mass production of microprocessor-based computers has shifted the computing paradigm from that of a

P. Robertson, H. Shrobe, and R. Laddaga (Eds.): IWSAS 2000, LNCS 1936, pp. 181–198, 2000.

calculator to the information and control devices that are commonplace today and will become ubiquitous in the near future.

While computer hardware has changed drastically in the past few years, computer software has struggled to keep pace. The centralized, monolithic programming model that was adequate, when treating computers as isolated entities, is poorly suited to distributed, multi-task-oriented computing. For computing to become truly ubiquitous, new distributed, multi-task-oriented programming methodologies must be developed. We believe that multi-agent technologies offer the capabilities needed. With these notions in mind, we are developing a distributed Port-Based Adaptable Agent Architecture (PB3A) to explore this non-monolithic programming model.

In this paper, the three levels of system adaptability are discussed in Section 2, the overall architecture is detailed in Section 3, the runtime environment is described in Section 4, some applications of the Port-Based Adaptable Agent Architecture are presented in Section 5, related work is described in Section 6, and conclusions and future work are laid out in Section 7.

2   Adaptability

As software systems grow in complexity, it becomes infeasible for humans to monitor, manage, and maintain every detail of their operation. From a human-computer interaction standpoint, it is desirable to build systems that can be assigned easily, perform intelligently (as evaluated from the perspective of the user), and complete tasks with little or no human intervention. Recognizing this need, the ultimate goal of PB3A is to aid in developing systems that are self adaptive. These systems analyze their performance and can dynamically reconfigure themselves to fit better to the current operating conditions and goals in a distributed environment. From a software perspective, three natural forms of adaptation arise.

The first form of adaptation is parametric fine tuning. Most software is written in terms of algorithms that manipulate data. The behavior of these algorithms depends on their parameters. Much research has been done on estimating the error of an algorithm and using that metric to modify the parameters. For instance, this could be changing the synaptic weights in an artificial neural network through backpropagation or the coefficients of an adaptive digital filter.

The second form of adaptation is algorithmic change. There is seldom one way to solve a given problem; every different approach to solve a problem or calculate a quantity gives rise to a unique algorithm. Two algorithms designed to address the same problem may behave differently based on the precise circumstances under which they are used. A system that is aware of the current operating conditions and the limitations of the algorithms it employs could dynamically choose and switch algorithms when conditions change. For instance, as lighting conditions vary, swapping a stereo vision algorithm for an HSI-based vision algorithm may improve performance.

The third form of adaptation involves mobility. In a distributed environment, computing resource availability varies both spatially and temporally. Certain nodes may have special-purpose hardware, more abundant memory and processing power, or lower data-access latency. Software that is aware of the resource conditions under which it operates could migrate to complete its tasks sooner or to make progress in case of failures.

The PB3A provides the primitives and methodologies by which all three forms of adaptation may be realized and initiated by the software itself when operating conditions warrant.

3   The Architecture

The Port-Based Adaptable Agent Architecture is a Java-based programming framework that aims to facilitate the development and deployment of self-adaptive, distributed, multi-agent applications. Unlike sequential programming models that require an application to be a single stream of instructions, PB3A utilizes a threaded programming model allowing simultaneous streams of instructions. To exploit the power of PB3A, a solution to a problem must be decomposed into a hierarchy of interconnected tasks. We consider a task to be some flow of execution that takes zero or more inputs, produces zero or more outputs, and may modify some internal state. We call these input and output points "ports", and refer to a fundamental unit of execution as a Port-Based Module (PBM).

In essence, a PBM clearly defines the boundaries, entry points, and exit points of the smallest unit of code in PB3A. The definition of tasks is recursive; a single task may be composed of multiple, possibly parallel, sub-tasks. To capture this notion, PB3A allows for the creation of Macros, a special type of PBM that is itself an interconnected collection of PBMs or other Macros. Also, the self-contained nature of the PBM, coupled with its completely specified port-mapping dependencies, allows not only for easy distribution and coordination of code modules onto a network of computers, but also for those modules to be mobile. More succinctly, PBMs can migrate from node to node during their execution. Where the PBM represents the most basic unit of execution, the Port-Based Agent (PBA) represents the most basic unit of self-adaptability. Thus, the self-adapting PBA is the cornerstone of our approach to managing software complexity.

The architecture is logically divided into two halves. On one half, there is the PBM task abstraction, detailed in Section 3.1. Derived from PBMs are three specialized categories: Macros, Port-Based Agents, and Port-Based Drivers, explained in Sections 3.2, 3.3, and 3.4, respectively. Since these derived categories are based on PBMs, they may be used anywhere PBMs can be used. Furthermore, a PBM may belong to multiple categories. The second half of the architecture concerns the support mechanisms used to maintain the PBM abstraction. These support libraries are referred collectively as the Runtime Core and are discussed in Section 3.5. Finally, the services that the Runtime Core provides are detailed in Sections 3.6 through 3.9.

3.1   Port-Based Modules

Each PBM has zero or more input ports, zero or more output ports, and possibly some internal state (see Figure 1). All ports are typed in the typical object-oriented programming (OOP) paradigm. A link is created between two PBMs by properly connecting an input port to an output port. Properly connecting an input port to an output port means obeying the OOP rules of inheritance. That is, information that the input port expects

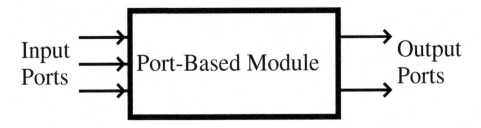

Fig. 1. A generic diagram of a Port-Based Module.

must be the same class as, or a super-class of, the information on the connected output port. A configuration can be legal if and only if every input port in the system is connected to at most one output port, however output ports may remain unconnected. An output port may map to multiple input ports. PBMs use a localized, or encapsulated, memory model. All state variables specific to an instantiation of a particular PBM, as well as all methods and static members, are contained within the PBM itself. This allows a PBM to be self-governing and independent of other PBMs.

3.2 Macros

The first PBM-derived category is the Macro. Since it is common to have repeated subsystems in a given application, groups of PBMs can be brought together in entities called Macros (Figure 2). Macros are composed of one or more PBMs and can be defined recursively by encapsulating other Macros. Any ports not connected to other PBMs inside the Macro are external input or output ports of the Macro. Once a Macro is defined, systems can be constructed from the Macro as if it were a PBM. Furthermore, any predefined system can be used as a Macro simply by designating its input and output ports. The PBMs comprising a Macro can execute on one machine, or they can disperse themselves across a network. Thus, a single Macro may execute on several computers simultaneously. In this manner, Macros facilitate the development of large-scale systems by providing multiple levels of abstraction and encapsulation.

3.3 Port-Based Agents

The next PBM-derived category is the Port-Based Agent (PBA). Where PBMs represent the most basic unit of execution, PBAs represent the most basic unit of self-reconfiguration and self-adaptability. In other words, a PBA is the smallest unit of code that can measure its performance and take steps to improve that performance. These steps may include internal parameter tuning, transferring processing nodes, spawning other PBAs, being replaced by a more suitable PBA, or modifying the internal reconfiguration of the PBA itself. In keeping with the modular theme, most PBAs should be Macros of many PBMs. A common PBA configuration consists of one or more PBMs processing data, one or more PBMs analyzing the performance of the PBA, and one or more PBMs deciding upon a course of action to improve performance.

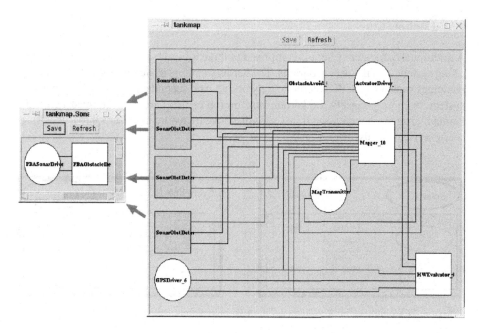

Fig. 2. Macros encapsulate one or more PBMs.

3.4   Port-Based Drivers

Though the PB3A is a high-level programming framework, low-level interactions must be considered. Since most incarnations of Java are inappropriate to interface with hardware, device drivers must be written in a language that can handle pointers, access registers, and perform other low-level, machine-specific interactions such as C or C++. To interface with devices, a machine-specific driver communicates through a platform-independent "resource port" to a Port-Based Driver (PBD). Presently, resource ports are TCP-based sockets. This allows a PBD to control a device from any computer that supports Java, irrespective of where the device is located physically. However, when the device driver and controlling PBD are located on separate machines, latencies can degrade the performance of the device, especially in real-time control applications. For this reason, the PB3A allows any PBM to specify its physical location so that network latencies can be avoided by using a shared-memory model for port information (this will be discussed in Section 3.5). Examples that use PBDs to control devices will be discussed in Sections 5.1 and 5.2.

Furthermore, legacy software also can be interfaced using a PBD. In this case, the legacy application can be considered the device. A PBD can issue commands to the legacy software, and results can be communicated back to the PBD through the resource port. There is an example of a large-scale system interfacing with legacy software using this methodology in Section 5.3.

3.5 Runtime Core

A traditional computer system is comprised of three logical parts: the hardware, the operating system, and the user programs. The hardware offers basic interfaces to computing resources such as the CPU, memory, networking, and secondary storage. The operating system, or more precisely the kernel, runs on top of this hardware. In most cases, the kernel manages resources and transforms disparate hardware interfaces into a consistent set of services for user programs.

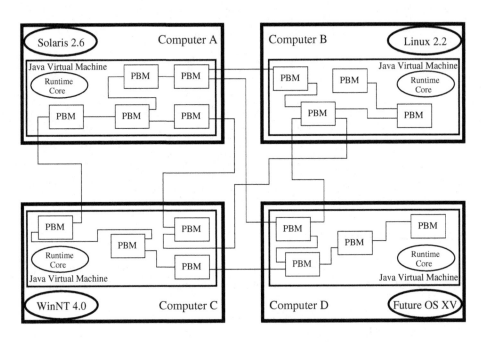

Fig. 3. The Runtime Core provides PB3A services.

In PB3A, the Runtime Core is the kernel that runs on top of one or more Java Virtual Machines (JVMs) and provides a consistent set of services to PBMs (Figure 3). The Runtime Core is written in Java and is platform independent, thus no modifications to the Runtime Core are needed when introducing a new computing environment. In a system involving multiple processing nodes, the Runtime Core instances on each node cooperate to manage the global state of the system. This global state includes the node where a PBM is executing and what port mappings have been established both locally and between nodes. In total, the collective Runtime Core presents a single, consistent computing interface that abstracts the heterogeneous, distributed computing infrastructure.

When a system begins to execute, a per-node daemon starts a JVM and Runtime Core on each of the nodes. Next, each Runtime Core receives its share of the global system configuration. Each share only contains information about the PBMs executing on that node and any PBMs whose ports are mapped to other PBMs on that node. For local PBMs, that information includes initial internal state and port-mapping data; whereas, for distributed PBMs mapped to local PBMs, only port-mapping data is included. From this configuration information, the Runtime Cores load all local PBMs. The Java byte-code for those PBMs may come from the local file system or be requested from a network host designated as the code server (see Section 3.8). Although all PBMs reside in the shared memory of a JVM on a node, each is self-contained and has no references to other PBMs, and consequently can have no effect on other PBMs. This memory-space protection is maintained by the JVM. Once all PBMs in the global system have been instantiated, the Runtime Cores begin mapping ports. Ports between PBMs on the same node map directly through shared memory. For mappings between two nodes, the Runtime Cores perform replication (see Section 3.6), and the mapping is created using a TCP-based socket. Once all port mappings are established, the Runtime Cores initialize each PBM with its initial state. Finally, a thread is created for each loop-based PBM and the Runtime Cores initialize the per-node event dispatch thread pools (see Section 3.7). This completes the distributed initialization phase and subsequently execution begins.

3.6 Ports

Current programming models do not allow for easy reconfiguration. The primary difficulties center upon dependencies and hidden interactions. The communication and coordination methods in the current programming models are known only to the sections of cooperating code and are hidden from the rest of the runtime system executing those sections of code. Reconfiguration in such a system requires altering memory addresses and potentially altering the way sections of various code communicate. Even multi-programming and multi-threading environments, where communication rules are more formalized, are not effective.

The PB3A solution to the problem is to formalize communication between cooperating PBMs and rigidly enforce the rules. That is, PBMs can only communicate with each other through type-specific ports. Each PBM is effectively treated as an individual unit that cannot access information in another PBM unless it is explicitly shared. Sharing data requires linking an input port to an output port of like or derived type. This connection results in an information pipeline where the link details are embedded in the ports themselves and are available only to the Runtime Core. The indirection and decoupling inherent in the input and output ports allows the Runtime Core to rearrange links arbitrarily without disturbing the PBMs. Consequently, swapping one PBM for another only requires instantiating the new PBM and implanting the ports, and possibly the state of the original PBM, into the new PBM. Some minor bookkeeping information in the ports must be updated, but the PBMs connected to the original PBM need not be disturbed.

The other significant advantage of ports lies in distributed and mobile code. Since the details of all port connections are managed by the Runtime Core, PBMs executing on different processing nodes do not need any special code to communicate. To establish port mappings between PBMs on two processing nodes, the Runtime Core of the input-side node issues a replication request to the Runtime Core of the output-side node if replication of that specific output port has not been previously requested. The output-side node's

Runtime Core keeps track of what output ports are replicated to where and sends port state updates to the appropriate nodes every time those ports change value. The consistency of this replication is defined on a point-to-point basis. That is, from sender to receiver, the changes are guaranteed to be delivered sequentially. However, when one output port is replicated to various processing nodes, no guarantees of consistency exist between the receiving nodes. Thus, two or more receiving nodes are not guaranteed to see the same value at the same time beyond the point-to-point consistency guarantee. This output replication allows PBMs to communicate as if they were running on the same machine, though with potentially increased latency. Furthermore, port communications hide the migration of a PBM between nodes from any PBMs connected to the migrating entity. Hiding port replication and migration frees a PB3A programmer to concentrate on the algorithms employed and information communicated, instead of how to communicate.

3.7   Port-Based Module Runtime Structure

The PB3A supports two different, though not mutually exclusive, runtime models for each PBM. A PBM may be threaded, event-driven, or both. A threaded PBM consists of a main method body that is executed within a loop controlled by the Runtime Core. The Runtime Core raises the lock of the PBM before executing the method body and releases the lock upon exiting. This guarantees that a threaded PBM will not be migrated while executing its main method body. After each iteration of the loop, and after dropping the PBM lock, the Runtime Core puts the thread to sleep for a PBM-specified amount of time. An event-driven PBM does not possess a thread of its own. Its event-dispatching method body executes only in response to changes on input ports of the event-driven PBM. Before executing a the event-dispatching method body of a PBM, the Runtime Core raises the PBM's lock. Upon completion of event-dispatching, the Runtime Core releases the lock. For PBMs that are both threaded and event-driven, the lock additionally prevents both sections of code from simultaneously executing. The event-dispatching facility itself is composed of multiple threads in a worker pool configuration so that events on different PBMs can execute in parallel.

3.8   Loading

As the maintainer of the PBM task abstraction, one of the Runtime Core's responsibilities is instantiating PBMs. The full specification of a PBM instance consists of Java byte-code, internal state, and port mappings. A PBM's internal state and port mapping data, along with its Java class name and PB3A instance name, are referred to collectively as the PBM's configuration. Loading is the process of instantiating a PBM based on its configuration. This process occurs at system startup and in response to requests issued by PBMs. To load a PBM, the Runtime Core must first retrieve the byte-code for the PBM's Java class. The Runtime Core locates this byte-code by first checking the local file system. If the byte-code is available locally, then the Runtime Core invokes the JVM to load the byte-code. Otherwise, the Runtime Core contacts a network host designated as the code repository, the ModuleServer (discussed in Section 4.1), and requests transmission of the byte-code via a network socket. Once the byte-code has been received, the Runtime Core invokes the JVM to load the byte-code. Next, an instance of the PBM class is instantiated and a member method is invoked to set the internal state of the instance to the data stored in the configuration. Finally, the Runtime Core establishes the port mappings of the PBM instance and may allocate a thread if the PBM is threaded.

3.9 Migration

PBM migration is the process of transferring an executing PBM from one processing node to another. Migration of a PBM involves capturing its configuration at the source node, transferring that configuration to the destination node, and reloading the PBM at the destination. Reloading the PBM from a configuration follows the same loading process discussed in the previous section, the primary differences concern capturing the state of an executing PBM and transferring that state across nodes. Just as a PBM has a method to set its internal state from its configuration, a PBM has a method that returns a memory reference graph representing its internal state, provided by the Runtime Core. When a request is made to migrate a PBM, the Runtime Core raises the PBM's lock and then invokes the internal state graph retrieval method. Raising the lock pauses the PBM and it cannot alter its internal state. The PBM's internal state graph, port mappings, Java class name, and PB3A instance name are then recorded in a configuration record. The Runtime Core of the source node then contacts the Runtime Core at the destination node and transmits the configuration record via a network socket. The transmission of the configuration record is conducted by Java Serialization. Java Serialization is a built-in language mechanism to convert any memory reference graph into a byte-stream. This byte-stream may be a file, a network socket, or a memory buffer. In addition to the configuration, the Runtime Core of the source will transmit any replication requests it has received for the migrating PBM's output ports. The destination Runtime Core then loads the PBM from its activation record and takes control of replication management from the source Runtime Core. The source Runtime Core is then able to deallocate local records and references of the migrated PBM.

4   Runtime Environment

The PB3A runtime environment consists of the ModuleServer, Launcher, NetExecutor, and NetController.

4.1 ModuleServer

The ModuleServer is the server side of PB3A's client-server code distribution system. Each PBM instance is composed of internal state, port mappings, and code. PBM code is a class (or set of classes) within Java's well-defined package name space. On client demand, the ModuleServer transmits PBM code to a remote host.

When a client needs PBM code to which it does not have access, the client connects to the ModuleServer. A separate server-side thread handles each connection, allowing multiple clients to make use of the server simultaneously. After connection, the client transmits the fully qualified name of each PBM code class. The ModuleServer resolves the name into a path in its local file system and then transmits the Java byte-code class file to the client. Using built-in Java mechanisms, the client can load the byte-code as a Java class. Then the PBM combines that code, internal state, and its port mappings to instantiate itself.

New PBM code can be added to the ModuleServer by simply copying their class files into a subdirectory of the ModuleServer's module path. The server does not need to be restarted for this new code to be recognized. Because the ModuleServer never loads the PBM code directly, new versions of existing PBM code can be added dynamically by overwriting the old class files. Again, the server does not need to be restarted.

4.2   ModuleManager

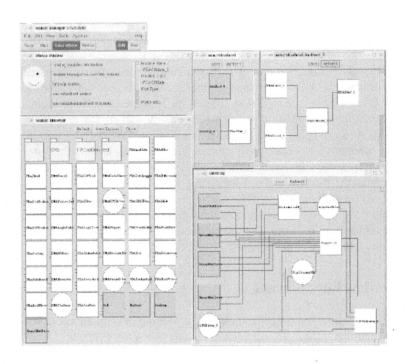

Fig. 4. ModuleManager visualizes PB3A systems.

Inspired by file browsers from graphical operating systems, the ModuleManager is a visual systems configuration tool, shown in Figure 4. Currently, the ModuleManager supports creating and editing system configuration files graphically. To create a new system, the user selects PBMs and then connects their input and output ports to form a configuration by pointing-and-clicking. A file browser-like interface allows users to search the local file system and the ModuleServer for PBMs. Essentially, the Module-Manager is a functional schematic editor for specifying data pathways in a PB3A system.

The ModuleManager allows the user to set special properties in the PBMs. The "Location" specifies on which host machine the PBM should begin execution. If this property is set to "local", then the PBM will execute on the machine that loaded the configuration. If the Location is a hostname, the PBM will execute on that host. Other properties that may be edited in the ModuleManger include the PBM's internal state. This editing can be done by the ModuleManger's built in State Editor via Java Reflection, discussed in more detail in Section 4.3.

After completing a configuration, the user may save the configuration to disk or send it directly to the Launcher for execution. The ModuleManager plays no part in this execution.

4.3   State Editor

Most PBMs have internal state and PB3A allows the editing of this state by the State Editor. When a PBM is selected in the ModuleManager, a set of properties is displayed. These properties include initial host, as well as several other items, and allows the user to edit the internal state of a specific PBM instantiation. The internal state of a PBM is the variables (primitives, objects, and arrays) declared outside the scope of any methods in the PBM (i.e., global variables). This information is obtained by Java Reflection. The State Editor queries the JVM for the names and types of state variables for a particular PBM class. Presently, Java Reflection only returns information on public, protected, or package-default members; information on private members of PBMs cannot be obtained in the State Editor. Next, the State Editor asks the JVM for the current values of the state variables for a specific PBM instance. The State Editor then presents this data graphically to the user, using any object-specific display methods, if necessary. To display primitive types (integers, doubles, etc.) all that is needed is a simple text box. However, some non-primitive objects, such as Bayesian Belief Networks or Hidden Markov Models, may be displayed in a more sensible, type-specific manner. The State Editor determines if the non-primitive object has a specialized display routine, which is a method written by the author of the object. If such a method exists, then the State Editor uses this method, otherwise the State Editor allows the user to open the object and view its members directly. This process can be repeated recursively through its embedded objects until only primitive types remain.

The author of a PBM need not put any hooks or access routines for the State Editor to gain access to its state variables. This makes the State Editor extremely versatile, and allows the State Editor to manipulate PBMs that have been dynamically added to PB3A.

4.4   Launcher

The Launcher comprises one of the two system execution entities in the PB3A. It contains a Runtime Core along with code to divide a global configuration into the smaller, node-specific configurations. The Launcher's local copy of the configuration mirrors the global configuration. This makes the Launcher responsible for synchronizing and managing changes to the global configuration. All requests that alter the global configuration are serialized by the Launcher.

During execution, the Launcher has a complete Runtime Core and is responsible for providing a PBM execution environment. The Launcher loads all PBMs from the ModuleServer or local file system, launches threads for threaded PBMs, provides event notification facilities, manages remote port replication, and responds to system reconfiguration requests.

Once the Launcher divides the global configuration into node-specific configurations, it contacts the NetController at each of the remote hosts. The Launcher then requests that NetExecutors be spawned to host that node's piece of the current, global system configuration.

4.5 NetExecutor

The NetExecutor is the second system execution engine in PB3A. Like the Launcher, the NetExecutor contains a Runtime Core and is responsible for providing a PBM execution environment. Immediately after spawning, the NetExecutor opens a network socket to the Launcher that initiated it. The NetExecutor then uses this network link to download from the Launcher the portion of the global system configuration that it must execute. Like the Launcher, the NetExecutor loads all PBMs from the ModuleServer or the local file system, starts threads for threaded PBMs, provides event notification facilities, manages remote port replication, and responds to system reconfiguration requests.

Currently, before NetExecutor can perform any action that would alter its local configuration, it must contact the Launcher and lock the global configuration. Since only one node may be locking the global configuration at a given time, this process guarantees that the NetExecutors provide Launcher with the information needed to serialize all system changes.

The Runtime Cores embedded in NetExecutors and the Launcher cooperate to manage the PB3A port-communication system. This local and remote port-access transparency frees the PB3A programmer to treat a distributed, heterogeneous network of processing nodes as if it were one large computer.

4.6 NetController

The NetController acts as a gateway daemon through which PBMs may enter a remote processing node. Whenever a NetExecutor or Launcher needs to start PBMs on, or migrate PBMs to, a remote node it must first ensure that a NetExecutor is running on that node. Upon receiving the global configuration name from a Launcher or NetExecutor, the NetController first determines if it has enough computing resources remaining to satisfy the request. If not, the NetController can reject the request. Otherwise, the NetController replies with the socket number of the NetExecutor, spawning a new NetExecutor if none are currently running the global configuration for that node. This process ensures that only one NetExecutor is designated for a given global configuration for each node. Moreover, this guarantees that if two PBMs from the same global system configuration are executing on a node, they will be executing in a shared memory space and port communications will work directly through memory references. If a Launcher loses contact with a NetExecutor, the Launcher can request the NetController to shut down the NetExecutor gracefully or forcefully.

5 Applications

We have used the Port-Based Adaptable Agent Architecture as the substrate for several applications that demonstrate some of the features of the architecture.

5.1 Robotic Mapping

Fig. 5. Robots used for mapping: Patton and Rommel.

In this scenario, two mobile robots, shown in Figure 5, are tasked to map a laboratory using ultrasonic sonars. One robot is endowed with a simple strategy to explore the laboratory, a Bayesian mapping algorithm, and a hardware monitor to detect any failures that would prevent the robot from completing its task, while the other robot sits idle. If the first robot has a hardware failure (such as a graduate student cutting the power to its motors) then the PBM monitoring the hardware issues a request to the Runtime Core to move the software to the idle robot. The Runtime Core then requests that all PBMs in the system (Figure 6) serialize their state so that any information collected by the first robot can be sent to the second robot. Next, the Runtime Core requests the ModuleServer to send the code for each PBM and the retrieved state information to the second robot. The system finally resumes execution on the healthy robot and continues mapping after the first robot fails. This transferring of software takes about five seconds once hardware failure is detected. Thus, this type of self-adaptive system can overcome crippling hardware failures and still complete its task.

5.2 Transferring Learned Knowledge

Another application where this architecture has proven very useful is in the transferring of learned knowledge from simulation directly to the real world. For this application, the

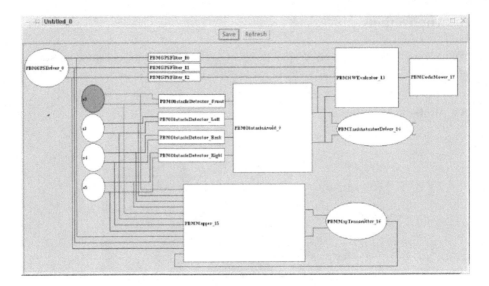

Fig. 6. Layout of the PBMs used for mapping.

Port-Based Adaptable Agent Architecture was combined with the mobile robot simulator RAVE, described by Dixon et al. [1]. RAVE provides interfaces and dynamic linking of libraries that allow the same robot code to execute on a simulated or real robot.

In this scenario, a mobile robot learns to move to a goal location while avoiding obstacles using a reactive control policy. The robot commences learning in simulation. The simulated robot is endowed with extremely simplified zeroth-order dynamics. Clearly, the dynamics of the real robot are more complex, and the parameters of the controller must be fine-tuned to account for this difference between the real and simulated robots.

When the task is learned satisfactorily in simulation a PBA triggers the Runtime Core to move the entire system from the simulated robot to the real robot. Since RAVE allows the same robot code to execute in simulation or on a real robot, the system can be immediately resumed on the real robot. After a few moments of learning on the real robot, the controller has sufficiently accounted for the difference in dynamics. The transferring of the controller code from the simulated to the real robot takes about two seconds. This form of self-adaptation, mobility, manifested by learning in simulation then finishing the learning on the physical system, allows for a drastic reduction in total time required to learn the task, while not suffering a decline in performance.

5.3   Traffic Optimization

PB3A was also used to develop a basic intelligent transportation system: an adaptive, decentralized signal controller for urban traffic. Each intersection has PBMs that collect sensor information, communicate with neighboring intersection controllers or traffic centers, and issue intersection signal commands. Different types of intersection controllers were designed: fixed-time controllers, periodically switching between red, yellow, and green lights; adaptive controllers based on local probabilities and queues; and learning techniques. A performance agent was developed to swap controllers depending on traffic conditions. The PB3A was applied in simulation to a small section in the urban area of the city of Pittsburgh called Penn Circle, as part of a Community Project to improve the traffic in the area. The goal was to study the traffic patterns and current intersection-controller quality compared to more advanced controllers. With PB3A, it was possible to deploy the whole system very quickly and connect it with the traffic simulator ARTIST developed by Bosch, using a PBD to interface with the simulator. Further developments will include the use of vehicle-to-vehicle communication, inclusion of bus schedules, emergency vehicle activity, and vehicle navigation features.

6   Related Work

The ideas underlying Port-Based Agents (PBAs) draw heavily on distributed-systems research, particularly the distributed operating systems research of the last dozen years.

The Sprite operating system, developed by John Ousterhout et al. [3] more than ten years ago, introduced the concept of process migration. Process migration allowed an executing instance of a program to be moved between workstations. The ability allowed a single Sprite user to harness the power of many workstations simultaneously and dynamically.

About the same time as Sprite, a group of researchers at the University of Tokyo created the Galaxy Distributed Operating System [4]. This project emphasized object access-level transparency for all resources. This ability to access system resources uniformly, independent of their locations, further simplified process migration. Recognizing that centralized object naming and locating schemes are inefficient for distributed systems, Galaxy employed distributed schemes to maintain global state. In this system, only processing nodes that require a given resource would cache the naming and locating information of that resource. The port-naming and locating mechanisms in the PB3A follow the same general scheme, thereby avoiding the centralized naming bottleneck and vulnerability.

In addition to drawing upon distributed operating systems, the PB3A resembles other mobile-object programming environments. One such system is the Emerald Distributed Programming Language [5] developed at the University of Copenhagen. The Emerald project created a distributed programming system for heterogeneous computer networks. This system operates in native code and native data representations on each individual platform, but marshals the data into platform-independent representations on transfer. In order to run an application across multiple platforms, the code for that application must be compiled for each platform. To deal with atomicity differences across various platforms, Emerald code utilizes "bus stops". An Emerald object may only be migrated from one node to the next when a bus stop is reached. Migrating the object at any other point runs the risk of leaving during a non-atomic operation on one platform that is atomic on another. To ease the programming effort, bus stop generation is built into Emerald compilers. PB3A ensures atomicity across heterogeneous platforms by using a similar locking scheme. All PB3A user code runs inside system-maintained locks and cannot migrate until those locks are obtained. The disadvantage of the Emerald system is that the introduction of a new platform may require altering the compilers and runtime libraries on all other platforms. Furthermore, the sharp behavioral differences among platforms may mean that a single application must be rewritten for each platform on which it may run. PB3A avoids both these disadvantages by using Sun Microsystems Java. Java's representation of code is platform independent and its behavioral specification, with the exception of some graphical user interface-related functionality, is uniform across all platforms for which Java is available.

Other agent-based systems include D'Agents, formerly Agent TCL, developed at Dartmouth College [2], Odyssey and Telescript from General Magic, TACOMA from University of Tromsø and Cornell University, and Aglets from IBM Research. These environments define agents to be code that can be installed and executed on remote hosts, with the ability to migrate to different hosts during execution. Whereas these systems emphasize the support infrastructure for agent programming paradigms and the communication mechanisms between agents, PB3A additionally focuses on the internal organization of agents, aims to explore recursively composed systems, and exploits self-adaptivity to cope with changing real-world operating conditions.

The port-based concept is derived primarily from port-based objects, first proposed and implemented by Stewart and Khosla in Chimera [6]. Port-based objects were designed for real-time control applications in a multi-processor environment with a single high-speed backplane. A link between two objects is created by connecting an output port of one object to a corresponding input port of another object. The informational scope within which the port-based objects exist is a flat, public data structure visible to all objects. This implementation is very efficient for monolithic systems, but it provides no concept of agency (see Wooldridge and Jennings [7]).

PB3A should be viewed as the natural evolution of the port-based concept. Where port-based objects were designed for multi-processor environments and for direct human-initiated reconfiguration, PB3A is being designed to utilize loosely coupled distributed computing infrastructures and self-initiated software adaptivity. The modern-day computing paradigm exemplified by distributed and self-adaptive systems absolutely requires the autonomy and self-awareness that are the hallmarks of agent technologies. Software composed from independent, self-aware agents that are able to alter their own structure, are best suited to complete tasks in the case of network latencies, node failures, and general operating condition variations that characterize real-world environments. PB3A's first advantage over Chimera is that PB3A uses dynamically loaded Java byte-code to avoid recompiling and relinking of the entire system when new objects are added. Specifically, to support distributed computing, PB3A augments the notion of the port to include cross-network links, employs an encapsulated memory model to make each PBM self-contained, and utilizes mobile Java byte-code along with the previously mentioned dynamic loading to provide code on demand to individual nodes of the network.

7   Conclusions and Future Work

We have created a distributed, agent-based architecture that facilitates the development of large-scale, self-adaptive systems. The Port-Based Adaptive Agent Architecture (PB3A) specifies a highly modular and decoupled agent-to-agent communication scheme via input and output ports and provides the necessary primitives for code migration. Furthermore, PB3A gives some specifications of how a Port-Based Agent (PBA) should be structured, giving agents the autonomy to become truly self-adaptive. Whereas previous research in this area has focused individually on mobility, software composition, or adaptability, we have presented a unified architecture. This unification allows more effective research into self-adaptive systems.

Another powerful notion in PB3A is the recursive definition of tasks. That is, a PB3A system may be composed of many agents. Each agent may be composed of many tasks which, in turn, may be composed of many sub-tasks, and so on. PB3A makes this logical, recursive system realization possible through the encapsulation of tasks in Macros.

The decoupled communication scheme between PB3A modules allows for their testing to be done in isolation. This gives rise to rapid prototyping and reliable systems to be designed and built extremely quickly.

Future work will allow the user to have a more interactive role in a PB3A system execution. Presently, once the system is started, the agents in the system determine when or if the system should adapt itself (moving agents to different nodes, swapping algorithmic modules, etc.). We will allow the user to adapt the system during execution by specifying any aspect of agents possible. Also, we will modify the State Editor to give the user the ability to view and modify the internal state of a Port-Based Module (PBM), in real-time, during its execution. Currently, the user may only use the State Editor to modify the internal state of a PBM before the system begins execution.

Also, the port and event systems will be made more sophisticated. We will embed environmental information into the ports of a PBM so that the PBM can make more informed decisions. Information such as network latencies, network failure rates, and CPU usage could prove useful to self-adaptive agents. Events will be expanded by allowing more types of events, rather than just input-port changes, and priorities will be given to different types of events.

Acknowledgments

We would like to thank Andrea Byrnes, Nathan Clark, John Dolan, Enrique Ferreira, Dmitry Frumkin, Jordan Harrison, Dan Heller, Jonathan Jackson, Jeff Lam, Rich Malak, Chris Paredis, Yatish Patel, Charles Tennent, and Niraj Tolia for their insight and help with this work.

This work was supported in part by DARPA/ETO under contract F30602-96-2-0240 and by the Institute for Complex Engineered Systems at Carnegie Mellon University. We also thank the Intel Corporation for providing the computing hardware.

References

1. Dixon, K.R., J.M. Dolan, W.S. Huang, C.J.J. Paredis, and P.K. Khosla. "RAVE: A Real and Virtual Environment for Multiple Robot Systems", *Proceedings of the IEEE/RSJ International Conference on Intelligent Robots and Systems*, 1999.
2. Gray, Robert. "Agent Tcl: A transportable agent system", *Proceedings of the CIKM Workshop on Intelligent Information Agents, Fourth International Conference on Information and Knowledge Management*, December 1995.
3. Ousterhout, John K., Andrew R. Cherenton, Frederick Douglis, Michael N. Nelson, and Brent B. Welch. "The Sprite Network Operating System", *IEEE Computer*, v. 21 n. 2, pp. 23 - 36, February 1988.
4. Sinha, Pradeep K., Mamoru Maekawa, Kentaru Shimizu, Xiaohua Jia, Hyo Ashihara, Naoki Utsunomiya, Kyu S. Park, and Hirohiko Nakano. "The Galaxy Distributed Operating System", *IEEE Computer*, v. 24 n. 8, pp. 34 - 41, August 1991.
5. Steensgaard, Bjarne and Eric Jul. "Object and Native Code Thread Mobility Among Heterogeneous Computers", *Proceedings of the 15th ACM Symposium on Operating Systems Principles*, pp. 68 - 78, December 1995.
6. Stewart, D.B. and P.K. Khosla. "The Chimera Methodology: Designing Dynamically Reconfigurable and Reusable Real-Time Software Using Port-Based Objects", *International Journal of Software Engineering and Knowledge Engineering*, v. 6, n. 2, pp. 249 - 277, June 1996.
7. Wooldridge, Michael and Nicholas R. Jennings. "Intelligent Agents: Theory and Practice", *Knowledge Engineering Review*, 1995.

An Architecture for Self-Adaptation and Its Application to Aerial Image Understanding

Paul Robertson

University of Oxford, Dept. of Engineering Science,
19 Parks Road, Oxford, OX1 3PJ, England, UK
(pr@robots.ox.ac.uk)

Abstract. Certain problems in which the environment is not well constrained do not lend themselves to a conventional open loop solution. Image understanding is such a problem domain. Image analysis programs are notoriously brittle. By using a self-adaptive approach for these problem domains we may be able to produce more robust and useful behavior. We describe an architecture that uses reflection to provide a mechanism for self-monitoring and self-modification and uses code synthesis as a means of modifying code dynamically in the face of changing assumptions about the environment of the computation.

Keywords: Aerial Image Analysis, Reflection, Code Synthesis, Agent Architecture.

1 Introduction

This paper provides an overview of the GRAVA [10] architecture and the rationale underlying its design.

This project began with the observation that a significant source of problems with interpreting visual scenes comes from our inability to precisely predict the nature of the environment in which the image interpretation programs are expected to operate. Unlike problems like adding up numbers which is unaffected by an outside environment, for visual interpretation problems we cannot be certain what the environment looks like. We believed that instead of having image analysis algorithms being applied "blind" that they should evaluate their performance and where necessary change the running system to accommodate the actual environment that they "observe". The need to reason about the computational nature of the system of which they are a part and to be able to make changes to that system suggested a reflective [3,8,11] architecture.

In the spring of 1998 DARPA introduced the term "Self adaptive software" to describe exactly the kind of problem described above. This project was later funded under the DARPA "Automatic Software Composition" (ASC) program.

A reflective architecture provides the mechanisms necessary to support two of the essential problems of self adaptive software – the mechanism for reasoning about the state of the computational system and the mechanism for making

P. Robertson, H. Shrobe, and R. Laddaga (Eds.): IWSAS 2000, LNCS 1936, pp. 199–223, 2000.

changes to it. Over the years there has been much work on reflective systems and the methods for their successful implementation are now well known [2,4].

Most work on reflection concentrates on how to provide these two mechanisms in the domain of interest so that a programmer may make use of them. The problem of self adaptive software goes a step further. Not only must we have mechanisms that support introspection and modification of the systems semantics, we must also have an implementation of the "programmer" of these mechanisms.

The components of self adaptive software include:

1. The ability to "monitor" the state of the computation. This includes some kind of model against which to compare the computation.
2. The ability to "diagnose" problems.
3. The ability to "make changes" to correct deviations from the desired behavior.

The reason that adaptation is sought is to achieve robustness. The ability to adapt to an environment that is not quite what was expected should enable a program to continue to function where it would otherwise break. Self-adaptation appeals to our intuitive notion that programs are often brittle. The underlying reason why self-adaptation is useful in building robust programs however is that the environment is often – or usually – impossible to model accurately.

When the environment can be modeled exactly it is possible to build programs that are rubust without the need for self-adaptation. It is the lack of absolutes in the world that makes self-adaptation attractive.

1.1   A New Kind of Computation

There are many useful ways of partitioning computation but the dimension that interests us in this paper is the dimension of predictability of the environment. A computation that depends upon a completely determined environment will be referred to as a type-1 computation and a computation that does not depend upon the environment to be completely determined we will refer to as a type-2 computation. Almost all of computer science has focussed on type-1 computations. When we try to accommodate environments that are less well determined the complexity rapidly increases to the point where the programs are difficult to maintain. Programs that perform input/output are examples of where this problem is frequently faced. Because the environment is not well determined a program that has to (say) read in a command string must face the problem of dealing with the full range of possibilities and respond to them appropriately. If we knew that a program would read a well formed command each time it would be easy. Here we restrict the problem by defining any input that does not fit the pattern of a correct input as being an error. Even with this simplification I/O programs are often huge and buggy.

Hypothesis: Most interesting computational problems are type-2.

In the previous century we have largely been concerned with the open loop absolute formulation of computing but it represents a small fraction of the types of computation that we are interested in. Nature provides countless examples of computational systems. They are almost without exception type-2 and they are robust. Now we wish to bring computation into the realm where nature has provided us with so many successful examples and we find that type 1 computation does not scale to the real world where absolutes disappear and guarantees are all but nonexistent.

Programs that have to interpret visual scenes are an extreme example of type-2 computations. The environment cannot be precisely specified and all scenes are legal. We wish to make sense of all visual scenes that the camera can capture.

Until recently we have built the theory of computation around the notion of type-1 computation and developed notions of program correctness around the assumption that the environment can be accurately and completely modeled. We have been able to do this because for the most part computation has occurred within the artificial environment of a computer separated from the outside world except for some input channels whose inputs have been rigorously specified.

While we have seemingly been able to do a lot with type-1 computation it is what we cannot do well that argues for a new theory of computer science that embraces the more broadly general view of computation that includes both type-1 and type-2 computation.

Even the simplest animals exhibit type-2 computations that are extremely robust. By comparison our ability to build robots that explore our unconstrained environment is hampered by a lack of understanding of how to build type-2 computations. Programs that interpret visual scenes suffer for the same reason.

When we have absolutes we can build a system that behaves perfectly. This is conventional programming. This is a rare occurrence in nature.

When success of a computation cannot be guaranteed for any reason we must:

1. Check how well the computation did.
2. Be prepared to take some constructive action if the computation didn't do well.

This formulation of an outline for type-2 computations is similar to a control system. Rather than simply assuming that the computation performs as expected, the result is measured against an expected behavior and when a deviation is detected a corrective force is applied and the computation retried in order to bring the result closer to the expected behavior – the set point. In this formulation type-2 computations consist of type-1 computations encapsulated in a control system. This allows us to benefit from everything that we know about building correct type-1 systems and requires additionally that we have mechanisms for:

1. Knowing the program intent.
2. Measuring how closely the program intent was met.
3. Applying a corrective force to bring the program behavior closer to the program intent.

Self-adaptive software is an attempt to build type-2 computations as systems that apply a corrective force by making changes to the program code. At the simple end of the spectrum of self-adaptive systems this can simply mean adjusting parameters upon which the program operates. At the other end of the spectrum it means re-synthesis of the program code.

The self-adaptive computation loop looks like this:

1. Synthesize a program based on an understanding of:
   a) What is intended.
   b) What the environment is like.
   c) How computational elements are likely to behave.
2. Monitor the behavior of the program measuring deltas.
   a) Measure how close the program is to achieving its intent.
   b) Measure what the environment is really like.
   c) Measure how computational elements are actually behaving.
3. Update our choices for computational elements based on empirical understanding of the system dynamics and re-synthesize (go to step 1 and repeat).

Program intent is described as a specification in some kind of language. A computational element is a module that may be selected to perform some operation called for by the specification. A computational element may have subordinate requirements of its own.

If the program specification is considered to be a theorem, the computational elements can be thought of as axioms or rules of inference (depending upon whether they transform a piece of specification into another or whether they simply satisfy a piece of specification).

The computational elements define a formal system and the goal of program synthesis is to prove that the specification is a theorem of the formal system defined by the collection of computational elements. The proof is actually a selection of the computational elements wired together as an executable program and it is guaranteed to implement the specification.

So far we have introduced the notions of type-2 computation and program synthesis abstractly. Our system attempts to apply these ideas to the task of robust aerial image interpretation. Parts of our solution are necessarily specific to the problem of image interpretation while other parts of our solution take the form of a general architecture, agent language, and synthesis engine that could in principle be applied to other problem domains. By discussing the abstract ideas of type-2 computation and program synthesis we have told only half of the story. A significant part of the problem involves the acquisition and application of models of the domain. Our approach to models and specifications has been corpus based. The model of the environment is extracted from a corpus of representative images while the specification for how the image should be segmented and labeled is learned by example from human expects. A human expert manually annotates an image corpus. The segmentations produced by the system are like those manually produced by the human expert.

Image segmentation is the partitioning of the image into disjoint regions, each of which is homogeneous in some property. It is an essential component of most image analysis systems and has been studied extensively Weska [12] Adams [1] Zhu and Yuille [13]. Despite its long history of research, current segmentation algorithms are inadequate and unreliable in real world conditions. It has been argued that image segmentation is not a low level process at all Marr [9] and that semantics are necessary in order to produce good segmentations.

We refer to semantic labels assigned to regions as "image content descriptors" and the process of generating them as "image labeling". An image content descriptor is a hypothesis about the content of that region (such as "urban area").

The Minimum Description Length (MDL) agent negotiation formulation described below permits us to generalize the region competition algorithm of Yuille and Zhu [13] and to permit agents with differing levels of semantics to participate in the segmentation. This allows segmentation, classification, and image parsing to proceed cooperatively.

By structuring the image interpretation architecture as a feedback loop with dynamic evaluation and circuit synthesis the system can draw upon a variety of capabilities (implemented as agents) and prior knowledge of the world (from an image corpus) in order to provide robust behavior over a range of image conditions.

Our approach to semantics is statistical/information theoretic. A corpus of hand annotated images is used as a source of prior knowledge about semantic relationships in representative images and as a mechanism for importing expert knowledge about the images in the corpus and specifications for the system behavior.

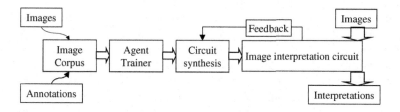

Fig. 1. Program Flow

Figure 1 shows the basic program flow for the system. Semantics are acquired from the image corpus containing representative images and expert annotations. Agents and meta-agents for image segmentation and interpretation are trained on the corpus allowing the circuit synthesis module to produce an image interpretation circuit that will interpret and segment images. Feedback allows agents self-knowledge to be used to monitor performance and to re-synthesize the interpretation circuit in order to track changes in image quality and content.

The corpus allows statistical information to be gathered that supports agent negotiation (agent architecture), expert knowledge extraction (circuit synthesis), and image parsing. We provide an overview of these components below.

In section 2 we describe the problem domain – image segmentation and labeling. Image interpretation is a special case of a general class of problems that we call "Interpretation problems". In section 3 we introduce the idea of interpretation problems. A key piece of the architecture is a novel agent architecture. The agent architecture supports competition among agents that attempt to find the global minimum description length interpretation. Section 4 gives a sketch of the agent architecture used in GRAVA. Section 5 provides an overview of the segmentation algorithm. The segmentation algorithm algorithm demonstrates the power of the MDL based agent architecture. Section 6 introduces the program synthesis engine.

2   The Problem Domain

As we have described above self-adaptive software involves several components:

1. A performance model;
2. A means of comparison; and
3. A mechanism for modifying the computation.

The goal of making self-adaptive software a reality involves finding ways of achieving each of these components and structuring a way of making them work together to produce a robust system.

We chose the problem of producing robust interpretations of aerial images as the test domain for our investigation into self-adaptive software.

Figure 2 shows an aerial image that has been segmented into regions. Each region has a coherent content designation such as *lake, residential*, and so on. The description that is formed by the collection of labeled regions is an interpretation of the image.

To produce such an interpretation several cooperative processes are brought into play. First the image is processed by various tools in order to extract texture or feature information. The selection of the right tools determines ultimately how good the resulting interpretation will be. Next a segmentation algorithm is employed in order to produce regions with outlines whose contents are homogeneous with respect to content as determined by the texture and feature tools. The segmentation algorithm also depends upon tools that select seed points that initialize the segmentation. The choice of tools to initiate the segmentation determines what kind of segmentation will be produced. Finally labeling the regions depends upon two processes. The first tries to determine possible designations for the regions by analyzing the pixels within the regions. The second looks at how the regions are related to each other in order to bring contextual information to bear on the process of selecting appropriate labels.

At any point a bad choice of tool for initial feature extraction, or for seed point identification, or for region identification, or for contextual constraints can

Fig. 2. Segmented Aerial Image

cause a poor image interpretation to result. The earlier the error occurs the worse the resulting interpretation is likely to become. For example a poor choice of tools for extracting textures from the image will result in a poor segmentation. The poor segmentation will result in poor region content analysis and so the resulting interpretation can be very bad indeed. The test for self-adaptive software is to determine how the program that consists of the collection of tools described above can be organized so that when a poor interpretation is produced the program self-adapts into a program that does a better job.

Figure 3 shows the dependency relationship between components of the system that we describe in this paper.

Image understanding requires models of the real world that can be used to produce a description of the image. We must be concerned with where these models come from and how to apply them to the task of image interpretation. In the case of a self-adaptive implementation the models must include an un-

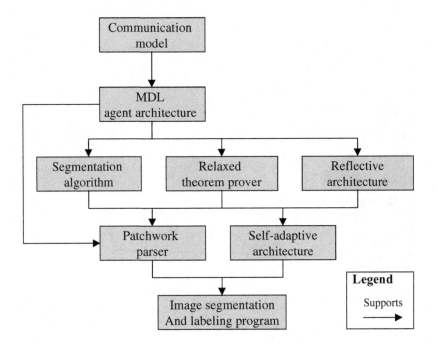

Fig. 3. Logical Components

derstanding suitable for estimating success of the interpretation and a model of how the parts of the program interrelate.

There are many ways of segmenting an image depending upon what is considered important for the task at hand. There is not one single *best* segmentation. Applications that wish to distinguish between different crop types may be interested in segmenting individual fields and assigning different labels to them depending upon their crop type. Other applications that are interested mostly in urban buildups may be happy to segment all fields as fields ignoring subtle differences caused by crop type.

In some applications the desired interpretation may be static but many applications will have different needs at different times changing dynamically as the application proceeds. A search program that attempts to find factories in images may at first be happy segmenting areas into industrial and agricultural regions and then with the industrial regions selected seek finer grained segmentation of the industrial region in order to search for the factory type that it is looking for. Systems involving mobile systems such as missiles or unmanned reconnaissance aircraft may have different interpretation needs depending on the phase of the flight. At other times weather conditions may dictate that only reduced levels of segmentation can be produced dues to deteriorated visibility. At a slower pace – but still dynamic for a satellite based Earth monitoring program – changes in seasons will affect the appearance of the landscape and the appropriateness of the various tools selected to interpret the image.

In summary, there are a large number of dimensions of change that can affect the performance of an image interpretation program of the form described above. To build a static solution to a dynamic program invites brittle program behavior. The self-adaptive software idea is to make the program monitor the various dimensions of change at runtime and when appropriate make changes to the running system so as to always do as well as it can under any given circumstance – and indeed to be able to estimate how well it has done at its task.

A major part of the self-adaptive problem involves mechanisms for implementing the self-adaptation itself but an equally important part of the problem concerns how models are build and maintained and how they are used in the monitoring and adaptation phases. Image interpretation it seemed to us presented an interesting case that could lead to an understanding of how self-adaptive solutions may be developed for image interpretation problems and perhaps interpretation problems in general.

3   Interpretation Problems

The problem of image interpretation belongs to an interesting class of problems that can broadly be charactarized as interpretation problems. Interpreting specifications of a segmentation is another example of an interpretation problem.

Our reflective architecture is based on the observation that for many problems a tower of interpretation problems can be constructed.

Consider the familiar problem of software development. In software development there are several layers of interpretation problem at work. Typically these are not automated, but the process in instructive because it is a familiar problem.

First the programs requirements are established. Typically these take on the form of a requirements document. The requirements say what the program should do at a very general level. It usually doesn't say much about how the program should operate or what it should look like.

The requirements document is *interpreted* to produce a specification that satisfies the requirements. The specification says how the requirements are to be achieved in the form of a program or suite of programs.

The specification document is *interpreted* to produce a design. The design shows at a fairly detailed level how the program components should work.

The design document is *interpreted* to produce a program — or suite of programs — that satisfied the design.

Finally the compiler interprets the program to produce the machine code that satisfies the program and the hardware interprets those instructions to produce the required behavior.

If a change occurs in any of these levels it must satisfy the level immediately superior to it and subordinate levels must be made to be compatible with the change. Since every part of the description was produced as a part of the interpretation of the higher level specification it is possible to *trace* the affects of the change up and down through the structure. The ability to track the path between components of a system and specifications and requirements that gave rise to them is called tracability.

At each stage a specification is interpreted by an interpretation procedure that brings some specialized knowledge to bear on the problem in order to produce a representation or description. The description thus generated becomes the specification of the lower level interpretation problem. The software engineering scenario described is a manual process although it may one day be automated.

The problem of self-adaptive software is to respond to changing situations by re-synthesizing the program that is running. To do this we reify the software development process within the domain of image interpretation programs. In our specific case, we must produce a segmentation that conforms to the specification implicit in the corpus.

The number of levels will vary from problem to problem. In principle there could be an arbitrarily large number of levels but in practice we expect most problems to have a small number of levels.

The level in the software development example described above that deals with the generation of machine code from a high level language description is of particular interest because our intuitions in this domain fit closely with the task of generating code from the corpus.

The compiler is an interpretation program that interprets the high level language source program and produces a description that draws upon knowledge built in to the compiler about the target machine. Nowhere in the high level source code are the details of the target machine represented. Indeed the code may be compiled with different compilers for different target machines. The compiler embodies various kinds of knowledge essential to producing a good representation of the source:

1. Knowledge of the high level language.
2. Knowledge of certain time and space considerations of certain patterns used in the source program and transformations into more efficient forms.
3. Knowledge of the target machine its instructions, registers, and efficiency considerations.

Of course the compiler may consist of several layers of interpretation problem in which the language is successively translated through intermediate languages until the target level is reached.

Typically a compiler is a carefully constructed program of considerable complexity in which various components perform the application of the domain knowledge (knowledge of the high level language and the target machine) to the task of translating the program. The task of the compiler can be presented in proof theoretic terms.

3.1   Compilation as Proof

The typical compiler can be thought of as the composition of several proof problems for example parsing, optimizing and producing machine code. The purpose of this discussion is to draw upon our intuitions of the compilation process and not to carefully model the behavior of a compiler. We restrict our discussion here to a single level of the compiler.

If we think of the task of the compiler as proving that the program can be computed by the target machine we can see that the resulting machine code is the axioms of the proof.

The knowledge in the compiler can be divided simply into two kinds

1. Knowledge of rules of inference and a procedure for recursively applying them in order to arrive at a proof.
2. Knowledge of the relationship between the source code and the target code in the form of rules.

In this model the compiler produces a tree structured proof. The leaves of the proof are machine codes. The machine codes are read off the fringe of the proof tree to produce the target machine language representation.

It is clear that various stages of the compiler fit this model. The parser is simply trying to prove that the source language is syntactically an instance of the set of programs defined by the high level language specification and the proof is the parse tree.

Of more immediate interest to us than the rationale for breaking up a compiler into a number of stages is the observation that each of these stages can be viewed as an interpretation problem as we have defined it above and that the interpretation problems form a tower.

4   Agent Architecture

In order to implement the interpreters necessary for solving the levels of interpretation problem required by our image understanding program we have developed a novel agent architecture.

Since the mid 1980's there has been growing interest in autonomous intelligent agents Giroux [5] Maes [7]. A key idea of these new architectures is that of "emergent functionality". The function of an agent is viewed as an emergent property of the interaction of the agent with its environment. Agents differ from purely algorithmic approaches in that part of their design depends on finding an interaction loop with the environment which will converge towards its goal. Where such interaction loops can be achieved significant robustness can be obtained. Our agent approach provides a way of building vision systems with such properties.

The GRAVA agent architecture is novel in that:

1. It supports meta-level agents that synthesize circuits of agents that mimic expert interpretation based on a corpus of hand annotated images.
2. It supports a novel agent negotiation mechanism based on a Minimum Description Length (MDL) formulation.

4.1 MDL Agent Negotiation

Image interpretation is fundamentally ambiguous. Interpretation involves finding the most probable interpretation. What we "See" is the most probable interpretation.

We have generalized this intuition in the form of a minimum description length or minimum entropy approach. In this approach agents compete to produce parts of a description of the image. The basis for competition is to seek to reduce the global entropy or to minimize the description length. This approach allows a natural interaction between agents of varying levels of sophistication and permits some analysis of the emergent functionality in terms of convergence to a solution.

The idea of minimum description length (Leclerc [6]) is that if a representation is optimally coded, the shortest description is the most probable one. This follows trivially because coding theory tells us that the most frequently occurring symbols should be encoded with the fewest bits. If we are looking for the most probable interpretation of an image it follows that we should seek the minimum description length. Part of the agent protocol for our architecture allows the agents to participate in the construction of the alphabet and to provide information that allows the entropy of the symbols in the working alphabet to be estimated.

There may be many agents at our disposal to generate the required description of the image. The architecture must provide for the agents to be harnessed in order to not only generate a description of the image but also to generate a description that meets the needs of the consumer. Figure 4 shows the components of the system. The agents are engaged in interpreting the image to form a description. The agents operate in an environment provided by a request from the consumer. The architecture provides selection of the appropriate agents as control over which agents are allowed to contribute to the generated description at various stages of its creation. These control activities are implemented as meta-agents whose operation can be summarized by the following control operations.

When the consumer makes (or modifies) a request, the meta-agents implement the following steps:

1. *Synthesize circuit.* The agents that are capable of producing the vocabulary of the description requested in the consumers request are selected from the pool of available agents. These agents themselves have pre-requisite input vocabularies which are used to select supporting agents from the pool. This

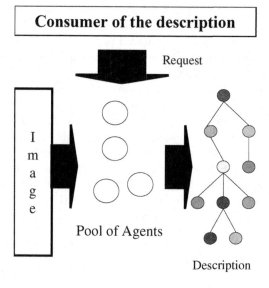

Fig. 4. Multi-Agent Interpretation Architecture

process is repeated until raw sensor inputs are reached. This process selects from the pool of agents those agents that may contribute to the requested description. This stage is similar to plan generation in other agent systems.

2. *Obtain vocabulary.* Once the circuit has been synthesized the agents in the circuit are asked for information about what vocabulary they consume/produce. The result is a global vocabulary that defines all of the symbols that may occur in the description of the image.

3. *Estimate entropy.* Having obtained the global vocabulary the entropy of each symbol is calculated. The entropy is the (possibly fractional) number of bits that would be required in an optimal coding of the vocabulary given the distribution of such features in real images that the agents have experienced in training (on the corpus). These entropies are used to determine the global description length as the segmentation and interpretation converges.

4. *Assign voting rights.* Once the entropies of the global vocabulary have been calculated the individual agents are informed of their strength when requesting an update of the global description. Agents use these strengths in order to compete to contribute to the global description. The strengths are determined so that agents whose contributions result in the smallest description length are preferred.

5. *Run!* The agents are allowed to operate on the description that begins as raw data and continues until no improvement in the description length has occurred for some number of iterations.

Since the goal of the agents is to produce a description, they operate by looking at the existing description for opportunities to improve (reduce the description length) the description. Often there are multiple agents that believe that they can improve the description at a particular place. If it were always the case that a local improvement in description length would guarantee a global improvement it would be sufficient to simply pick the agent that offers the greatest improvement locally. Generally however the locally best improvement does not guarantee the globally best improvement. As a result we employ a Monte-Carlo agent selection approach in which the agents that are competing for an update of the description are chosen at random weighted by their voting strength calculated above. This process continues until a complete description has been generated. The process then begins from the raw data again and the resulting description is compared to the previous one. The best description is retained. This process repeats until the description length of the resulting description fails to improve after some number of iterations.

5   Semantic Segmentation

The segmentation algorithm is a good example of the MDL agent architecture in action. The algorithm extends work by Leclerc [6] and Zhu & Yuille [13].

Marr [9] argued that segmentation was not a well founded problem for a variety of reasons but principally because it did not seem possible to find low level processes that could account for the apparent ability of human vision to perceive regions.

Our view of segmentation is that contrary to the common view that segmentation is a low-level process we take segmentation to be a cooperative process with all levels of processing. Where other algorithms pick *a priori* methods for determining things like curvature characteristics, we let such things be driven by the semantics.

The image interpretation problem is viewed from the communication theory view as one of intelligent compression. We wish to throw away all information that we are not interested in and then package up the result in such a way as to minimize the message length. Most image compression algorithms decide what to retain on the basis of being able to reproduce a good approximation to the original image as perceived by a human viewer. Lossy compression may however throw away some crucial detail for certain tasks even though the reconstructed image looks like a close approximation to the original. We are not interested in image reconstruction for human viewing but would like to reconstruct a semantic rendition of the image for whatever purpose the interpretation system is engaged.

Compression algorithms like MPEG are designed as architectures that permit special purpose methods to be plugged in to achieve the compression. Our approach to image segmentation is similar. We provide a basic low-level base level segmenter – a knowledge free segmenter – that makes few assumptions and discards nothing. We also provide an architecture that permits semantic agents that cooperate with the segmenter to be plugged in.

The choice of which agents are used in performing the segmentation and what inputs are made available to the segmenter determine the nature of the resulting segmentation.

There are a number of important structural issues regarding segmentation.

1. Region contents.
2. Region size and shape.
3. Region neighbors.

Size and shape includes the characteristics of the outline of the region. Different regions will want different outlines depending on semantic attributes. For example a leaf outline might have a smooth curved outline or an outline with points of high curvature depending on the leaf type. Low level algorithms such as Zhu & Yuille [13] prefer smooth outlines for all region types.

5.1 Architecture for Segmentation

Segmentation should be facilitated by image interpretation and image interpretation is facilitated by segmentation. The idea of the architecture is to allow the two processes of interpretation and segmentation to proceed cooperatively – each influencing the other and finally converging upon the best interpretation and segmentation that can be achieved.

When we know what a feature in an image is, we can know what is salient about that feature – and therefore what must be a part of the description. What is salient is not just a function of the feature. It is also a function of what we want to do with the description. It is semantics that allow us to decide what can be omitted from an image description. Without semantics we cannot discard any information. Our algorithm is called semantic segmentation because it allows semantics to govern what is retained in an image description. Leclerc's list of criteria for image partitioning insisted on a lossless representation. That is because the descriptions had no idea of salience and therefore had to retain everything. Our algorithm and architecture doesn't define what is salient, but provides a framework within which salience can be specified.

The image interpretation problem is one of efficiently communicating a description of the image content that allows sufficient reconstruction of the image for the purposes that the application demands. One way of reducing the description length for communication is on the basis of shared information. If the transmitter and the receiver share knowledge that shared knowledge need not be part of the transmitted message. If an image contains a chair it is not necessary or useful to transmit every detail of the chair. We can represent it as a "chair". To be useful it is probably necessary to parameterize "chair" to specify enough details for a useful reconstruction. We may want to specify what kind of chair it is – swivel office chair, arm chair etc. It may be necessary to provide its size position and orientation too. "Chair" in this example is part of the description language, it is image content semantics, and it is a parameterized model. Sometimes it may be structurally decomposed and other times it may be a single level model.

Where the "chair" model – or models in general – come from is not important. They can be learned from data, or they can be manually constructed. What is important for our purposes is that there is a mechanism for establishing the probability of the parameterized model occuring in the image given whatever prior information is available.

5.2 MDL Agent Formulation of the Algorithm

A semantic element or model is implemented as an agent that attempts to describe a region of the image in terms of the model that it represents. Such a description consists of the name that uniquely describes the model and a vector that parameterize the model. The agent also produces an estimate of the probability of the parameterized model appearing in the image.

An agent has the responsibility of having regions of the image represented as compactly as possible. To achieve this, once an agent instantiated a representation of a region of the image it begins to search for other agents that can represent the region more efficiently. To do this it invokes feature finders that may infer the applicability of an agent. This is somewhat like the opposite of the region growing algorithms. Rather than regions trying to grab pixels from its neighbors, our algorithm has regions attempt to give away its pixels in order to produce a smaller description.

We want higher level semantics to influence segmentation but we don't want every interpretation agent to have to have built-in support for segmentation. We prefer to have a general segmenter that knows as much as is necessary about maintaining a segmentation and as little as possible about built-in assumptions that lead to a segmentation. For this reason, in order to ground the cooperative process between segmentation and interpretation we define a base level segmenter that gets the process started.

Figure 5 shows the flow of the semantic segmentation algorithm. Initially a single region is initialized that contains the whole image. Its description length is computed based on the null semantics representation of the base segmenter (described below).

The first step (*1) is to attempt to find regions that can be introduced that can reduce the description length. If no such opportunities can be found the algorithm terminates. New regions can be null semantic regions (like the original region) or can be semantic regions.

In the second step (*2) each region attempts to reduce the description length by giving away boundary pixels to neighboring regions. This is repeated until no more reduction can be achieved by giving pixels away to neighbors. If no reduction occurred during this step the algorithm terminates.

The third step (*3) attempts to reduce the description length by merging neighboring regions. When neighboring regions are merged the total boundary cost is decreased but the cost of representing the internal pixels may increase if the regions are not similar.

The above three steps are repeated until the algorithm terminates in step *1 or step *2.

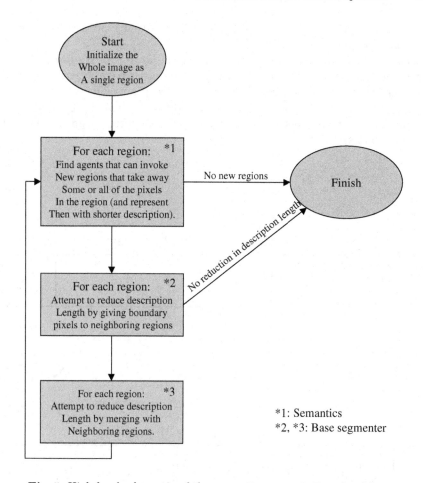

Fig. 5. High level schematic of the semantic segmentation algorithm

Step *1 is complicated by conflicting opportunities to introduce new regions (the potential new regions overlap). These cases are handled by Monte-Carlo decision points. Step *1 corresponds to seed point selection when the new regions are are null semantics base level regions.

Step *1 introduces semantics by allowing agents that implement semantics to reduce the description length.

Steps *2 and *3 implement the base level segmenter.

5.3   Base Level Segmentation

The problem of defining the base segmenter is to define a compact and useful representation of the image in terms of regions. The purpose of designing the message format is to enable us to compute the message length that would be required to communicate the image. We don't actually need to construct the message – or to communicate it.

The image is to be represented as n regions $R_0..R_{n-1}$. We begin the image representation with n the number of regions. In order to represent a region it is necessary to describe the pixels that the region contains. One way to do that is to represent the boundaries of the region. Given the boundaries of the region, the pixels can be described in order from top left to bottom right staying within the boundaries.

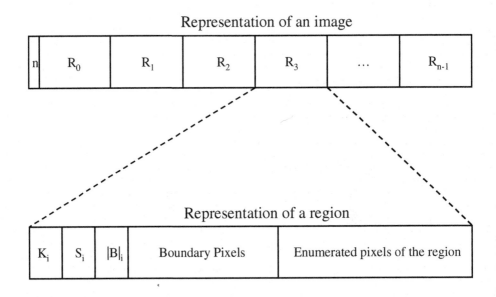

Fig. 6. Base Description Language for Images

We may have many different approaches to representing regions so the first thing that we represent is the kind K of region that we are going to transmit.

$$DL(K) = -log_2 P(K) \tag{1}$$

We begin by specifying the representation for the base region type that makes no assumptions about the shape or contents of the region. Having determined that the region is a base region we specify how many borders $|R|$ the region R has.

$$DL(|R|) = -log_2 P(|R| = n) \tag{2}$$

Next we describe each boundary of the region. The first boundary is the outer boundary. If there are subsequent boundaries they are all internal and contain embedded (subtractive) regions. For each boundary $B_i \in R$ we define an (arbitrary) starting pixel S_i.

$$DL(S_i) = -log_2 \frac{1}{p} \tag{3}$$

We specify the number of pixels $|B_i|$ that comprise the boundary.

$$DL(|B_i|) = -log_2 P(length(B_i = k)) \tag{4}$$

Then for each boundary pixel in order we describe the position as a relative move from the previous pixel $M_{i,j}$. Since there are 7 possibilities at each step (a boundary cannot double back on itself) the length move can be represented as:

$$DL(M_{i,j}) = -log_2 P(M_{i,j}|M_{i,j-1}, Mi, j-2..., M_{i,j+1}, M_{i,j+2}, ...) \tag{5}$$

The conditional probabilities can be learned from a corpus of representative boundaries. This is a knowledge free estimate of smoothness constraints for the boundary of the region. Making the representation too sparse requires too many outlines to obtain a good estimate. We use the following in our implementation:

$$DL(M_{i,j}) = -log_2 P(M_{i,j}|M_{i,j-2}, Mi, j-1, M_{i,j+1}, M_{i,j+2}) \tag{6}$$

This determines the position and shape of the region as well as the number of pixels in the region. It also allows us to define a unique ordering of the pixels. Given such an ordering we can represent the individual pixels in the region without knowing more about the region than its bits.

Our intuitions about regions are that they are homogeneous.

If they are homogeneous, we mean that all the pixels of a region are taken from the same distribution. We can estimate that distribution by building a histogram of the pixels in the region. Then the coding length of a pixel whose intensity is p is given by:

$$DL(Pixel_{i,m}) = -log_2 P(intensity = p|region = R_i) \tag{7}$$

5.4   Region Splitting

Figure 7 shows a region splitting in action. On the left a region is growing around the two islands. At this point the islands are part of the background region. Twenty iterations later the growing (lake) region has expanded past the islands and the islands have split away from the background and are now separate regions.

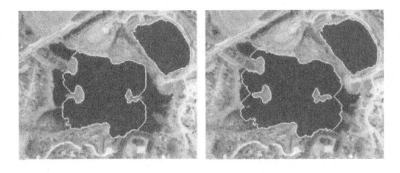

Fig. 7. Region Splitting

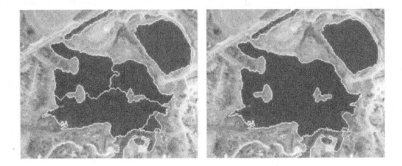

Fig. 8. Region Merging

5.5   Region Merging

Figure 8 shows a region splitting in action. On the left a number of regions have grown to accommodate the lake. In the next iteration (the right image) the regions internal to the lake have been merged. It is more compact to represent them as a single region than as separate regions.

Next we give an overview of the segmentation algorithm.

1. The algorithm begins with the entire image as a single region. The description length is calculated. Each region is represented by an agent.
2. each agent (initially only one) seeks to reduce the description length of its region. There are two ways of doing this.

   a) The agent can give away pixels of its region to a neighboring or internal region.
   b) The region can spawn new regions thereby giving up the pixels contained in those new regions. In order to spawn new regions, feature detectors may be run over the region to find support for viable internal regions.

These steps are done in turn as follows. First for each region in the image the agent attempts to give away boundary pixels to neighboring and internal regions. The pixels can be given away if the description length is decreased more for the giving region than it is increased for the acquiring region. This process is repeated until convergence. Convergence occurs when there are no opportunities for any existing region to give away pixels. Initially this point is reached immediately because there is only a single region and therefore no region to give pixels away to.

Upon convergence the agent for each region solicits agents to produce sub-regions. The addition of sub-regions must reduce the global description length. Once new agents and regions have been initialized the prior attempts to reduce global description length are performed. The cycle is repeated until no new agents get introduced.

6   Circuit Synthesis

Fig. 9. Image Interpretation Channel

The goal of the system is not simply generate a good description and segmentation of the image but to generate a description and segmentation that is similar to ones generated by a human expert. This situation is modeled as a problem of communicating the expert's intent to the program. the human expert provides specifications in the form of an annotated corpus that defines what the image interpretation programs should produce from the image. The coding of specifications as annotations and subsequent decoding by synthesizing a circuit of agents that can reproduce the annotations given an image is modeled as transmission through a noisy channel (see Figure 9). The goal of the circuit synthesis module is to maximize the mutual information between the behavior of the produced circuit and the specifications.

6.1   Learning by Example

The purpose of the program is to segment an image in a way that is as similar as possible to an expert segmentation. This formulation of the segmentation problem is different from the way segmentation problems are usually defined. Typically segmentation programs are judged subjectively by looking at the resulting segmentation and judging how well major regions have been identified.

For a segmentation to be useful it needs to be able to make distinctions that later stages of processing are interested in because ultimately the success of the image interpretation problem depends upon the usefulness of the segmentation. For our purposes the success of the segmentation is defined as being the closeness of the segmentation to that of a human segmenter.

In general we can think of the segmentation problem as being one of producing a segmentation that satisfies a specification for what the segmentation should be. In our case the specification takes the form of the corpus of hand annotated images. There is a great similarity between the task of building annotations to mimic those of an expert and what is known as learning by example.

6.2   Generalizing the Problem Description

The task of synthesizing a program from a specification is as we have discussed above similar to the problem of compiling a program and the characterization of the problem as one that is essentially a theorem proving problem suggests a way of building a general architecture. Before we can do that however there is one level of relaxation that is necessary.

In compiling a program into machine code, we generally deal with certainty. The high level language that is being compiled is not ambiguous and the machine code can be relied upon to perform as expected. In the case of image interpretation or interpretation problems in general the source specification may be ambiguous and the rules are not guaranteed to succeed. Instead we have a way of characterizing the likelihood of succeeding. Thus the compiler is a very special case of a more general problem. It is this aspect of the problem that makes a self-adaptive software solution important.

In the compiler example we were able to represent the rules as models that take an input and produce a description.

To generalize the problem we add two capabilities:

1. A post-test to test the effectiveness of the generated description.
2. A measure of utility of the rule.

Before, if the code could be generated it was guaranteed to produce the correct result. We must have a way of evaluating the result to establish its effectiveness. Furthermore we must have a way of recovering from cases where the test is negative.

In the simple compiler case any rule that could generate code from the source language was as good as another.

In the deterministic case a proof is a proof. In our generalized version of the problem some proofs are better than others. Specifically the proof that has the highest overall likelihood of succeeding is the best proof. It is ridiculous to call the task theorem proving or the result to be a proof when the result has only a likelihood of succeeding. Henceforth therefor we refer to the generalization of theorem proving a *support generating*, the result of applying such a procedure a *support*, and the procedural embodiment of the process a *support generator*.

Each node has a probability associated with it. This probability is the probability that the node will succeed in its task. Each node contains a test procedure to determine whether it has succeeded in practice. Viewing the support as a program the probability that the entire program will succeed is given as follows.

$$P(rule_n = success | P(sub_0)\&P(sub_1)...\&P(sub_m))$$ (8)

In some systems only terminal nodes (nodes that produce leaves) may have probabilities less than 1.0 while other systems may allow any node to have a fractional probability of success.

We can represent each leaf of the tree as a code of length $-log_2(P(leaf_i))$. The description length of the proof then is given by:

$$DL(support) = \prod_{s \in support} -log_2 P(s)$$ (9)

The support generator searches for rules that generate a valid supports and the description length is calculated for each. The Monte-Carlo algorithm selects the best support by taking enough samples to find the shortest description length support. The resulting program is produced trivially from the support tree. At runtime when a test fails probability assignments for the leaves are updated and the synthesis engine runs again with probabilities that reflect the knowledge of the environment known at runtime. The support that has the shortest description length generates the program most likely to succeed based on what is known about the environment at the point in time when it is generated.

7   Conclusions

Many problems in artificial intelligence can be characterized as finding the most probable interpretation from an ambiguous set of choices. Speech understanding natural language understanding, visual interpretation are obvious examples of problem areas with those characteristics. Typically what is the most probable interpretation is something that depends upon context that is only available at runtime. The GRAVE architecture supports a self-adaptive approach to this class of problems.

A reflective tower representing different levels of specification and an interpretation function that converts specifications into executable code by using a support generator (relaxed theorem prover) as a code generator allows reflection to identify precisely the piece of code responsible for a deviation in performance from the intended behavior and allows that piece of code to be dynamically re-synthesized so as to produce a modified piece of code that reflects the best that is known about the environment at that point in time.

This model has proven effective at dynamically mutating an image segmentation program so as to produce the best interpretations.

The applicability of this architecture is restricted to problems that can be construed as interpretation problems. Nevertheless we believe that there are a significant number of interesting problems that fit within those confines and that the GRAVA architecture provides a mature architecture for building self-adaptive programs at least for image interpretation problems but likely also for other problems that can be cast as interpretation problems.

Little is known about the stability of systems built this way and there are as yet no known guidelines for building systems that are intended to be stable. More work remains to be done in this area.

8 Acknowledgements

Effort sponsored by the Defense Advanced Research Projects Agency (DARPA) and Air Force Research Laboratory, Air Force Material Command, USAF, under agreement number F30602-98-0056. The U.S. Government is authorized to reproduce and distribute reprints for Governmental purposes notwithstanding any copyright annotation thereon.

The views and conclusions contained herein are those of the authors and should not be interpreted as necessarily representing the official policies or endorsements, either expressed or implied, of the Defense Advanced Research Projects Agency (DARPA), the Air Force Research Laboratory, or the U.S. Government.

References

1. R. Adams and L. Bischof. Seeded region growing. *IEEE Trans. on PAMI*, 16(6), 1994.
2. Alan Bawden. Reification without evaluation. In *Proceedings of the ACM Conference on LISP and Functional Programming*, pages 342–351, 1988.
3. C. Smith Brian. Reflection and semantics in a procedural language. Technical Report 272, MIT Laboratory for Computer Science, January 1982.
4. Jim des Rivieres and C. Smith Brian. The implementation of procedurally reflection languages. In *Proceedings 1984 ACM Symposium on Lisp and Functional Programming, Austin, Texas*, pages 331–347, August 1984.
5. Sylvain Giroux. Open reflective agents. In J. P. Muller M. Wooldridge and M. Tambe, editors, *Intelligent Agents II Agent Theories, Architectures, and Languages*, pages 315–330. Springer, 1995.
6. Y. G. Leclerc. Constructing simple stable descriptions for image partitioning. *Int. J. of Computer Vision*, 3:73–102, 1989.
7. Pattie Maes. Situated agents can have goals. In Pattie Maes, editor, *Designing Autonomous Agents*, pages 49–70. MIT/Elsevier, 1990.
8. Pattie Maes and Daniele Nardi. *Meta-Level Architectures and Reflection*. North-Holland, 1988.
9. D. Marr. Early processing of visual information. *Phil. Trans. R. Soc. Lond. B*, 275:483–524, 1976.
10. P. Robertson. A corpus based approach to the interpretation of aerial images. In *Proceedings IEE IPA99*. IEE, 1999. Manchester.
11. Paul Robertson. On reflection and refraction. In Akimori Yonezawa and Brian C.Smith, editors, *Reflection and Meta-Level Architecture, Proceedings of the 1992 International Workshop on New Models for Software Architecture*. ACM, 1992. Tokyo.

12. J. S. Weska. A survey of threshold selection techniques. *Comput. Graph. Image Process*, 7:259–265, 1978.

13. S. C. Zhu and A. L. Yuille. Region competition: unifying snakes, region growing, and bayes/mdl for multiband image segmentation. *IEEE Trans. on PAMI*, 18(9):884–900, 1996.

Self-Adaptive Multi-sensor Systems

Steven Reece

Robotics Research Group, University of Oxford,
Parks Road, Oxford, OX1 3PJ, UK.
reece@robots.ox.ac.uk
WWW home page: http://www.robots.ox.ac.uk/~reece

Abstract. Our ability to devise safe, reliable multi-sensor systems is
critical in an age where sensor platforms are increasingly complex. The
difficulties inherent in the design and verification of complex systems
necessitates intelligent reconfiguration of sensors and their signal processing tools online. This paper introduces a self-adaptive (i.e. deliberative)
approach to flexible model-based image understanding. The methods described in this paper use qualitative reasoning to maintain probabilistic
models of qualitative sensor-centred scene descriptors.

1 Introduction

Many advanced systems now make use of
large numbers of sensors in applications ranging from aerospace and defence, through robotics and automation systems, to the monitoring and control of process and power
generation plants. The primary purpose of
using multiple sensors is to provide a more
accurate and more comprehensive understanding of the system and its operation. However, multi-sensor systems can be complex and
the system designer must choose which sensor combinations to include and which signal processing tools to use to interpret and
classify the sensor data. System robustness
is hard to guarantee as it is virtually impossible to anticipate all the possible operation
scenarios. Further, the human designer, who
is familiar with the intricacies of vision and

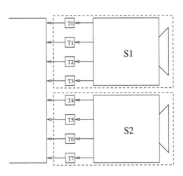

Fig. 1. Sensor data flow from sensors S_i through signal processing
tools t_j.

acoustic sensing modalities, is less familiar with system sensor modalities such
as infrared and ultrasound. Ambient conditions can affect sensor output and, for
the sensor data to be interpreted correctly, significant experience or knowledge
of the physics of the sensing process must be available.

To illustrate the strange ways that some sensors see the world Figure 2 shows
the 2D ultrasonic time-of-flight image of a specular (near) rectangular room.

P. Robertson, H. Shrobe, and R. Laddaga (Eds.): IWSAS 2000, LNCS 1936, pp. 224–241, 2000.

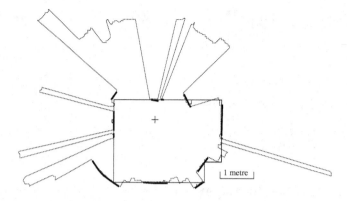

Fig. 2. Sonar placed at the cross-hairs scans a room which is rectangular with one corner missing (shown in profile), courtesy J. Leonard. The dotted line shows the range values for a complete 360 ultrasound scan of the room.

Almost all range values returned by the sonar do not correspond to the actual range to the room walls. However, parts of the sonar data, which are marked in bold in the figure, behave predictably as the robot moves and the properties of these *sensor centred cues* can be explained directly from the physics of the sonar sensing process. [1] Figure 3 shows how lighting and temperature conditions can affect infrared images. There are many surprising sensor centred features in infrared images (such as heat shadows). The important point here is that all these affects can be explained by the physics of the environment and the physics of the senor modality.

It is our aim to design and build self-adaptive sensor platforms which are able to adapt models of the environment and sensing processes for the purpose of image understanding. The motivation behind our project is summarised thus:

1. robust autonomous image understanding systems require reliable information. Most existing systems use models of the environment and these models are based on fixed ontologies often including detailed descriptions of specific features in the environment. Thus, existing systems require extensive human coding (one estimate for the complexity of the problem is that a single scenario in fleet battle management requires 20,000 rules [11]).
2. systems must adapt their software and hardware so that it is correct, useful and sufficient in unforeseen environments. Similarly, the sensing system must adapt its sensors and signal processing algorithms to ever changing tasks and environments. It must be able to choose appropriate sensor and signal processing tool combinations and also must be able to reason with concepts which emerge from multi-sensor data in various environments.

---

[1] The bold structures are called "Regions of Constant Depth" [9]. No familiarity with these structures are required for this paper.

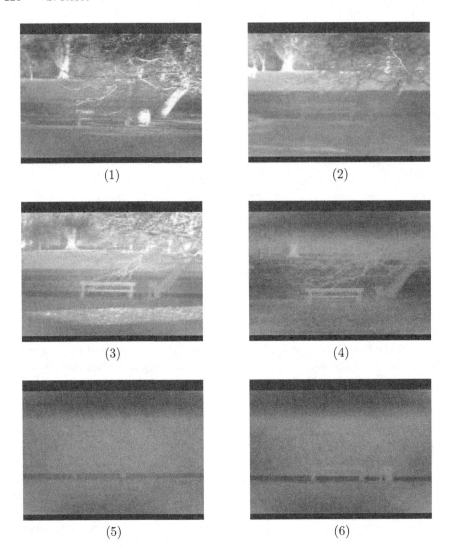

Fig. 3. A park setting (including bench, tree and path) seen through a 4.0 to 6.0 micron infrared camera on a bright day (1, 2 and 3), a dull day (4), a rainy day (5), and at night (6). Images were obtained with an Inframetrics InfraCAM infrared camera, courtesy British Aerospace.

3. robust image understanding systems must therefore be encoded with generic knowledge so that they can infer environment specific knowledge. The physical laws governing of the environment and sensing processes are the only invariants.

This paper describes an image interpretation system which has, as its core, a procedural image concept formation algorithm which is able to adapt sensor signal processing tools and an expert system for interpreting the sensor data. The expert system is able to adapt its knowledge of the behaviour of the signal processing tools by composing models from generic physics-based model fragments of the sensing process. We are evaluating self-adaptive multi-sensor methods via an application in near-infrared aerial image understanding.

2 Towards Robust Near-Infrared Aerial Image Interpretation

Aerial image understanding is an important component of intelligent data gathering, but a huge amount of manual labour is involved in the interpretation of the data. Image understanding programs are notoriously unreliable in unconstrained environments and many existing systems are sensitive to changes to their environments. Where robustness and predictability are crucial these programs can degrade ungracefully when novel environments are encountered.

A number of architectures have been proposed to alleviate image understanding problems [15] which use either application-specific knowledge or sophisticated mathematical image analysis techniques. Alternatively, instead of manually building highly complex programs that apply knowledge, a *reflective* approach uses software that is able to reason about its computational intent and state in order to assemble the sensors in such a way as to be consistent with the task of the system [15].

It has been argued that knowledge-based (i.e. expert system) reflective software can be unwieldy and lead to systems with unpredictable performance as it is difficult to guarantee that the knowledge-base is consistent and complete [15]. An alternative is to learn rules from some apriori labelled image bank. However, this approach requires that the image bank be complete and, again, it is not obvious how this can be guaranteed. Yet a further alternative is to use generic expert knowledge, that is basic rules of physics, from which expert rules can be built online and autonomously. This approach uses domain-specific "differential equations" derived from the physics rules and then simulates them to generate relevant context-specific expert system type rules which describe the expected behaviours of the system.

Qualitative Reasoning (QR) is a field of Artificial Intelligence which investigates the most general approach to model building and model simulation of physical laws. By *qualitative* we mean a range of data types including the usual quantitative engineering representations. These are nominal, ordinal, interval and point type representations: *Nominal* information encodes the presence or absence of a property; *Ordinal* values encode the most basic relationship between properties, such as whether one spatial region is rougher than another; *Interval* values encode the weakest quantitative knowledge using lower and upper bounds on the property value and *point* values encode specific quantitative values. Both parameter values and process models can be represented by the full range of qualitative information types. Each data type can be represented within the interval calculus [12] so that the nominal and ordinal types are semantically grounded in quantitative mathematics. Much QR research has been aimed at extending point-valued techniques commonly used in quantitative engineering to all representations [1,7,13].

In our infrared aerial image domain qualitative descriptions of physical parameter values are obtained from raw observations by statistical signal processing tools. These tools are basic, generic algorithms for extracting some statistic of the observation such as, for example, the average spectral energy or texture information. Many such tools can be encoded by humans. The next section introduces some simple signal processing tools for multi-spectral near-infrared aerial image interpretation.

3   Simple Signal Processing Tools

A multi-spectral sensor records reflected radiation at a ground resolution of 20m in three, discrete wave bands - 0.50 to 0.59 microns (green light), 0.61 to 0.68 microns (red light) and 0.7 to 0.8 microns (very near infrared). Figure 4 shows the 512×512 grey scale rendering of an near infrared image of Edinburgh. [2] We aim to construct an automated image segmentation and segment recognition algorithm. It is envisaged that the algorithm would be supplied with a large corpus of simple signal processing tools. The algorithm would then select a subset of these tools appropriate for its task. The task is to partition the image into spatial regions and then, when traversing the same scene, to determine when a spatial region boundary has been crossed. This is the *localisation* problem.

Simple or complex signal processing tools may be used which measure statistics (mean, mode, variance, entropy, histogram etc) of observables (luminosity, texture, shape, size etc). In the aerial image interpretation domain image statistics are determined from the reflected radiation energy $I(w)$ at pixel w. The statistics are evaluated over window areas of size 40×40 pixels. Each tool determines some statistic for $I_a(w)$ over subsets of the discrete spectral bands and outputs an ordering ($\succ$) of the various spectral bands - green (G), red (R), near-infrared (I) and non of these (B). The tool ordinal output is determined by some statistic S which is calculated for each of the spectral bands $a, b \in \{G, R, I\}$. In general, $a \succ b$ whenever $S_a > S_b$.

Some tools operate on the *binary spectral domination image* $B(w)$. The binary domination image for a spectral band is the set of pixels at which the intensity of the band exceeds that for all other bands. For all $a \in \{G, R, I\}$:

$$B_a(w) = \begin{cases} 1 & \Longleftrightarrow \quad (\forall b \in \{G, R, I\}) \ I_a(w) \geq I_b(w) \\ 0 & \text{otherwise.} \end{cases}$$

The white areas in Figure 5, part (a) depict the binary domination images for our image of Edinburgh.

---

[2] Multi-spectral aerial images were provided by the European space agency satellite SPOT.

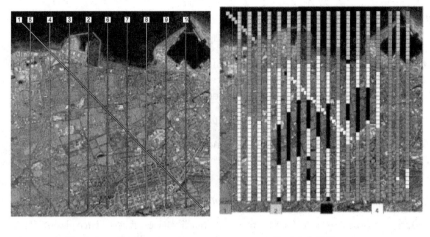

Training Stripes   Spatial Segments

Fig. 4. Aerial image segmentation of Edinburgh into roughly - sea, coast, suburbs and parks.

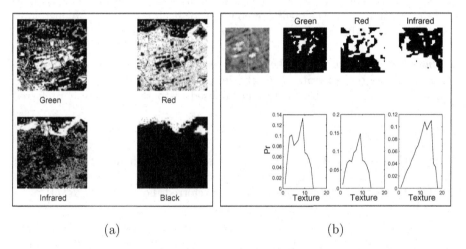

(a)   (b)

Fig. 5. (a) Binary domination images from the SPOT near-infrared multi-spectral data of Edinburgh. Also, (b) binary domination sub-images and corresponding texture histograms.

Luminosity Spatial Extent Tool (LD): the luminosity spatial extent tool returns an ordering of $\{G, R, I, B\}$. A spectral band is preferred if it exhibits the greatest intensity over the majority of the pixel window. For $a \in \{G, R, I\}$ the tool determines the extent of domination of each band:

$$S_a = |\{w \in W : \mathrm{B}_a(w) = 1\}| .$$

For $a, b \in \{G, R, I, B\}$:

$$a \succ b \iff S_a > S_b .$$

Luminosity Variance Tool (LV): the luminosity variance tool returns an ordering of $\{G, R, I\}$. A spectral band is preferred if the variance of its intensity value over the window W exceeds that of other bands. For $a, b \in \{G, R, I\}$:

$$a \succ b \iff \sigma_{w \in W}(I_a(w)) > \sigma_{w \in W}(I_b(w)) .$$

Luminosity Mean Tool (LM): the luminosity mean tool returns an ordering of $\{G, R, I\}$. A spectral band is preferred if the mean luminosity value over the window W exceeds that of other bands. For $a, b \in \{G, R, I\}$:

$$a \succ b \iff E_{w \in W}(I_a(w)) > E_{w \in W}(I_b(w)) .$$

Texture tools are used to evaluate the distribution of structure sizes within an image, including empty space (i.e. black) structures. The texture tools are based on Galloway's *Primitive Length Encoding* [4] and operate on the binary domination images. The image is examined for neighbouring pixels of the same type (either filled or empty) which fit some structuring element - in this case a square of size d pixels. The number of image pixels $N(d)$ with neighbourhoods that can contain the structuring element are counted for each $d \in [1, 512]$. A histogram over values of d, called the *texture histogram*, records the values $V(d) = N(d) \times d^2$.

Texture Entropy Tool (TE): the texture entropy tool returns an ordering of $\{G, R, I\}$. This tool operates over the individual spectral band texture histograms. The band with the greatest normalised histogram entropy is preferred. For $a, b \in \{G, R, I\}$:

$$a \succ b \iff Entropy(V_a(d)) > Entropy(V_b(d)) .$$

Texture Mode Tool (TM): the texture mode tool returns an ordering of $\{G, R, I\}$. This tool operates over the individual spectral band texture histograms. The band with the greatest histogram mode is preferred. For $a, b \in \{G, R, I\}$:

$$a \succ b \iff \mathrm{argmax}_d(V_a(d)) > \mathrm{argmax}_d(V_b(d)) .$$

To illustrate the operation of the five tools described above, Figure 5, part (b) shows the binary domination images and texture histograms for a 40×40 spatial segment drawn from near the centre of the Edinburgh image at location (300, 300). The luminosity spatial extent tool yields 45%, 48% and 7% domination for each of infrared, red and green frequency bands. The band ordering is $R \succ I \succ G \succ B$ which could indicate a suburban area.

The qualitative sensor output is called a *sensor cue* and is a transfiguration of a set of quantitative observations made by the sensor. The sensor cue is a tuple comprising the tool descriptor, a representation of the observations and a label denoting the interpretation of the representation. So, the sensor cue for the luminosity spatial extent tool output above is:

```
(:tool 'ID :rep '(R I G B) :interp 'IR-R-G-B-ordering) .
```

4 Reconfigurable Sensors and Signal Processing Tools

Sensor selection is necessary when the number of sensors on platforms is prohibitively large for data processing [3]. Further, the preponderance of available signal processing tools requires that the sensors themselves are tailored to various tasks by selecting appropriate signal processing tools [5,6]. The sensor system should reconfigure itself so that it is *complete* (i.e. apriori no objects are excluded) and this can be achieved in one of three ways: by *learning* when to reconfigure according to context; by *recognising* that a sensor (or tool) is not performing to specification or by *reasoning* about the problem domain.

Learning which sensors to use in various situations requires only basic statistical information obtained by observing the likely success rates of sensors. Such methods are generic, although they do require guaranteed complete experience of the problem domain. A more sophisticated statistical approach is to reason explicitly about each sensor but in such away that the reasoning is independent of the problem domain. Many sensors have generic (domain independent) performance signatures. For example, some indication of the performance of the Kalman filter can be determined by continuously monitoring its innovation profile. Doyle's SELMON system [3] uses a number of sensor-independent information measures to determine a *sensor importance score* - an importance ordering on the set of sensors. These scores, along with causal models, determine when and which sensor output is presented to the human system monitor.

This paper considers systems which learn when to adapt their tool sets. There are three adaptation tasks for such a system: the tools are adapted to the image concepts; models of the image concepts (which we will call *cue-segments*) are adapted by (re-)clustering image cues from homogeneous spatial regions and then tool sets are adapted to recognise the distinctions between the clusters. A set of signal processing tools is applied to windowed data and the set of sensor cues returned by these tools is termed the *cue-sub-segment* label. Different image spatial locations may yield the same cue-sub-segment label (i.e. the same sensor cues). Sub-segments are clustered to form image *cue-segment* models.

Definition 1. *Assume access to sensors* S *and signal processing tools* T. *Each sensor and tool is identified by a numeric index.*

- *A simple qualitative sensor cue from signal processing tool* $t \in$ T *is denoted* q_t. *All possible qualitative outputs from a sensor-tool* $T(i)$ *are collectively denoted* $C_{T(i)}$.
- *A cue-sub-segment* ss *is an n-tuple formed from the qualitative output from* n *signal processing tools* $T \subseteq$ T $(|T| = n)$: $ss \in C_{T(1)} \times \ldots \times C_{T(n)}$.
- *A cue-segment* S *is a set of cue-sub-segments* $S = \bigcup_i ss_i$.
- *The function* tools(S) *returns the signal processing tools which observe the cues in cue-segment* S:

$$tools(S) = \{t : q_t \in S\} .$$

An observed cue admits only a subset of all possible cue-sub-segments. When cues are randomly distributed between cue-sub-segments the number of cue-sub-segments admitted by n observed cues is an exponential decreasing function of n (see Figure 6). Figure 6 also shows the average number of cue-segments admitted by m cue-sub-segments when the cue-sub-segments are randomly clustered into cue-segments. Combining these two graphs we get the number of cue-segments admitted by various numbers of observed cues. The number of admitted cue-segments undergoes a phase-change as the number of observed cues increases. The reason for this phase-effect is that cues, when shared between different admitted cue-segments, are uninformative. The phase-change occurs when the cue-sub-segments with a preponderance of inter-segment shared cues are eventually filtered. The phase-effect phenomenon is not restricted to randomly clustered cue-segments. The optimal tool/segment combination would exhibit a cue-segment admittance phase-change for the smallest number of observations. To realise optimality the image should be segmented into highly correlated cue clusters and the algorithm to do this is described in the next section.

5   Image Segmentation

Sensor-tool combinations draw out sensor-centred features from the image such as "heat islands" in the infrared spectrum and "regions of constant depth" in ultrasound images [13]. These features are instances of sensor-specific concepts which collectively form a physics-based ontological lexicon of scene descriptors. Contrast this view with ontologies commonly found in the literature which use high level feature descriptions such as "field", "airport", "river", "football stadium" etc. In this section we show how infrared aerial images can be segmented into infrared-specific spatial features.

The localisation task requires that the aerial image is partitioned into recognisable regions. Of course, a segmentation is only valuable if the signal processing tools can discriminate different regions. Since the choice of tools is unknown by the human system designer a dynamic, sensor-centred segmentation method is required. A sensor-centred segment is a homogeneous collection of image pixels.

There are two possible approaches to clustering. We can either cluster the spatial sub-segments directly based on neighbourhood and cue variation relationships or we can cluster the sensor cues themselves and then form spatial segments to correspond, in some way, with the clustered cues. The latter method is used in this paper as it is more efficient; there are 142 different spatial sub-segment types to cluster in the Edinburgh image but only 39 different cues.

The segmentation method first determines the expected joint frequency $Pr(x,y)$ of pairs of sensor cues, x and y, within a window (of size 40×40 pixels) which traverses the image along a number of stripes. [3] $Pr(x,y)$ is the likelihood that two sensor cues are observed in the same sample window (see [14] for details).

---

[3] The raw quantitative sensor data is initially subjected to COMOC morphological filtering to reduce the number of different sensor cues.

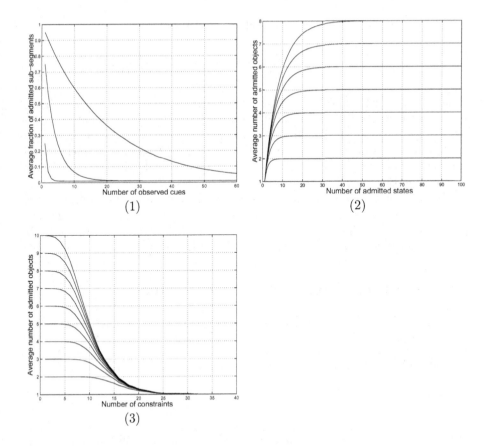

Fig. 6. (1) Typical exponential decrease of number of cue-sub-segments admitted by increasing numbers of observed cues; (2) Average number of cue-segments represented by cue-sub-segment ensembles of various sizes; (3) Average number of cue-segments admitted by different numbers of observed cues.

$Pr(x, y)$ can be used to calculate the *fidelity* (or *correlation*), $F(G, x) = \frac{Pr(G|x)}{Pr(G)}$, between groups of sensor cues G and individual sensor cues x. For optimal localisation, image spatial segments should be maximally distinct and, in turn, segments should be formed from maximally distinct groups of sensor cues. In [14] we show that the most appropriate segmentation G which maximises the expected log likelihood $\log \frac{Pr(x|G)}{Pr(x|\neg G)}$ also maximises the difference between the cross-entropy of $Pr(x \mid G)$ and $Pr(x \mid G)$ and the entropy of $Pr(x \mid G)$. When C is the set of all possible cue clusterings then:

$$G = \text{argmax}_{G \in C} E_{G \in \mathsf{G}, x} \left(\log F(G, x) - \log F(\neg G \mid x) \right) . \tag{1}$$

Once cue clusters have been formed using Equation 1 image spatial locations can be classified by mapping them onto the cue clusters. Cluster $G \in \mathsf{G}$ is the model for a spatial location with neighbourhood W when:

$$G = argmax_{G \in \mathbb{G}} \sum_x Pr(x \mid W) \log \frac{Pr(x \mid G)}{Pr(x \mid \neg G)} \; .$$

When extra constraints are applied to the segmentation task, such as image spatial segment extent limitations, the cue clusters can be manipulated further to conform to these constraints. Cue clusters that yield spatial segments which are too large can be split and those which yield spatial segments which are too small can be merged. A cluster G can be split into maximally distinct sub-clusters by applying Equation 1 to the restricted set of cues G.

Figure 4 shows the result of grouping sub-segments in the Edinburgh image. The image is segmented into sea, dock area, city and includes the large scale park structures in the middle of the city. The probabilistic model was built by sampling along stripes 1 to 10 which are shown in Figure 4.

6   Signal Processing Tool Selection Criteria

Cue-segments can be reduced in size because sensor cues may be ignored when they are either uninformative or they are redundant.

— *Inter-cluster discrimination*: ignore cues with weak fidelity:

$$\frac{Pr(G \mid z)}{Pr(G)} \approx 1 \; \supset \; Pr(z \mid G) \approx Pr(z \mid \neg G) \quad [\; or \; Pr(G) \approx 1 \;].$$

— *Intra-sub-segment cue redundancy*: ignore cue when significantly correlated with other cues in cluster:

$$\frac{Pr(z_1, z_2)}{Pr(z_1)Pr(z_2)} > \text{correlation upper limit} \; .$$

When all cues from a sensor are ignored then the sensor is redundant and can be deselected from the sensor suite. Intra-sub-segment cue redundancy often offers many alternative ways in which the sensor suite can be reduced in size. The set of all possible reduced cue clusters for segment i obtained by filtering cues with weak fidelity and redundant cues is denoted S_i. Members of S_i are called *reduced segments*.

Definition 2. *When a and b are two segments, S_a and S_b are alternative reduced segments for a and b respectively and t is a set of tools $t \subseteq \mathrm{T}$ then t is a sufficient tool suite STS for distinguishing a and b when:*

$$STS(t, a, b) \iff (\exists s_a \in S_a, s_b \in S_b) \; t \supseteq tools(s_a) \; \cup \; tools(s_b) \; .$$

A sufficient sensor suite t is a *minimal sensor suite* if there is no other sufficient sensor suite that is a subset of t.

Definition 3. *When a and b are two segments in an aerial image, $t \subseteq T$ and $t' \subseteq T$ are sufficient tool suites then t is a minimal tool suite STS_* when:*

$$STS_*(t,a,b) \iff \neg(\exists t') \, t' \subset t \, .$$

Two heuristics are available to choose between possible reduced segments. They are used when minimal adaptation of tools between spatial segments is required or when static, minimal but globally sufficient tool ensembles are required.

Definition 4. *When $\tau = \{\text{"}S_i \to S_j\text{"}\}$ is the set of all possible aerial image segment transitions, t_{ij} is a sufficient tool set for the transition $S_i \to S_j$ then $t \in T$ is a global tool suite if:*

$$(\forall \text{"}S_i \to S_j\text{"} \in \tau)(\exists t_{ij} \subseteq T) \; STS(t_{ij}, S_i, S_j) \, \wedge \, t \supseteq t_{ij} \, .$$

When t and t' are global tool suites then t is a minimal global tool suite when:

$$\neg(\exists t') \, t' \subset t \, .$$

The *minimal change tool suite* is the minimal set of tools which can be used for the recognition of aerial image segment transitions and also require minimal change between spatial regions.

Definition 5. *When $\tau = \{\text{"}S_i \to S_j\text{"}\}$ is the set of all possible aerial image segment transitions, t_{ij} and t'_{ij} are minimal tool suites for the transition $S_i \to S_j$ then $t \in T$ is a minimal change tool suite if $t = \bigcup_{i,j} t_{ij}$ and for all other tool suites $t' = \bigcup_{i,j} t'_{ij}$:*

$$\sum_{\text{"}S_i \to S_j\text{"} \in \tau, \text{"}S_j \to S_k\text{"} \in \tau} |t_{ij} \setminus t_{jk}| + |t_{jk} \setminus t_{ij}| \leq$$

$$\sum_{\text{"}S_i \to S_j\text{"} \in \tau, \text{"}S_j \to S_k\text{"} \in \tau} |t'_{ij} \setminus t'_{jk}| + |t'_{jk} \setminus t'_{ij}| \, .$$

To illustrate the efficacy of the reduced sensor suite Figure 7 shows a tri-segmented image of Brighton. In part (a) the full range of signal processing tools is used for each cluster. In part (b) a reduced set of tools is used chosen from 15 possible tool suites consistent with a fidelity lower limit of 1.2 and a correlation upper limit of 3.

7 A Case for Compositional Model-Based Qualitative Reasoning

Qualitative models are less sensitive to changes in environmental conditions than more refined (quantitative) models. For example, whereas a temperature change will affect radiation temperatures, the spectral band intensity and texture tool sensor cue values will be largely unaffected. Thus, $Pr(x, y)$ is robust to small environmental changes. Further, since a qualitative value encompasses a range

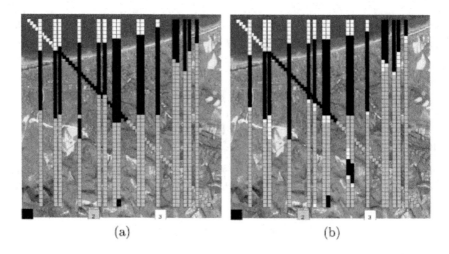

(a)   (b)

Fig. 7. Segmented image of Brighton, including segments 1 (city), 2 (South Downs) and 3 (English Channel): (a) full sensor suites $1 = \{LD, LV, LM, TE, TM\}$, $2 = \{LD, TE, TM, LM\}$ and $3 = \{LD, TE, LV\}$ and (b) reduced sensor suites $1 = \{LD, TE, LM\}$, $2 = \{LD, TE, LM\}$, $3 = \{LD\}$.

of quantitative values, $Pr(x, y)$ will be generally larger for qualitative representations than for more refined representations. The signal to noise ratio of an estimate for Pr obtained by window sampling as described above is proportional to $\sqrt{\frac{Pr}{(1-Pr)}}$. Thus, increasing the coarseness of the representation increases the signal to noise ratio and therefore localisation using qualitative representations is less sensitive to noise.

However, probabilistic models of qualitative representations may not generalise when physical ambient conditions change significantly (for example from day to night or the weather can change). Figure 8 shows the contrast between daytime and nighttime thermal images (reproduced from [10]). The signal processing tool cues are markedly different at night compared to daylight sensing. The water in this scene (note the large lake at right and the small, lobed pond in lower centre) appears cooler (darker) than its surroundings during daytime and warmer (lighter) at night. Note also the contrast in texture of the built up area in the upper left corner of both images.

Thus, logical sensor models are necessary for interpreting tool cues in different environmental conditions. However, modelling dynamic cooling behaviour and other physical processes is difficult since collecting the necessary data and constructing and validating reliable models is prohibitively expensive [2]. Models are often imprecise and can be qualitative in nature (but general enough to describe a wide range of quantitative behaviours). For example, a (partial) qualitative model is given in [10]:

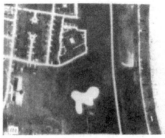

Fig. 8. Daytime and nighttime thermal images, Middleton, Wisconsin. (a) 2:40 P.M. (b) 9:50 P.M. September 17, 1971; 600 m flying height, 5 mr IFOV (Courtesy National Centre for Atmospheric Research. Also in [10]).

"Water normally appears cooler than its surroundings on day time thermal images and warmer on night time thermal images, except for the case for open water surrounded by frozen or snow-covered ground where the water would appear warmer day and night".

Most thermal scanning operations, such as geologic and soil mapping, are qualitative in nature [10]. In these cases, it is not usually necessary to know absolute ground temperatures and emissivities, but simply to study relative differences in the radiant temperatures within a scene. However, expert systems which reason with qualitative rules can be large and difficult to build and it is almost impossible to guarantee completeness. Alternatively, we can envisage a system which, through task orientated deliberation, composes appropriate models from generic model fragments online.

Our research is aimed at developing such a system. We envisage an adaptive qualitative reasoning system which is able to build appropriate time-dependent models, reason with them (via simulation) and then refine them using probabilistic domain specific information. Research into *compositional modelling* [8] is ongoing and is aimed at automating the model building process. The compositional modelling problem is a derivative of the familiar frame problem - to determine which aspects of the world should be explicitly in the model and which should be omitted. The remainder of this paper will demonstrate the value of qualitative models built from simple generic physical rules. We will endeavour to construct expert rules to describe the diurnal luminosity cycle which will aid in the interpretation of Figure 8. The expert rules will be generated using QSim [8] which is a QR simulation program. The basic building blocks of QSim (and all QR systems for that matter) are [17]:

- *Constituents* (i.e. processes, components) are described by local variables and their values which are inferred from constraints on their derivatives.
- *Qualitative values* capture ordinal, interval or point relationships between quantities. A *qualitative value* is an open interval of the reals or a single real value. The *quantity space* of a parameter is the set of possible qualitative values the parameter can take and is generally an exhaustive and mutually

exclusive set defined over the extended real line (i.e. $R \bigcup \{-\infty, \infty\}$). The ordinal relationships between landmarks can be supplemented with (possibly incomplete) knowledge of their quantities in the form of bounding intervals [12,8] and fuzzy intervals [16].

- *Qualitative constraints* (i.e confluences, or the Qualitative Differential Equation (QDE)) describe consistent value assignments for sets of parameters. QDEs are abstract representations of the system's ordinary differential equations (ODE). For example, M^+ describes the set of monotonically increasing functions. QDEs combine to describe the laws of physics and the laws of mathematics.
- *States* are assignments of qualitative values to variables consistent with the qualitative constraints.
- *System Behaviours* are described by a sequence of states. *Simulation* is the process of inferring system behaviours from QDEs and an initial state.

The QSim program is able to simulate a dynamic process from the qualitative differential equations describing the process.

Example Application: The Diurnal Luminosity Cycle There now follows a brief example of how qualitative reasoning can be used to guide the choice and interpretation of signal processing tools, specifically the luminosity spatial extent tool. The rate of change of radiant energy L depends inversely on the inertia of the radiating material. Further, the radiant energy is a monotonically increasing function of the body temperature (BT) of the material which, for simplicity, we will assume depends directly on the incident sun light intensity:

$$\left| \frac{dBT}{dt} \right| = M^-(inertia) \qquad \text{and} \qquad L = M^+(BT) \ .$$

The first QDE tells us that the magnitude of the radiation temperature change over time is an inverse function of the material's thermal inertia. The second QDE describes the monotonic increasing relationship between the temperature of the object and its luminosity. Ambient temperature, and thus object temperature is assumed to increase from dawn until noon and then decrease through sunset.

Using generic mathematical rules relating the signs of values and their derivatives, such as:

$$add(+, +) = + \qquad \text{and} \qquad sgn(|A| - |B|) = sgn(A - B) \times sgn(A + B) \ ,$$

the requirement that diurnal behaviours are cyclic and an initial state:

$$T = midnight \ ,$$
$$sgn(L_{water} - L_{soil}) = + \ ,$$
$$sgn(inertia_{water} - inertia_{soil}) = + \ ,$$

QSim is able to generate the state sequence shown in Figure 9. This state sequence corresponds to the diurnal cycle description in [10] and reproduced here.

The table in Figure 9 represents an expert system type description of the diurnal cycle: between midnight and dawn the radiation temperature of soil and water decreases steadily and the difference $D = L_{water} - L_{soil}$ is positive and increasing. Between dawn and noon, both L_{water} and L_{soil} increase. Their difference D decreases through *crossover* at state 4. Between noon and the following midnight L_{water} and L_{soil} decrease continuously and D increases steadily through crossover at state 8. This is one of three behaviours predicted by QSim. The other two describe behaviours with no crossovers; when the temperature curves meet but do not cross and when they do not meet at all.

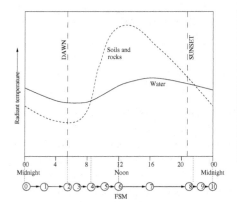

State	Time interval	L_{water}	L_{soil}	D
0	MIDNIGHT	DEC	DEC	+ INC
1	(MIDNIGHT DAWN)	DEC	DEC	+ INC
2	DAWN	DEC	DEC	+ INC
3	(DAWN NOON)	INC	INC	+ INC
4	(DAWN NOON)	INC	INC	0 DEC
5	(DAWN NOON)	INC	INC	− DEC
6	NOON	INC	INC	− DEC
7	(NOON MIDNIGHT)	DEC	DEC	− INC
8	(NOON MIDNIGHT)	DEC	DEC	0 INC
9	(NOON MIDNIGHT)	DEC	DEC	+ INC
10	MIDNIGHT	DEC	DEC	+ INC

Fig. 9. Generalised radiant temperature variations for soils and rocks versus water. Correspondence between the QSim generated state sequence and observation, courtesy [10].

From the QSim generated system behaviour we are able to generate a number of relevant expert rules which are related to the current operation of the system. Such rules explain how the sensor cues should be interpreted, they guide the sensing process and inform of sensor operation limitations. For example:

- *Image interpretation*: water is the most luminous at night and soil during the main part of the day.
- *Sensing strategy*: |D| is maximum near dawn and noon - ideal times for object discrimination.
- *Infrared sensor operation limit*: luminosity contrast between water and soil is low at some time in the morning and evening.

8   Conclusions

Our research is aimed at developing a sensor management and monitoring system which is able to guide the reconfiguration and interpretation of sensors and their image processing tools. This paper introduces a self-adaptive approach to flexible model-based aerial image understanding. Primarily, the proposed system selects a subset of sensors and their signal processing tools to understand images in novel environments. -

Image primitives are obtained by a clustering algorithm which clusters significantly correlated cues which maintains maximum (Bayesian) discrimination between clusters. Adequate minimal tool sets can then be determined for spatial segment recognition. However, static probabilistic models are insufficient and logical environment models are required. The difficulty in designing complete models means that some sensor process models must be inferred from the physical laws of nature online. We believe that Qualitative Reasoning is a promising approach to this problem since this expert system derivative is able to work with incomplete information and is also able to extend its database to novel environments.

9   Acknowledgements and Disclaimers

Effort sponsored by the Defence Advanced Research Projects Agency (DARPA) and Air Force Research Laboratory, Air Force Material Command, USAF, under agreement number F30602-98-0056. The U.S. Government is authorized to reproduce and distribute reprints for Governmental purposes notwithstanding any copyright annotation thereon.

The views and conclusions contained herein are those of the authors and should not be interpreted as necessarily representing the official policies or endorsements, either expressed or implied, of the Defence Advanced Research Projects Agency (DARPA), the Air Force Research Laboratory, or the U.S. Government.

References

1. G. Chen, J. Wang, and L. S. Shieh. Interval Kalman Filtering. *IEEE Transactions on Aerospace and Electronic Systems*, 33(1):250–259, January 1997.
2. E. Davis. Qualitative Simulation and Prediction. *IEEE Expert*, 12(3):102–103, 1997.
3. R. J. Doyle, U. M. Fayyad, D. Berleant, L. K. Charest Jr, L. S. Homem de Mello, H. J. Porta, and M. D. Wiesmeyer. *Sensor Selection in Complex System Monitoring Using Information Quantification and Causal Reasoning*, pages 229–244. MIT Press, 1992.
4. M. M. Galloway. Texture Classification Using Gray Level Run Length. *Computer Graphics and Image Processing*, 4:172–179, 1975.
5. T. Henderson and E. Shilcart. Logical Sensor Systems. *Journal of Robotic Systems*, 1(2):169–193, 1984.
6. T. Henderson, E. Weitz, and C. Hansen. Multisensor Knowledge Systems: Interpreting 3D Structure. *The International Journal of Robotics Research*, 7(6):114–137, 1988.
7. M. Hofbaur. Analysis of Control Systems using Qualitative and Quantitative Simulation. In *Eleventh International Workshop on Qualitative Reasoning, Tuscany*, pages 115–120, 1997.

8. B. Kuipers. *Qualitative Reasoning, Modelling and Simulation with Incomplete Knowledge*. MIT Press, 1994.
9. J. Leonard and H. Durrand-White. *Directed Sonar Navigation*. Kluwer Academic Press, 1992
10. T. M. Lillesand and R. W. Kiefer. *Remote Sensing and Image Interpretation*. John Wiley & Sons, 1994.
11. V. Lynn. Strategic Computing. In *Artificial Intelligence Symposium*, 1984.
12. R. E. Moore. *Methods and Applications of Interval Analysis: SIAM Studies in Applied Mathematics*. SIAM, 1979.
13. S. Reece. *Qualitative Model-Based Multi-Sensor Data Fusion: The Qualitative Kalman Filter*. PhD thesis, Robotics Research Group, Department of Engineering Science, Oxford University, 1998. Also available at http://www.robots.ox.ac.uk/~reece.
14. S. Reece. DARPA Project F30602-98-0056 Report. Technical report, Dept. Engineering Science, Oxford University, England, 1999. Also available at http://www.robots.ox.ac.uk/~reece.
15. P. Robertson. Adaptive Image Analysis for Aerial Surveillance. *IEEE Intelligent Systems and Their Applications*, 14(3):30–36, 1999.
16. Q. Shen and R. R. Leitch. Fuzzy Qualitative Simulation. *IEEE Transactions on Systems, Man and Cybernetics*, 23(4), 1993.
17. P. Struss. Model-Based and Qualitative Reasoning: An Introduction. *Annals of Mathematics and Artificial Intelligence*, 19:355–381, 1997.
18. J. Sztipanovits, G. Karsai, and T. Bapty. Self-Adaptive Software for Signal Processing. *Communications of the ACM*, 41(5):66–69, may 1998.

Results of the First International Workshop on Self Adaptive Software

Robert Laddaga, Paul Robertson, and Howie Shrobe

MIT AI Lab

We began the workshop with three goals in addition to hearing and commenting on each other's papers. Those goals were to define self adaptive software, to point out some useful research directions, and to attempt to categorize and partition the space of interesting applications of self adaptive software. We addressed the first goal rather well, and the second to the degree that some research directions are clear, given the elaboration of the definition of self adaptive software. We were not able to cover the third goal in the time we had. In this concluding paper, we present the findings of the workshop concerning the how self adaptive software can be defined and researched.

The approach we took was to view self adaptation as a complex feature, and identify its component features. We produced the following diagram:

Self Adaptivity Components

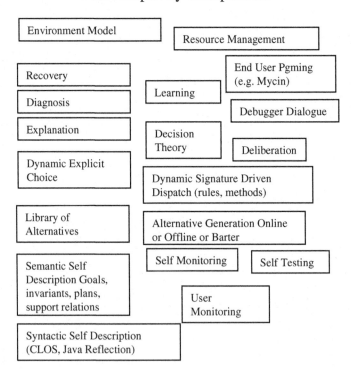

P. Robertson, H. Shrobe, and R. Laddaga (Eds.): IWSAS 2000, LNCS 1936, pp. 242-247, 2000.

The simplest sort of self adaptivity requires only a library of alternative functions (or procedures or methods), and some simple form of explicit choice at runtime among alternatives.   One form of elaboration is using dynamic signature driven dispatch, where some kind of matching is done on context or call parameters, in order to determine the appropriate method or rule to be invoked on any given occasion. This type of system is common today, in the form of Dynamic Object Languages (e.g. Common Lisp), and in rule based systems.

Alternatively the simplest model can be elaborated by adding some kind of self monitoring, to determine if there is a need to switch to an alternative method. Self monitoring can be elaborated with self testing, where the system proactively looks for problems at runtime. A third form of monitoring is accepting advice from the user, when the user determines that things are not going well. Such advice could be as simple as "try something else", or could be a fairly complex dialogue.

These three separate threads, alternatives, dynamic dispatch and self monitoring, can also all be combined, and provide a first level of useful self adaptation. This is the crucial middle of the diagram, and represents technologies that are relatively well in hand, at least for laboriously constructed self-adaptive programs. What we mean by well in hand is that dynamic dispatch, and libraries of alternate algorithms, at least for some application domains already exist. It is a relatively trivial matter, given today's available memory to make such libraries accessible at run-time. We also already know how to evaluate some of our system functionality. The laborious part is in hand coding transducers to fix input-output mismatches in calling chains of alternative algorithms, and hand coding the evaluation of performance of alternative algorithms at run-time.

The next phases of elaboration involve improving the base from which we operate. In the lower part of the diagram, we see semantic and syntactic self-description. These involve the incorporation in running code of what was once design time information about our programs and systems. Semantic self description includes goals, plans, designs, and semantic dependencies of both the overall system and each function, method or module. Syntactic self description includes necessary dispatch, calling and storage requirements.

In addition to significant elements of semantic and syntactic self description, we also need the appropriate reflective programming technology so we can use the descriptions to revise structural and behavioral features of our programs or systems. With these three capabilities in place, all the features indicated in blocks above this base, including the base functionality middle blocks, can be implemented with enhanced functionality. The more semantic and syntactic description we provide, the greater the possible self adaptivity.

We now move to the upper left quadrant of the diagram. We begin with explanation. By this we mean the ability to usefully characterize the behavior of the program, both when it is working well, and when the program is misbehaving. This involves the coordination of self monitoring behavior with the high level functional and goal descriptions of the program, and related library alternatives. If we combine the explanation capability with some sort of natural dialogue management (audio, text or graphic based), we can provide behavioral and alternative behavioral explanations to human users or designers.

A level above simple explanation of behavior, is diagnosis of crucial dependencies during correct and incorrect behavior, and the ability to in some cases extend that to diagnosis in terms of a causal analysis. Where explanation tells us behaviorally what happened, and what went wrong, diagnosis allows us to single out the functions or modules that are at the root of the misbehavior.

Without explanation or diagnosis, we are flying blind when self monitoring indicates that we have a problem. We can dynamically select alternatives at random, or with little information about what might help, but this won't permit rapid return to correct behavior. With explanation and diagnosis, we have exactly the information needed to make informed choices about which methods or modules to swap out, and which are the most promising alternatives.

Note that the next box up in the diagram is labeled "recovery". Recovery largely consists of noting a functional or performance discrepancy, diagnosing the problem, and replacing the failing components with correct components. Our diagnosis, explanation and dynamic alternative choosing blocks cover this behavior reasonably well. However, recovery also involves determining and repairing or remediating side effect damage, rolling back operations as needed and finding a clean place to restart operation. This sort of behavior is well understood in database operation, were the practice is common, but not well understood or practiced in general software.

The block labeled "environmental model" covers application or domain specific models of the program's or system's environment. These would include physical models for embedded systems, statistical models of behavior, and models of relations among external states, program inputs and program outputs. Where the rest of the self adaptive framework provides the description of the structure and functionality of the program or system itself, the environmental models provide description of structure and behavior of the world with which the program deals.

We turn now to the upper right quadrant. By deliberation, we mean the ability to reason from evidence and values to a specific course of action. Deliberation can take many forms, including voting schemes, deductive inference, reasoning by analogy, case-based reasoning, and others. One particular form of deliberative choice has been singled out for a box of its own, because of its generality and popularity, both in practice and research. That method is decision theory, in which probabilities are used to weigh evidence via a common metric, and utilities are used to weigh preferences by a common metric. With decision theory, all evidence is commensurable, as are all preferences. A common form of decision theory is Bayesian Decision theory, in which actions are undertaken to maximize the expected utility of results.

One of the most important tools for the software developer is an interactive debugging tool. Current debugger technology provides a text and graphical based presentation of evidence concerning program behavior. The evidence presented is based purely on general behavioral properties of programs in a specific language, and some structural properties of the programming language implementation. Given an ability to diagnose and explain behavior, as well as modify it in experimental ways, one could imagine building a debugger dialogue tool, capable of communicating with a programmer in terms of high level expressions about the goals and methodology of a program or system. The tool could further engage in dialogue about probable causes, diagnostic hypotheses, experiments designed to narrow in on a conclusive diagnosis, and having diagnosed a problem, suggest alternatives.

The next two blocks denote very advanced capabilities: learning and end user programming. By learning we mean that programs and systems will record failures and attempted fixes, and learn better approaches. This would also include generalizing principles from specific experience. Human assisted learning would also be a possibility, given the dialogue capabilities we have posited before. Those same dialogue capabilities make end user programming possible. Self adaptive software knows a great deal about itself, its organization and structure, and its alternative capabilities. We imagine a partnership in which users indicate how they would like programs to work better, and programs indicating what changes they could make, and the resulting dialogues producing better outcomes for the user.

Finally, we discuss resource management. One significant problem that self adaptive systems will need to deal with is management of their own computational and communication resources. So, for example, they will need to trade off time to compute and configure a better solution against the time needed to compute solutions with old or new configurations. Of course resource management is, in general, a portion of the solution to many real world problems, and as such, contributes to the environmental models component of self adaptive systems.

We also had some additional comments about research directions. One general issue is about analysis and assurance. Research is needed first on what kinds of assurance can be provided, for example verification, verification taking environment into account, and analysis of stability, for self adaptive software.

One of the interesting problems for libraries is to determine the kinds of meta data needed. Examples are notations of data dependent computational efficiency or accuracy, or resource requirements and bounds. Further examples are identification of clusters of properties that form descriptive languages for application domains, and the event ordering and structural constraints. There are also language issues, such as the extent to which existing languages such as PRS and UML can be useful. Finally, it would be good to know to what extent these meta data items can be computed dynamically. For example, the meta data description could be a program that answers a context dependent question at run time, with the context provided as an argument.

Self adaptive software is a significant paradigm shift for software engineering. The old paradigm, which originated in the 60s and 70s assumes that it is necessary and possible to reason thoroughly, totally, completely, and definitively about everything the program will do. Having demonstrated correctness, we run open loop afterwards. In order to accomplish these goals, we seriously limit the programming languages we use, with static typing, and limitations on control structures. (An uncharitable interpretation would be that we make our languages impoverished enough to be safe.)

The new paradigm begins by assuming that part of the world isn't under our control, and that vigilance is necessary. Therefore we must dynamically monitor for undesirable states, and run closed loop to bring the system in to compliance. This requires static proof that dynamic features prevent unacceptable behavior (possibly bounded statistically), and providing higher likelihood of achieving good things. To do this we need to make our programming languages rich enough to be safe.

The new paradigm also requires that we acknowledge that constraints and requirements change also. Software must adapt to that kind of change as well.

We close with a few subset diagrams, indicating a portion of self adaptive software represented by rule based systems developed in the seventies, and forward looking views of recovery based systems targeted for robustness, and fully autonomous systems.

An Interesting Subset:
Adaptable Computing (c. 1978)

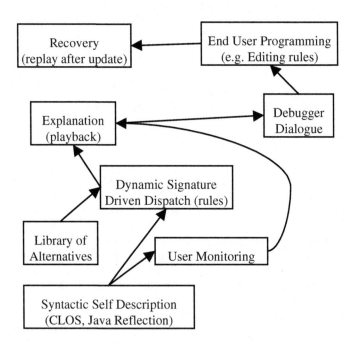

Stay out of Trouble Layer

Recovery (replay after update)	Debugger Dialogue
Semantic Self Description Goals, invariants, plans, support relations	Self Monitoring
	User Monitoring

Syntactic Self Description
(CLOS, Java Reflection)

Autonomous Robustness

Recovery	Resource Management
Diagnosis	
Explanation	

Explicit Choice

Library of Alternatives	Self Monitoring
Semantic Self Description Goals, invariants, plans, support relations	Self Testing

Syntactic Self Description
(CLOS, Java Reflection)

Author Index

Lecture Notes in Computer Science

For information about Vols. 1–1910
please contact your bookseller or Springer-Verlag

Vol. 1941: A.K. Chhabra, D. Dori (Eds.), Graphics Recognition. Proceedings, 1999. XI, 346 pages. 2000.

Vol. 1942: H. Yasuda (Ed.), Active Networks. Proceedings, 2000. XI, 424 pages. 2000.

Vol. 1943: F. Koornneef, M. van der Meulen (Eds.), Computer Safety, Reliability and Security. Proceedings, 2000. X, 432 pages. 2000.

Vol. 1944: K.R. Dittrich, G. Guerrini, I. Merlo, M. Oliva, M.E. Rodriguez (Eds.), Objects and Databases. Proceedings, 2000. X, 199 pages. 2001.

Vol. 1945: W. Grieskamp, T. Santen, B. Stoddart (Eds.), Integrated Formal Methods. Proceedings, 2000. X, 441 pages. 2000.

Vol. 1946: P. Palanque, F. Paternò (Eds.), Interactive Systems. Proceedings, 2000. X, 251 pages. 2001.

Vol. 1948: T. Tan, Y. Shi, W. Gao (Eds.), Advances in Multimodal Interfaces – ICMI 2000. Proceedings, 2000. XVI, 678 pages. 2000.

Vol. 1949: R. Connor, A. Mendelzon (Eds.), Research Issues in Structured and Semistructured Database Programming. Proceedings, 1999. XII, 325 pages. 2000.

Vol. 1950: D. van Melkebeek, Randomness and Completeness in Computational Complexity. XV, 196 pages. 2000.

Vol. 1951: F. van der Linden (Ed.), Software Architectures for Product Families. Proceedings, 2000. VIII, 255 pages. 2000.

Vol. 1952: M.C. Monard, J. Simão Sichman (Eds.), Advances in Artificial Intelligence. Proceedings, 2000. XV, 498 pages. 2000. (Subseries LNAI).

Vol. 1953: G. Borgefors, I. Nyström, G. Sanniti di Baja (Eds.), Discrete Geometry for Computer Imagery. Proceedings, 2000. XI, 544 pages. 2000.

Vol. 1954: W.A. Hunt, Jr., S.D. Johnson (Eds.), Formal Methods in Computer-Aided Design. Proceedings, 2000. XI, 539 pages. 2000.

Vol. 1955: M. Parigot, A. Voronkov (Eds.), Logic for Programming and Automated Reasoning. Proceedings, 2000. XIII, 487 pages. 2000. (Subseries LNAI).

Vol. 1956: T. Coquand, P. Dybjer, B. Nordström, J. Smith (Eds.), Types for Proofs and Programs. Proceedings, 1999. VII, 195 pages. 2000.

Vol. 1957: P. Ciancarini, M. Wooldridge (Eds.), Agent-Oriented Software Engineering. Proceedings, 2000. X, 323 pages. 2001.

Vol. 1960: A. Ambler, S.B. Calo, G. Kar (Eds.), Services Management in Intelligent Networks. Proceedings, 2000. X, 259 pages. 2000.

Vol. 1961: J. He, M. Sato (Eds.), Advances in Computing Science – ASIAN 2000. Proceedings, 2000. X, 299 pages. 2000.

Vol. 1963: V. Hlaváč, K.G. Jeffery, J. Wiedermann (Eds.), SOFSEM 2000: Theory and Practice of Informatics. Proceedings, 2000. XI, 460 pages. 2000.

Vol. 1964: J. Malenfant, S. Moisan, A. Moreira (Eds.), Object-Oriented Technology. Proceedings, 2000. XI, 309 pages. 2000.

Vol. 1965: Ç. K. Koç, C. Paar (Eds.), Cryptographic Hardware and Embedded Systems – CHES 2000. Proceedings, 2000. XI, 355 pages. 2000.

Vol. 1966: S. Bhalla (Ed.), Databases in Networked Information Systems. Proceedings, 2000. VIII, 247 pages. 2000.

Vol. 1967: S. Arikawa, S. Morishita (Eds.), Discovery Science. Proceedings, 2000. XII, 332 pages. 2000. (Subseries LNAI).

Vol. 1968: H. Arimura, S. Jain, A. Sharma (Eds.), Algorithmic Learning Theory. Proceedings, 2000. XI, 335 pages. 2000. (Subseries LNAI).

Vol. 1969: D.T. Lee, S.-H. Teng (Eds.), Algorithms and Computation. Proceedings, 2000. XIV, 578 pages. 2000.

Vol. 1970: M. Valero, V.K. Prasanna, S. Vajapeyam (Eds.), High Performance Computing – HiPC 2000. Proceedings, 2000. XVIII, 568 pages. 2000.

Vol. 1971: R. Buyya, M. Baker (Eds.), Grid Computing – GRID 2000. Proceedings, 2000. XIV, 229 pages. 2000.

Vol. 1972: A. Omicini, R. Tolksdorf, F. Zambonelli (Eds.), Engineering Societies in the Agents World. Proceedings, 2000. IX, 143 pages. 2000. (Subseries LNAI).

Vol. 1973: J. Van den Bussche, V. Vianu (Eds.), Database Theory – ICDT 2001. Proceedings, 2001. X, 451 pages. 2001.

Vol. 1974: S. Kapoor, S. Prasad (Eds.), FST TCS 2000: Foundations of Software Technology and Theoretical Computer Science. Proceedings, 2000. XIII, 532 pages. 2000.

Vol. 1975: J. Pieprzyk, E. Okamoto, J. Seberry (Eds.), Information Security. Proceedings, 2000. X, 323 pages. 2000.

Vol. 1976: T. Okamoto (Ed.), Advances in Cryptology – ASIACRYPT 2000. Proceedings, 2000. XII, 630 pages. 2000.

Vol. 1977: B. Roy, E. Okamoto (Eds.), Progress in Cryptology – INDOCRYPT 2000. Proceedings, 2000. X, 295 pages. 2000.

Vol. 1979: S. Moss, P. Davidsson (Eds.), Multi-Agent-Based Simulation. Proceedings, 2000. VIII, 267 pages. 2001. (Subseries LNAI).

Vol. 1983: K.S. Leung, L.-W. Chan, H. Meng (Eds.), Intelligent Data Engineering and Automated Learning – IDEAL 2000. Proceedings, 2000. XVI, 573 pages. 2000.

Vol. 1984: J. Marks (Ed.), Graph Drawing. Proceedings, 2001. XII, 419 pages. 2001.

Vol. 1987: K.-L. Tan, M.J. Franklin, J. C.-S. Lui (Eds.), Mobile Data Management. Proceedings, 2001. XIII, 289 pages. 2001.

Vol. 1989: M. Ajmone Marsan, A. Bianco (Eds.), Quality of Service in Multiservice IP Networks. Proceedings, 2001. XII, 440 pages. 2001.

Vol. 1991: F. Dignum, C. Sierra (Eds.), Agent Mediated Electronic Commerce. VIII, 241 pages. 2001. (Subseries LNAI).

Vol. 1992: K. Kim (Ed.), Public Key Cryptography. Proceedings, 2001. XI, 423 pages. 2001.

Vol. 1995: M. Sloman, J. Lobo, E.C. Lupu (Eds.), Policies for Distributed Systems and Networks. Proceedings, 2001. X, 263 pages. 2001.